Call Me Woman

Ellen Kuzwayo grew up in the country, but has lived most of her life in the city. She has been a "disgruntled schoolteacher", social worker, mother, wife, and in her sixties returned to study at the University of the Witwatersrand for a higher qualification in social work. Today she is active in the community life of Soweto. She is president of the Black Consumer Union of South Africa, and the Maggie Magaba Trust. She was chosen Woman of the Year in 1979 by the Johannesburg newspaper *The Star,* and was nominated again in 1984. She has helped to make two films, "Awake from Mourning" and "Tsiamelo: A Place of Goodness," both of which have had international distribution.

aunt lute books is a multicultural women's press that has been committed to publishing high quality, culturally diverse literature since 1982. In 1990, the Aunt Lute Foundation was formed as a non-profit corporation to publish and distribute books that reflect the complex truths of women's lives and the possibilities for personal and social change. We seek work that explores the specificities of the very different histories from which we come, and that examines the intersections between the borders we all inhabit.

Please write or phone for a free catalogue of our other books or if you wish to be on our mailing list for future titles. You may buy books directly from us by phoning in a credit card order or mailing a check with the catalogue order form.

Aunt Lute Books
P.O. Box 410687
San Francisco, CA 94141
(415) 558-8116

Call Me Woman

Ellen Kuzwayo

Preface by Nadine Gordimer
Foreward by Bessie Head

aunt lute books
SAN FRANCISCO

First United States Edition
10-9-8-7-6-5-4-

Aunt Lute Books
P.O. Box 410687
San Francisco, CA 94141

Originally published in Great Britain by The Women's
Press Ltd. 1985
Typeset by M C Typeset, Chatham, Kent, Great Britain
Printed and bound in the United States

Library of Congress Cataloging-in-Publication Data
Kuzwayo, Ellen.
    Call Me Woman / Ellen Kuzwayo : preface by Nadine
Gordimer : foreward by Bessie Head.
    Originally published : London : Women's Press, 1985.

        p. :   cm.
    ISBN 1-879960-09-5 : $9.95

    1.   Kuzwayo, Ellen.   2.   Social reformers — South Africa — Biography.
3.   Women, Black — South Africa — Social conditions.   I. Title.
HQ1800.5.Z75K89 1991   305.4'88968'092 — dc20   91-29170
[B]   CIP

I dedicate this book to my loving mother

Emma Mutsi Tsimatsima, formerly
Merafe, born Makgothi

and to my sons
Matshwene Everington Moloto
Bakone Justice Moloto
Ndabezitha Godfrey Kuzwayo

and the Youth of my Community.

Contents

Acknowledgements

My thanks to:

The Maggie Magaba Trust and Zamani Soweto Sisters Council for their moral support and willingness to make their contribution when it was needed, and for their sisterhood.

Harry Oppenheimer for making it possible for me to start writing this book – through the sponsorship he gave me.

John and Jane Moores for their sponsorship to complete the book, their warm friendship and generous family hospitality.

Elizabeth Wolpert, for her continued encouragement and moral support and for her patience to listen with a critical ear to my work; and both her and her family for providing their home as a base to work from during my stay in England, and where I met many old and new friends from all over the world.

My sons and their families for their deep understanding and acceptance of all my efforts and commitments.

Nadine Gordimer for accepting my first request to assess my work and her encouragement: 'Ellen I am pleasantly surprised by what you have written – go ahead and allow no one to interfere in your style of work!'

Bessie Head for graciously dropping everything to meet me at very short notice when I was passing through Serowe.

Ros de Lanerolle and The Women's Press team for accepting to publish my book on first request, and their tremendous support, guidance and patience.

Marsaili Cameron, my editor, whose sensitivity and understanding helped me through the process of writing this book.

Robin Lee for his professional contribution and support at the beginning when I struggled to see my direction.

The University of Witwatersrand for giving me free office space to write the book.

The Universities of Fort Hare, Natal, Ngoya and the Witwatersrand for their cooperation in supplying me with research material.

I want to thank all the people I interviewed for their cooperation and willingness to work with me at all times.

All my sisters in exile. I am so aware of their painful separation from their families and country.

Last but by no means least – Dorcas Kepi Ramphomane, my personal secretary. For her commitment, support and understanding – particularly at the moment when I was under pressure against time and production of work.

Preface
Nadine Gordimer

Ellen Kuzwayo is history in the person of one woman. Fortunately, although she is not a writer, she has the memory and the gift of unselfconscious expression that enable her to tell her story as no-one else could.

It is a story that will be both exotically revealing and revealingly familiar to readers. Ellen Kuzwayo's life has been lived as a black woman in South Africa, with all this implies. But it is also the life of that generation of women anywhere – in different epochs in different countries – who have moved from the traditional place in home and family system to an industrialised world in which they had to fight to make a place for themselves. Perhaps the most striking aspect of this book is the least obvious. It is an intimate account of the psychological road from the old, stable, nineteenth century African equivalent of a country squire's home to the black proletarian dormitories of Johannesburg. Living through this, Ellen Kuzwayo emerges not only as a brave and life-affirming person; she represents in addition a particular triumph: wholeness attained by the transitional woman. In her personal attitudes, her innate fastidiousness, her social ease, she seems one of the last of the old African upper-class-Christianised, at home in European culture but not yet robbed of land and pre-conquest African culture. Yet in her break with the traditional circumscription of a married woman's life, her braving of her society's disapproval of divorce and finally her move to the city, she cast away all props. Not only did she learn to stand alone and define herself anew in response to the terrible pressures of a city ghetto; she did so without killing within herself the African woman that she was. Ellen Kuzwayo is not Westernised; she is one of those who have Africanised the Western concept of woman and in herself achieved a synthesis with meaning for all who experience cultural conflict.

That this conflict, in her case, was rawly exacerbated by racist laws in South Africa is self-evident. Yet Ellen Kuzwayo's evolution as a politically active woman, all the way to the final commitment to the black struggle that brought her to prison, is shown to stem from the same instinct to turn toward freedom – and pay the price – that enabled her to become a whole and independent being as a woman. It all began that night she spent sleeping in a graveyard in escape from the tyranny of a bad marriage; from that graveyard she was reborn, as a woman and as a black person.

Her simple but highly observant narrative brings statistics alive. What it means to be black in segregated Johannesburg is conveyed concretely, as if one absorbed it for oneself in a Soweto street. Whether she is doughtily defending the black women whom economic necessity makes into illicit liquor sellers, or explaining the economics of the women potters of her childhood who bartered the vessel for the amount of grain it would hold, her approach is fresh and vivid. And her total honesty is very moving. She is not afraid to reveal an aspect of racism not often admitted by its victims: the moral ambiguity oppression brings. In a touching self-examination she confesses that the conditions of black ghetto life have changed her strong moral convictions about crime. We in turn have to ask ourselves what kind of society brings a woman of this one's strict integrity to say 'I am shocked that as I become older . . . I find that my attitude has been changing. Now, when I read in the press about the theft of thousands of rands by blacks . . . I often express the desire that they are not discovered.'

We are shocked, too; not by Ellen Kuzwayo, who 'would never (herself) take anyone's belongings', but by South Africa.

This book is true testimony from a wonderful woman. For myself, she is one of those people who give me faith in the new and different South Africa they will create.

Nadine Gordimer
June 1984

Foreword
Bessie Head

When the [Afrikaner] Nationalist government first came to power in 1948, they were welcomed in a strange way by black people:

'We prefer the Boer,' they said.

This was said not with any affection for the Boer [Afrikaner], but because he would be a kind of clarifier of the situation in South Africa. The Boer was preferred to the hypocritical English of whom it was said they smiled at you with their front teeth and chewed you with their back teeth. The Boer would hate nakedly, would express his evil and prejudice nakedly and would be a blunt, brutal final death on the land. There would be no half measures. Indeed this was so. With the triumph of Afrikaner Boer power, notices of separate amenities for white and black appeared overnight in public places; a day previously black people had sat wherever they pleased in a bus. Now they were abruptly informed by the driver to move to the back of the bus. It was to be a history of skin colour; skins were to be constantly legislated for, the white skin being a passport to paradise and many privileges; the black skin being a kind of rhinoceros hide at which are hurled tear gas, batons, bullets and ferocious police dogs.

The autobiography of Ellen Kuzwayo puts aside the rhinoceros hide, to reveal a people with a delicate nervous balance like everyone else. No calculation is ever given to the price black people have had to pay for thirty-six years of Boer rule. The documentation of human suffering in this book is terrible. It is as though a death is imposed on people by the ruling white race and black people constantly struggle to survive under this pall of doom. But at the end of the book one feels as if a shadow history of South Africa has been written; there is a sense of triumph, of hope in this achievement and that one has read the true history of the land, a history that vibrates with human compassion and goodness.

Ellen Kuzwayo's lifespan covers two major eras. First comes the era of her youth when, for black people, she could still feel southern Africa as one cultural unit of traditional moral codes and values and where most black people were rural people who lived on the land as farmers. Her family benefits from a special form of land tenure common to many Barolong clans at the turn of the century whereby the chiefs had divided the land into private farms while technically owning a final protecting right over these farms. In reality the old order has been disrupted and she represents a new generation that is an harmonious blending of traditional courtesies and Christian values. Her youth and education in such institutions as Lovedale College equip her for the beautiful contribution she makes during her lifetime. As a young girl she is taught to serve, not only her immediate family circle but also the passer-by on the highway who might be hungry. Colleges such as Lovedale and Fort Hare were under the control of missionaries and the education was of a high quality. From this educated class of black people, both men and women, there are the first stirrings of political activity, but with a very broad base. It was felt that tribalism was a danger to the black community and that the leadership should be chosen on the basis of merit and not ethnicity. The women accepted a two-fold role, to liberate themselves from a traditional heritage of inferiority and to support the men on issues of national liberation.

The abrupt break Ellen Kuzwayo experiences from an early rural background to the broken disjointed chaos of the slums and shacks of the townships of Johannesburg follows a pattern experienced by many black people. The men are forced off the land to earn money in the mines to pay poll tax. Starving women of the rural areas follow the men to the city and survive precariously, brewing beer or working in domestic service. Of Johannesburg, Soweto, she writes:

'. . . it is not easy to live and bring up children in a community robbed of its traditional moral code and values; a community lost between its old heritage and culture and that of its colonists.'

All the headline news is here, the desperate eruptions in Soweto, the bashings, the shootings, the bannings, the detentions and the mass murder of school children in Soweto during the 1976 unrests. Since the rhinoceros hide is put to one side one often puts the book down in agitation, finding it impossible to believe that people could endure such terrific suffering. The truth is the human physical frame cannot endure unnatural states of torture, unnatural states of detention. Ellen Kuzwayo's son, Justice Bakone, is involved in a black consciousness literacy programme. For this community service he is banned to a desolation in Mafikeng and only allowed to speak to one person at a time. He breaks down inwardly. He finds solitude impossible to bear.

During Mrs Kuzwayo's own detention for five months in 1976, we learn that there are two forms of detention for political prisoners. She was detained under Section 10 and allowed newspapers, letters and fresh food from outside prison. Then there's Section 6. One just walks into it and is bashed about by the security police from wall to wall, knocked to the ground, and so on. This is done to young girls aged twelve. One day she heard the terrified inmates of Section 6 sing their Sunday school song: 'Amazing Love'. I cannot see a Lord in the sky who will provide that amazing love, but I can see people providing it for people. That's what this book is all about. Books like these will be the Bible one day for the younger generations.

Bessie Head
1984

Ellen Kuzwayo's career

29 June 1914, birth of Ellen Kate, only daughter of Phillip Serasengwe and Emma Mutsi Merafe

c.1916 her parents divorce; she is brought up on her grandparents' (Jeremiah and Segogoane Makgothi) farm at Thaba Patchoa with her mother, aunts and cousins

1920 Death of both grandparents

1921 Mother marries Abel Tsimatsima; they continue living on farm

1922 Birth of half-sister, Maria Dikeledi

1927 To Thaba'Nchu to live with her mother's youngest sister, Blanche, while she attends St Paul's School, where she passes standards 5 and 6

1930 To boarding school, St Francis' College, Mariannhill, Natal

1930 Mother dies

1932 To Adams College, Durban

1933 Graduates as lower primary school teacher; step-father remarries to Aunt Blanche

1935 Graduates as higher primary school teacher

1936 To Lovedale College; first visit to natural father in Pimville, Johannesburg

1937 First teaching post at Inanda Seminary in Natal; nervous breakdown, returns to live with step-father and Aunt Blanche

1938 Teaches at St Paul's School, Thaba'Nchu

1938 Aunt Blanche forces her to leave home; she moves first to live with her father in Johannesburg, then to Heilbron to live with Aunt Elizabeth; remains until 1940

1939 Maria marries Thari Pilane, son of Chief Ofentse Pilane of Saulspoort

1940 On a visit to Maria, meets Ernest Moloto

1941 Marriage to Moloto and lives in Rustenburg

1942 Birth of son, Everington Matshwene

1944 Birth of second son, Justice Bakone

1946 Seriously ill following miscarriage, marriage breaks down; temporary residence with mother-in-law in Legkraal; on return, flees to Johannesburg to live with father, leaving sons behind

1946 Secretary of Youth League of ANC

1947–53 Teaches at Orlando East, living first with father, then with uncle in Orlando

1947 Divorces

1949–51 Involvement in film *Cry the Beloved Country*, plays a Skokian Queen

1949 Meets Godfrey Kuzwayo (G.R.)

1950 Marries G.R.; they live in Kliptown

1951 Birth of third son, Godfrey

1953–5 Trains as a social worker at Jan Hofmeyr School of Social Work; fellow students include Winnie Mandela and Pumla Finca

1956 First post as social worker for Johannesburg City Council

1957–62 Working for Southern African Association of Youth Clubs, Johannesburg

1958 Eldest son comes to live with Ellen, following the divorce of his father from his second wife

1961 First visit to London

1963 Appointment at YWCA Dube centre

1964–76 General Secretary of YWCA Transvaal region

1964 Second son comes to live with Ellen illegally

1965 Death of second husband, G.R. Kuzwayo

1966 Bakone expelled from Fort Hare for political involvement

1968 Bakone again expelled from Fort Hare

1969–71 involvement of Bakone in black consciousness movement, forms friendship with Steve Biko and Barney Pityana

1969 E. to New York as representative of YWCA congress

1971 Bakone banned to Mafikeng

1972 Bakone marries

1974 E's family dispossessed of farm under Group Areas legislation

1976 E. accepts post in School of Social Work, University of Witwatersrand; following Soweto unrest, is appointed a member of Committee of Ten, and becomes a founder Board member of Urban Foundation

1977–8 Detained for five months at Johannesburg Fort; released March without having been charged

1978 Appointed consultant to Zamani Soweto Sisters Council (umbrella body of Soweto women's self-help groups)

1979 Appointed Chairwoman of Maggie Magaba Trust

1980 Appointed Treasurer of A re Godiseng Chelete Basadi;
awarded Diploma in Advanced Social Work Practice
1984 Appointed first President of Black Consumer Union

Principal legislation affecting the black community, and chronology of major events

1910 Act of Union; Britain hands over the administration of South Africa's four provinces to the local white population, leading to further restrictions on black people and the removal of all parliamentary rights

1912 African National Congress (originally named Native National Congress) formed

1913 Native Land Act; attempts to issue women with passes on the same basis as men lead to massive protests

1936 Native Land and Trust Act fixes the distribution of land on a permanent basis, with 13 per cent being allocated to the African majority

1943 ANC Youth League formed

1950 Group Areas Act passed to continue and extend racial segregation; Suppression of Communism Act passed, providing for the banning of activists and outlawing many forms of opposition to apartheid

1951 Bantu Authorities Act provides for setting up bantustan structures

1952 Defiance Campaign against Unjust Laws launched by ANC and South African Indian Congress

1955 Freedom Charter adopted by the Congress of the People

1956 20,000 women protest in Pretoria against the extension of passes to African women

1956–61 Treason Trial of 156 leaders of the Congress, all eventually found not guilty of high treason; bus boycotts in Alexandra, Johannesburg and Evaton on the Rand

1959 International anti-apartheid movement is launched in response to ANC call for a worldwide boycott of apartheid; Pan-Africanist Congress formed

1960 Sharpeville massacre; ANC and PAC banned

1961 South Africa leaves Commonwealth; launch of armed struggle against apartheid

1962 United Nations General Assembly calls for sanctions against South Africa

1963 Voluntary arms embargo instituted by UN Security Council

1964 Nelson Mandela, Walter Sisulu and six other colleagues are sentenced to life imprisonment at the close of the Rivonia Trial

1966 UN General Assembly condemns apartheid as a 'crime against humanity'

1973 Wave of strikes by black workers

1976 Internal Security Act passed, introducing even harsher measures than those already in existence under the Terrorism Act and other legislation; protests against Bantu Education by school students in Soweto develop into a nationwide uprising

1977 Steve Biko dies in detention; banning of 18 black consciousness and other anti-apartheid organisations; mandatory arms embargo imposed by UN

1980 Launch of renewed national campaign for the release of Nelson Mandela; countrywide boycotts of apartheid education by school and college students; wave of industrial and community-based protests

1981 Countrywide resistance to the regime's celebrations of 20 years of the apartheid Republic

1983 Formation of United Democratic Front as umbrella grouping for anti-apartheid organisations throughout South Africa

1984 Nationwide resistance to the introduction of a new constitution, incorporating a tricameral parliament, which continues to exclude the African majority from all political power including citizenship rights

PART ONE

Soweto

1
Coming Back Home

Section 10(i)(a)

6761/78

Johannesburg Fort
P/Bag 748
Johannesburg
26–09–78

Darling Mama,

It was so wonderful to see that familiar handwriting. 'Twas like I've really come back home. Thank you Mama for the message, so soothing, so inspiring. And needless to say, the Baby Oil and swabs. I think that's exactly what I needed – real cleansing – what the intellectuals would call spade work on my face. I'm happy to tell you that my face looks much better. Brighter, feels fresh and alive. Like Sis Gladys said when she first saw me, 'Ungathi uvuka emlotheni' ('As if you'd slept in an ash heap').

Except for the natural consequences following the denial of basic human needs, viz. Fresh Air, Sunshine, Essential Vitamins, Communication, Love, Movement, Security, to name but a few, I remained unscathed. Mama, I'm happy to tell you that it's wonderful to be out of a situation where you suddenly believe it is a privilege to be alive. Where your life ceases to be your God-given Right. The inhumanity of man against man is as old as man himself. It dates as far back as Cain and Abel, Judas Iscariot and Jesus Christ . . .

I don't have to tell you how life is at the Fort. You've been here before and should be acquainted with the daily routine. All I can say is I am at home. Enjoying the clean, peaceful atmosphere prevailing in this place.

I deliberately create a mental block when I have to think of psychological problems, insecurity etc. that must be affecting my child. You are a social worker, you know what effect bearing my absence from him must be having on him. But like I was taught: Take it to the Lord in Prayer . . ..

3

It's good to read papers again and be able to catch up with many issues. Among others, I have since learnt I'm now a Plural. I've had to catch up fashion-wise too, so don't you worry, I've got a pair of tight-fitting pants too. They call it *Potsotso* I hear. I hear everything has gone so crazy: they wear flared dresses/skirts with petticoats longer than dresses, pencil heels with white ankle socks, *onderbaait-jies* [waistcoats] on top of jackets. Everything seems so reversed. I really got lost when Lindy (little sister) wrote to me last week in an earnest attempt to help me catch up with the syllabus.

How is the family: Buti Ntshwene and fam., Bakone & Tembu Bobo? Give them my regards. I thought Ousi Matantase would be having yet another grandchild by now. I think I must write to T.J. and ask for 'conception leave', then I can come back and have the baby here. Do you think he'll get a treat? [i.e. a shock].

So long K, stay as sweet as you are. I'm keeping courage, for that's my duty and my obligation.

Lovingly,

Debs

N.B. Pardon the scratching Tu! [Please!]

Where is home for a black person in South Africa? For Debra Nikiwe Matshoba, the writer of this letter, home in September 1978 was the Johannesburg Fort, where she was in detention under Section 10 of the Terrorism Act, perhaps the most cruel of the security laws of the country. This was her second term of detention. Earlier she had been held under Section 6, where you are held incommunicado, or in solitary confinement. Now she was under Section 10, where she was allowed contact with the outside world, and she found this a much more acceptable detention; hence her sharing in paragraph three: 'All I can say is that I am at home. Enjoying the clean, peaceful atmosphere prevailing in this place.'

Debra was a member of the Young Women's Christian Association youth club when I was General Secretary of the Association from 1964 to 1976. She was an active and committed member, and in the course of time became Chairman [sic] of the Youth Department of the YWCA. In these early years, although a cheerful person and an asset to the Association in many ways, Debra did not display any special courage or strength. These qualities surfaced at the time of her detention when she was no more Debra Matshoba but Debra Mabale, married and the mother of a lovely bouncy boy aged between two and three years.

When she wrote this letter to me, in reply to a message of support I had sent her shortly after my own release from prison, her husband was also in detention and the care of her child was out of her control. What strength, what courage, to write a letter so carefree yet strong, casual but meaningful, joyful but very sad. She writes, 'I deliberately create a mental block when I have to think of the psychological problems, insecurity, etc. that must be affecting my child.' Think for a moment of what lies behind these words. And humour too, during a period so full of different strains and tensions. 'I'm now a Plural' – a strange sentence, I'm sure, to anyone unfamiliar with South African society, but it made me laugh. The government, for as long as I can remember, has always had a special department to administer matters pertaining to the black people in South Africa. The first one, during the United Party rule of the 1930s and 1940s was known as the 'Native Affairs Department'. When the Nationalist Party took over in 1948, they changed the name to the 'Bantu Administration Department' in an attempt, I suppose, to establish themselves and to make their presence and image felt. I can only suspect that the short spell of life this tag enjoyed was because the black people ridiculed the name, as the word 'bantu' means 'people' regardless of their status, religion, sex or race. Then came the 'Department of Plural Relations', followed now by 'Co-operation and Development'. Over a century, black people have had at least three different labels: 'Natives', 'Bantu' and even 'Plurals'. Does it make sense to you? I hope it does.

Other changes in fashion brought Debra an easier way of laughing. I always enjoyed her reflections on the difficulties of keeping up with the ever-changing styles of dress outside. The only reference she makes which may be incomprehensible outside this country is the comment about asking 'TJ' (the Minister of Justice) for 'conception leave'. This is a sick joke about the migrant labour system, whereby many black men spend their working lives in cities, compelled to leave their wives behind in the country. The few weeks a year spent at home are referred to as 'conception leave'.

It is a letter I treasure. Here, in a few words, are the strength, calibre and outstanding personality of many black women – women who have been detained under extremely brutal and frightening conditions but who have emerged like tested steel, their character and courage somehow untouched by bitterness and deep-seated frustration.

Debra had another home apart from Johannesburg Fort. She lived at Kagiso, an African township in the Krugersdorp district in the western areas of Johannesburg. Kagiso is about 18 miles from Soweto and both these townships fall under the jurisdiction of the West Rand Administration Board, an extension of the government at local level. What kind of home was that? This township has many things in common with Soweto, my own home. Our poverty is the same; our unemployment problem is the same; our insecurities are the same; our harassment is the same; our anger is the same.

Some call it a ghetto. Is it a ghetto? You can size it up for yourself. I have lived here for the last 27 years. With all its imperfections and shortcomings, and they are many, it is home to me. Soweto is a huge complex, spread over 32 square miles of endless, monotonous rows of predominately three-roomed, matchbox-like houses; all dull greyish colour. In recent years it has been interspersed here and there by some beautiful and comparatively large homes built by private owners on 99-year leases. It is situated approximately 18 miles south-west of the glittering centre of Johannesburg. The name 'Soweto' is derived from this geographic location, its full name is 'South Western Townships'. It is made up of at least 20 townships, each divided by just a street, and very difficult to distinguish one from the other, even by the residents of Soweto themselves.

I have seen it established and develop to its bursting maturity. Over the years I have seen the miseries caused by its appallingly inadequate facilities: very unreliable electrification, for example, and continually bursting water pipes, even during the severe droughts of the 1980s. Its very streets are in a pitiful state, except for the few main tarred arteries which carry the heavy commercial traffic, including police and army vehicles, and which link together the municipal offices. These offices are under the management of a small number of white officials who live in beautiful Johannesburg and have to travel every day to work. Other commuters into Soweto include doctors and schoolmasters, along with a few other notables who man the prisons and other related institutions. Most commuting, however, is done in the other direction, away from Soweto into Johannesburg.

This is Soweto, an immense jungle born out of a few scattered locations of the early 1920s which housed the first black job-seekers who were drawn to the small mining town of Johannesburg from the late nineteenth century. Among these communities I remember

Pimville, Western Native Township, Sophiatown and several others which mushroomed on the outskirts of some of the areas of Johannesburg during its early years.

Orlando East, established in 1930, was the beginning and foundation of the present Soweto. This township marked the introduction of the systematic implementation of the 'Group Areas' legislation – legislation which defined 'no-go' areas for black and coloured people and so cemented the system of apartheid. From its failure to provide basic community needs, such as proper electrification, adequate sewerage and rainstorm drainage, as well as well-built, tarmacadamed streets, the residents of that community have always looked on it as a permanent camp and overnight dormitory for the supposedly 'temporary' labour force for the ever-growing city of Johannesburg. Black people have always been aware of the authorities' rationale that blacks are sojourners in the cities of South Africa who come to work temporarily and return 'home' in due course to some 'homeland'. It is a strange view to say the least – particularly when the 'homelands' are completely foreign and unknown to the vast majority of the black people involved, who have been born and brought up in the cities. This way of thinking, however, has made it impossible over the years for the South African authorities to recognise and accept the universal truth that the place and date of any person's birth determines that person's citizenship, domicile and nationality in any normal country.

It was Orlando East, then, which received the first black people to be gradually removed from inner Johannesburg under the cloak of 'clearing the slums' from the city. In this way, the section of the population earning the lowest wages was removed at least 10 miles away from their place of employment. No thought was given by the authorities as to what this extra distance from the city would eventually mean in terms of rands and cents to the people removed. No thought was given, either, to the likely effects of such 're-settlements' on the peace and stability of the country.

As the Group Areas legislation took its course in the 1950s, the authorities became so relentlessly committed to its implementation that they disregarded the values associated with basic human rights. Where then were the 'western' standards which the rulers of this country claim to uphold? Where were the Christian principles which are propounded from pulpits every Sunday? They dispossessed all the black Sophiatown residents of their homes without one thought for those who held title deeds for the land where their houses stood.

All residents were removed with their tenants to new, smaller and poorer structures on 30-year leases. Similar 'removals' from other parts of Johannesburg were effected. Such forced removals resulted in all those people congregating and settling in this massive area of Soweto, which has a population estimated at 2–2½ million, congested in these 32 square miles. Such 'removals' have become the order of the day and the way of life for the remover and the removed alike.

In this complex children are born and families live, under very difficult conditions. It is from here that the majority of parents leave every morning, some of them as early as four o'clock, and come back home late in the evening. Many arrive home as late as half past seven in the evening because of inadequate railway and bus services as well as limited, unsafe taxi services. Most parents leave their children sleeping; they can only hope that they will adhere to the instructions and guidance they leave them.

The 'ideal' that mothers should not accept employment or at least not full-time employment until their children are of a particular age is a luxury in a community where the average monthly wage for men is between 200 and 350 rands a month. (This is the official figure; my own experience leads me to think it a very generous estimate.) Within the first week of the month, this meagre wage dwindles fast into rent and electricity accounts which never come to less than R75. The basic monthly food bill comes to at least R95; and this is a true example of living from hand to mouth: the food in such a home is mainly mealie-meal [maize porridge], one vegetable a week, fresh or sour milk every other day, and other basic needs like fuel, water, soap. The cheapest monthly third-class ticket to work is R15. The rest must cover essentials such as medical charges, children's school uniform, school and book fees, as well as shoes and warm clothes in winter for the family. The replacement of other necessities, such as household linen, becomes a luxury. There is never money left for entertainment, and there may also be endless admonishment from the priest for unpaid church dues.[1]

Poverty on this scale co-exists with a white standard of living that is among the highest in the world. The truth is that South Africa contains at least two social systems. Take education, for example. From its inception, the so-called National Education system has catered almost exclusively for the white population of South Africa. There were a few exceptions: my grandfather, Jeremiah Makgothi, for example, along with several others who received their education during those early years at one mission school or another proved that, given an opportunity, they were quite capable of achieving what boys and girls of their age group in other racial groups were capable of achieving. My grandfather qualified as a teacher and taught both black and white children in the same classroom in Thaba'Nchu in the Orange Free State towards the close of the nineteenth century, and the heavens did not fall down.

Just stop and think where South Africa would be today in terms of demonstrating to the international scene the realities of different racial groups living as one nation in one country, if the early rulers of this country had not become greedy, mean and both selfish and self-centred at the turn of the century and started on discriminatory legislation which has left the whole country in a state of total fear and mistrust, with a future 'too ghastly to contemplate', to quote one-time Prime Minister J.B. Vorster, one of the greatest advocates of the evil system of apartheid.

The education system established exclusively for the white people of South Africa catered fully for the needs and interests of the school population of that community, at least at primary and high school levels. Children coming out of that community of industrialists, professionals, competent well-to-do tradesmen, wealthy merchants in different spheres, small and big business men, had their school fees and books paid for by the state, which also provided them with school meals of one type or another. Except for those children on scattered farms, whose parents organised a school bus, the majority of white children lived within walking distance of their school. When this was not the case, their parents owned at least one car and could easily drop them and pick them up from school when necessary.

Contrast at this point the tensions, fear and uncertainties that black children were, and are still, tormented with. It is very revealing to ponder for a short while over the drop-out rates in the black schools, caused by the inability to pay school and book fees, by the need for school uniform and, at other times, by the complete absence of hard cash to pay bus fares to and from school, or to buy the simplest, cheapest sandwich to eat at school. It may be difficult to believe that during the early 1950s the government saw fit to cancel the school meals scheme which had been in existence for a good while prior to the state's takeover of black education from the missionaries. But it is true. What shame on a country which professes to be Christian.

How can we forget that some of the parents of these black children worked for some of those very wealthy white people? Many of these white families owned more than one car and a very luxurious home; in some cases they even had a car for their children. All these may be noble things to have and do; but they would have been nobler if these employers had paid a living wage to their employees to enable them to afford a better education and home for their families and hopefully a better future for themselves as well as peace and stability for the South African people as a whole.

The discriminatory system of education provided for blacks over generations has changed names in a chameleon-like way according to the whims of each so-called Minister of Education. These changes have been ridiculous at times and extremely annoying at others. As a little girl I started my schooling under the impoverished 'Native Education Department' which some time along the way put on a new cloak – 'Bantu Education' – for a few years, before it assumed yet another cover – this time, 'Department of Education and Training'. The only thing that has remained constant is the government's determination to provide nothing that could rightfully be called national education.

Changes of name have never made any difference to the long-standing problems of the education received by black children in South Africa. These include: overcrowded classrooms; the low standard of the average teacher, both at primary and high-school levels; and the very poor salaries of black teachers over a very long period. The government has talked for a long time about bringing the salaries of people holding the same qualifications up to the same level; but such talk has been repeated too often for too long with no action for anyone to take the talk seriously. In addition, the improvements in teachers' salaries have come too late to make any meaningful impact on the ever-escalating cost of living in recent years.

It is usual in Soweto to find teachers over-burdened with huge classes of 50 to 60 pupils, where they will not find it possible to identify a slow or retarded pupil, let alone have the opportunity to give such a pupil individual attention. The appallingly poor state of the majority of schools, with broken window-panes, unhinged doors and cracked walls, all not conducive to healthy learning, has left much to be desired over many years. The wicked inadequacies and deficiencies of the education system in Soweto led directly to the street unrest of 1976, a dreadful time which I describe in Chapter 3.

All these unwholesome conditions in the homes, schools, places of employment and many other areas affecting the lives of black people have over the years helped to swell a very dangerous mood of tension, anger and great anxiety. Those feelings have been aggravated by the endless arrests of black men, women and children for not having on their person a 'pass' when ordered by police to produce one. In recent years when the authorities have been confronted by the evils arising from 'influx control' legislation, implemented to control the flow of people into industrial urban areas, they have argued that this notorious document is issued for the safety and protection of blacks. The truth is the opposite. Its apt description, in short, is that it is the cornerstone of apartheid together with the hideous Native Land Act of 1913, described by the South African novelist Bessie Head as '[creating] overnight a floating landless proletariat whose labour could be used and manipulated at will, and [ensuring] that ownership of the land had finally and securely passed into the hands of the ruling white race.'[2] It is impossible to go into depth about all this legislation. To blacks the two laws are hell because they break up families, uproot communities and corrupt values and mores as well as destroy the whole culture of black people.

All this is Soweto, my home. Before I turn to take a closer look at the lives of the women, men and children who live, and have lived here, let me go back in history a little. Why do over two million people call this place home? How and why did they come to Johannesburg in the first place? How did black women and men become so dependent on the 'golden city' and, as a result, so vulnerable to legislation by the white rulers?

After the discovery of gold in 1886 on the Witwatersrand and of diamonds in Kimberley, people from different communities streamed into the Johannesburg of that time, which was more or less a temporary mining camp. Men flowed to the mines from the rural areas, and ended up as underground mineworkers. They were employed and housed by the mines in mine compounds; they left their families behind to be cared for by the senior woman in every home. Yet in spite of this process, the close of the nineteenth century found the black people of South Africa living under more favourable conditions than at the present day. They lived on land which they owned and which they tilled and cultivated to grow crops. Part of this land was used as grazing fields by those communities which reared domestic animals. With those families which remained in the care of housewives while husbands had gone to earn money in the cities, the whole responsibility fell on the shoulders of the senior woman in the family. However, she had the security of cultivating the land, looking after the sheep, goats, cattle and chickens owned by the family. Old and tested farming methods, the settled, stable communities, the common code of ethics observed, the heritage of communal living of black people; all these, together with the complete absence of removals of communities, or 're-settlements' as they are commonly described by the powers of today, gave the families of migrant labourers some security and stability in compensation for the very meagre wages of their husbands in the mines and the long absences of the men from home.

The struggle of these women was heightened in the 1930s when community land was declared 'Trust Land' and removed from the control of black people, culling of cattle was introduced, and communities were forced to move willy-nilly from one area to another. The endless, complex legislation which accompanied all these new and foreign developments gnawed at the very fibre of the stable code of ethics at the heart of the black people's lives. The pangs and strains of those far-reaching changes fell on the shoulders of the women of the rural communities where fathers, sons, brothers, uncles and husbands had left to sell their labour in the towns and cities of South Africa in order to earn hard cash to pay poll-tax, the scourge of generations in the black community.

Poll-tax was also extended after the colonists found that the 1913 Native Land Act did not immediately provide them with the results they wanted. They had banked on the now landless natives rushing to the mines and so providing an inexhaustible source of cheap labour; but these hopes were frustrated when many natives remained in the country to carry out their farming in the best way they could under the new, harsh conditions. The introduction of poll-tax at this time forced the men either to pay the tax in hard cash or go to prison. The only answer was to leave the country and sell their labour in the mines. The whole burden of looking after the homestead, livestock, ploughing and the family was shifted to the womenfolk in the villages. It has stayed that way to this day.

The black woman, who through the centuries had been viewed by the white state as unproductive in industry, as totally dependent on her male counterpart, as helpless, unintelligent to the point of being useless and stupid – the woman who much against her will had resigned herself to being labelled a 'minor' by the state – was suddenly plunged into a situation of accepting numerous roles of responsibility. Without warning, training or any sort of preparation, she became overnight mother, father, family administrator, counsellor, child-minder, old-age caretaker and overall overseer of both family and neighbourhood affairs in a community which had been totally deprived of its active male population.

The long period of nine months spent by mine labourers away from home began to take its toll on the life-style of the communities of these miners. The absence of a father in the home, particularly where there were male children, denied the children a model of how men lived in the family and community, as well as male guidance and support. It is both difficult and shocking to imagine what effect this inhuman situation had on the lives of the wives of these men, as well as on the offspring of such a community. The loss of companionship and normal fulfilment of husbands' and wives' duties and requirements in any family for three-quarters of the year for several continuous years, the frustration and hardships resulting from such absence, are frightening to imagine.

Overnight, the values of the past became legend to the point of being ridiculed as old-fashioned and out-dated. People began to question certain long-standing practices which had been taken as the law and the truth and thus become the cornerstone of the moral fibre of the black community. The absence of their men from home for long periods did not make any sense to their families. Some women were very bitter and torn by the absence of their husbands who had gone to the 'golden' or 'diamond' cities, some for good. The drastic changes in the way of life of their communities, brought about by the complex foreign legislation in their land of birth, without any consultation with those they saw as their leaders, left black people without direction or a pattern to follow: a tragic state of affairs for any people.

They were bewildered and deeply upset by the complete disregard of the government for the black leaders. With the coming of the white man to South Africa, the titles of *Kgosi*, *Morena* and *Nkosi* (all meaning king) were reduced to 'Chief', an inferior status commanding far less dignity and respect. With the passing of time, these once recognised and respected heads of communities, whose power was equal to that of kings in other parts of the world, were subtly and gradually undermined. As the legislation took root in the black communities, the status of these heads was reduced to irrelevancy and meaninglessness, most of them being seen as puppets who could be easily replaced by a man chosen by the government – and the government's choice, of course, would not be based on line of birth or on the will of the people.

All these factors posed very serious questions and problems for the womenfolk in rural areas. The responses came in an endless flow of black women to the cities in search of their husbands, and fathers of their children, even, at times, in search of their missing sons.

The first census in this country, in 1896, reveals that during that time there was a population of 102,000 in Johannesburg, and that half of that population was black. The ratio of men to women was 12 to one.[3] The years that followed saw many more women enter cities, although they did so despite some stringent influx regulations. With their lack of education and their unfamiliarity with a foreign language and culture, black women found themselves at a great disadvantage when they tried to sell their labour in the cities. The first problem they were faced with was accommodation: the first few who came solved it by being employed in domestic work, where they were provided with a room, usually somewhere at the back of the employer's dwelling place.

The problem of accommodation was real. This gave rise to multi-racial communities in areas like Vrededorp which were then known as 'coolie' or 'Kaffir' locations, and the Burghersdorp brickfields. Despite the unhygienic conditions in these locations, they provided shelter for the many homeless newcomers to Johannesburg in those years. The emphasis of life was shifted to basic material needs with little regard given to the cultural and moral values which hitherto had been the cornerstone of healthy, wholesome living in the rural setting.

Like the men, the black women benefited temporarily from these slum dwellings; but the question of unemployment still remained unanswered, as there were not enough white homes to absorb the ever-growing numbers of black women who were pouring into the cities in search of domestic work, the only employment open to them. They saw this as the only suitable response to the scourge of rural impoverishment.

As we shall see in the next chapter, the problem was to call forth a number of partial solutions, some legal and some illegal. But the attempts at solutions have led in their turn to further intolerable problems. The black people of South Africa have been evicted and to this day have still not attained their rightful homes.

References

1.The minimum 'Household Subsistence Wage' was calculated to be R272.77 for a family of five in March 1984, according to the Institute of Planning Research, University of Port Elizabeth.
2.Bessie Head's Foreword to *Native Life in South Africa* by Sol T. Plaatje (Ravan Press, Johannesburg, 1982) This powerful indictment of the beginnings of apartheid was first published in London in 1916.
3.Pauline Morris, *A History of Black Housing in South Africa*, p.17 (Robprint, Johannesburg, 1981).

2
Hunger Knows No Laws

It is not easy to live and to bring up children in a community
deprived of its traditional moral code and values – a community lost
between its old heritage and that of its colonisers.

The black people of the whole of Southern Africa had a very
strong code of traditional moral values, most of them enshrined and
intertwined in their languages. These languages were very rich in
proverbs. It is striking to observe how many proverbs were held in
common by societies which lived at a great distance from each
other. The same sayings, for example, were familiar to the Basotho
of Lesotho, locked in the southern tip of Southern Africa, and to
the Bapedi people in the extreme north of Southern Africa.
Similarity of proverbs runs through all the different communities of
South Africa; Zulus, Batswana, Xhosas, Swazis, Tshongas and
several others. Proverbs to a very great extent were regarded as an
undefined code of law. Many are frequently used to this day and
still retain their social and ethical importance. The few examples
given below in Setswana are used in all black communities south of
the Sahara.

'*Motho ke motho ka motho yo mongoe*' means 'No man is an
island'. The communal way of life of the black people of this region
is based upon this saying. In the black community a neighbour is
seen as very important and so is the neighbourhood. In my own
neighbourhood of Soweto, Orlando West Extension, as I walk
down my street, I acknowledge the adults, youths and everybody in
that street, without making any special effort or wasting any time.
The recognition of the person you meet is generally wrapped up in
an informal 'dumela', 'saubona', 'molo', 'absheni', all words of
greeting, very simple and casual, yet very far-reaching in their
meaning as far as the relationship between the people is concerned.

In Soweto, houses are not allocated according to the class or
status of residents. It is not unusual for Dr X to find himself having

as his neighbour Mr Y, the road-digger. This is the accepted way of life in Soweto, it is a reality. When tragedy hits Mr Y's family, without thinking twice Dr X puts his jacket on and goes to stand by his neighbour, even if just to hold his hand. In the case of death, he may do this several times until after the burial. This is us as a people, as a community. If there is death in my immediate neighbourhood, on my return from work, after doing one or two household chores, it is common practice for me to find out from my nextdoor neighbour if she has been to call on the bereaved family. If not, we may go together, or I may join the women of my street to be with that family for half an hour or so.

Many proverbs carry great social and ethical meaning: '*Se epele monkaoena mosima, etla re gongwe o wele mo go ona,*' for example. This lacks an equivalent in English so I am compelled to translate it: 'Do not lay a trap for your neighbour, lest you fall in it yourself.' Another is '*Di tloga ba apari di ya ba folleding*,' which means 'Pearls worn by princesses today may be worn by their maids in future.' And then everywhere is found this universal one: '*Moja morago Kgosi*', meaning 'He who laughs last, laughs longest'.

These very meaningful statements are gradually falling out of use and losing their original meaning because of the unending forced movement of the black communities. This state of affairs has been aggravated by the continued discriminatory legislation levelled against the black people of South Africa, legislation which has uprooted communities, separated families, estranged siblings and left the black nation landless, homeless, stateless and dispossessed of all its heritage.

The continued unsettling of communities in later years through migratory labour, combined with the effects of influx control legislation which makes it illegal for the children and wives of migrant labourers to be with their fathers and husbands in the cities, has led to a situation where the black people of this country sometimes seem reduced to a nation of villains and scoundrels. The women often find themselves literally left 'holding the baby' as they are left at home with complete responsibility for looking after the aged and the young as well as for the general upkeep of the home. This responsibility is a heavy one; and very few women have escaped at some time in their lives, in one form or another, confronting the pain, reality and challenges of this task.

In Part 2 of this book, I shall describe in detail how my own life and the lives of my children have been affected by the laws and restrictions imposed on the black people of South Africa. For the moment, let me give an example of how family life can be disrupted and destroyed and children made the helpless victims of inhuman laws.

As a comparatively well informed woman in my community, I hoped, after divorce, to enable my young sons to leave Rustenburg, where they had a miserable existence after my departure, and come and live with me in Johannesburg. From the early stages of my planning I had always counted on the help of my own father who was a civic leader of ability in Pimville, one of the black townships which fell under the jurisdiction of the 'Non-European Affairs Department' of Johannesburg City Council. I had seen him many a time successfully negotiate 'legal status' for so-called 'illegal residents' in Johannesburg. At that time – in the 1950s – there was talk about the laws being made even more stringent for entry into the cities and urban areas in this country.

In addition to my father's ability as a civic leader, I was also counting on the Children's Act legislation which in general provided that children of a certain age be placed in their mother's care. Using my father, I set the ball rolling in applying for my two sons to come and live with me. They were aged four and two years, respectively. All efforts with my father on my side failed for the two-year-old. I appealed in vain. The reality then came home to me: that Children's Act was intended for white children only; further, black children are not children in the eyes of the government.

The loophole which allowed my elder son to settle in Johannesburg was that, as custom demanded, I had come to my father's home to have my first child. This custom is both considerate and sensible: black people believe that a young mother must go to her home for the birth of her first child, so that her parents can support and nurse her during the new experience of childbirth. For this reason my first son was born at Bridgeman Memorial Hospital, a maternity hospital of repute in those years. (Like many others, it disappeared under the heavy wheels of Group Areas legislation.) The younger one, however, had not been born in Johannesburg; and all efforts to bring him to the city failed. That is why, at some time during this fruitless struggle, we agreed that he should come to Johannesburg to live with me, his mother, in my new home, illegally, 'influx control' or no 'influx control'.

That is how desperate we were. Think of it. A young child denied by the state his right to receive his mother's tender loving care –

care which would help him grow and mature into a worthy citizen of the community. Very many mothers and children in Soweto, for a variety of reasons and under different circumstances, have at one time or another come face to face with this problem. In trying to solve it, some of them have met with some success; but the majority have knocked their heads against a hard granite wall. This fact has resulted in many of the children of such families becoming so deeply hurt and frustrated that, in desperation, they have ended up lawless and work-shy. In some cases they have graduated as hard-boiled criminals – not from choice, but because of force of circumstances.

Legislation which separates communities, categorises huge numbers of people as underdogs and dispossesses citizens has terrible effects on the mores and values of the disadvantaged communities. Large numbers of people have been persistently degraded and driven to crime. In the early years of my life, I had very strong, clear, sharp feelings against crime. As a young girl, for example, I was very critical about thieves, about burglars, about shop-lifters, about everybody who took from others that which did not belong to them. I am shocked that, as I have become older, and much as I would never take anybody's belongings without their permission, I find that my attitude towards these offenders, some of them committing very serious offences, has been gradually changing. Now when I hear, or read in the press, about a big burglary or the theft of thousands of rands by blacks, young or old, men or women, I often express the desire that they will not be caught. I suspect that I am not the only one to find myself changing in this way. It is a change forced on me, certainly not chosen, and it is one I bitterly resent. In the South African situation, I have often had cause to halt and reflect: Who is robbing whom in this country?

Take a mother in domestic service from 6.00 a.m. to 6.00 p.m. or even later, earning barely R80 a month. Is not this a case of exploitation? Would it be surprising if such a mother, with full family responsibilities and the best intentions in the world, should be tempted to make good her needs by stealing from the employer?

Who in this case is the first to display tendencies of theft? Is it employer or employee?

Even as I write this chapter, I want to say in no uncertain terms that crime at all times, and of any kind, is appalling; regardless of who commits it and against whom it is committed. Having said that, I wish to invite the readers of this book to look without prejudice beyond such acts as rape, theft, murder, and others in the category of crime. I would like us to ask ourselves in all sincerity whether hereditary tendencies in individuals are the only explanation for degenerate human behaviour. Have we ever taken into consideration the effects of what we might call 'institutionalised crime' against the black people in South Africa? In my view, institutionalised crime is even more powerful and dangerous than the crime committed by individuals, because such crime is continuously reinforced with one piece of legislation after another to ensure its effectiveness. When crimes are committed through legislation, who can bring the criminal to justice?

The monster that is institutionalised crime takes refuge in its invisibility and in very cleverly worded formulations which conceal its real meaning and sting. It remains hidden for a time because of the cunning way its formulators and interpreters present it to trusting, simple-minded communities whose knowledge and understanding of legal language is always very limited, even amongst the so-called educated black people. Over the years these people have received sufficient education in English and Afrikaans to allow employers to communicate with their employees, but planned by those in authority to fall short of allowing them to understand the implications and ramifications of such legislation.

Go back 70 years when the government of this country passed the hideous law known as the 1913 Native Land Act. This is the fundamental law that underpins apartheid, that designates 87% of the land for whites and only 13% to the vast black majority. The passing of this Act, only three years after Britain had handed political control of the country to the white minority, stimulated the first national black campaigns by the newly founded African National Congress. Over the years, this law has uprooted, outlawed and dispossessed thousands of communities and individual private owners of their heritage, of their rightful possession of land in the country of their birth. Today the families of such communities have been separated and fragmented; and their wealth of cattle, sheep, goats, horses, pigs and poultry has vanished like mist from the surface of the earth. Their children have become more and more emaciated and more vulnerable to endless social diseases, such as tuberculosis, kwashiorkor (a new arrival of the 1950s) gastro-enteritis, dysentry, cholera, long-forgotten bubonic plague, typhoid, and many others; diseases which have maimed tens of thousands and killed at least twice that number. Lime Hill, one of the notorious government resettlements of the 1960s, was exposed in the press at the time as a graveyard for infants and toddlers.

The laws regarding influx control, Group Areas and so-called resettlement of black people were passed under the cloak of the 'security' of the country; in fact, all such laws are formulated to oppress the black people and to deny them freedom of speech, movement and domicile. What greater crime can you ask for? If this is not crime, there has never been life.

In an effort to save themselves as a people, they have sometimes responded in 'criminal' ways to the terrible degradation and humiliation heaped on them. It is a response which white people would also have shown if they had found themselves victims in a similar situation. Why, then, must we be seen as inhuman and ruthless when after years – scores of years – of negotiations and consultations with the rulers of this country, negotiations which have passed unrewarded, we are driven to fight back? The fact and gospel truth is that we are driven to fight with our backs against the wall in an effort to save ourselves from a tragic situation of dispossession and peril.

As I have said, it is not easy to live and to bring up children in a community robbed of its traditional moral code and values: a community lost between its old heritage and culture and that of its colonists. You need to experience the problem to understand its magnitude and seriousness. My limited saving grace in this situation was that I picked on the few values which to me were basic for my daily living as a person and for the very existence of my family, particularly when I battled through life as a widow after my second husband's death in 1965. Before that, I had always been a working woman. I maintained that as one of my basic principles in life; another was to keep and maintain a home in the best way I could afford, to make it *my* home in its structure and tone, for the benefit of my children and myself as well. As a child brought up with a strong Christian background, I clung to the values, ethics and beliefs of that heritage, particularly after my husband's death, when suddenly the Church as an institution did not seem to hold much hope for me.

I shall tell my own story in detail in Part 2 of this book. Now I should like to turn and look at how other black women have managed to survive the horrible conditions thrust on them.

First of all, what about the large numbers of women, whom the first chapter described as flocking to the cities during the early years of the century? What means of survival did they find?

The new 'industry' of washerwomen was born from the desperate need of these black women. The more affluent white families introduced several specialised categories of domestic work: the general worker who carried the major work load in the house, as a cook and general overseer; the cleaner/washerwoman; the ubiquitous nanny (a term used to describe the child-minder). All these jobs were done by women, some of whom received training in their tasks from the mistress of the home. The majority of such workers became extremely proficient in their jobs after several years of service.

Many women remained with their employers for 20 years or more. Some, even now, have served one family for two generations, moving on to the son's or daughter's new family. Some of these workers grew old in one job, earning low wages equivalent to R5 to R10 a month with no provision for a pension at retirement.[1] Most of these early black domestic workers lived all their lives on the employers' premises. If they had husbands or male friends, they lived with them on those premises.

On several occasions, during my time as a social worker, I received urgent phone calls from the city, making enquiries about accommodation for the aged in Soweto. Such requests were invariably from wealthy white employers who had disregarded their responsibility for making provision for their employee's retirement whilst these women were still healthy, strong and relatively young. Such requests could not be met and I still wish to know what happened to such old mothers.

Through my involvement with voluntary welfare work, I have met many old women in similar circumstances. Some of them have been sent by their employers to the notorious 'transit camps' in Soweto. Some employers had made promises to maintain them but have never come back to honour such undertakings. The 'transit camps' are set aside by the West Rand Administration Board for destitute black people in the district of Johannesburg, theoretically as staging posts, on their way to 'resettlement' in a black 'homeland'. Some come from hospitals; some have become 'redundant' to the domestic services or in industry; while others have for one reason or another lost their homes, or never had any, and have ended up homeless, jobless and penniless. The community of Soweto over the years, through different churches and women's organisations, has rendered outstanding service by collecting for these people clothing, food, kitchen utensils and some basic household products like soap, Vaseline and the like. There are two of these camps in Naledi, each housing about 20 to 25 people, men, women and children.

I have listened to heart-breaking stories from some of the inmates there, old men and women, who live under appallingly congested conditions. Most of them receive a negligible amount from a pension fund; and some depend on pitiable savings to provide them with day-to-day supplies. Their salaries, which should have been such as to make it possible to save for rainy days, were so low that they literally lived from hand to mouth. These old people had served their employers with loyalty and showed great love for their employers' children. In return, they were dismissed from their work and discarded to transit camps to be forgotten and to wait for their death with regrets and great bitterness. I was deeply touched by some of these mothers who reported that their employers had solemnly promised to maintain them during their stay at the camp with food and some small allowance, but that the last time they saw their employers was when such arrangements were made; or when the employers dumped them at the 'Native' (or 'Bantu' or 'Plural') Commissioner's office.

These are some examples of the sufferings and endless struggle borne by some of these great mothers of South Africa who have brought up and nurtured children of all communities, sometimes at the sacrifice of their own children. I quote one such mother: 'Struth God, the children I brought up, some of them are doctors today, yes; but not one of them thinks of me today.' Indeed, thousands of black mothers could echo this same statement. Some have cared for white babies from their birth, up to those babies' own child-bearing age. Some have cared for them whilst their parents were out at dinners, bridge games, cinemas or other entertainments of their choice, coming back home at midnight, or long after. For some of these gracious black mothers, this was a weekly duty, for others it was twice a week; for the rest, it could have been, or is, a daily event, depending on the different interests of the parents. I know of cases of black mothers who have remained with white infants aged two to three months over varying periods from one to six months while the parents were overseas on some mission or another. Indeed, some of the leading white men and women in this country are the products of the ingenious hands and minds of the black

'nurse', 'nanny' or 'mother' who has been, and is still, underpaid for
one of the outstanding responsible human services: that is, bringing
up children. This is a task she has undertaken with pride,
responsibility, love, loyalty and respect for both the child and the
parents. Yet how has she been rewarded?

But what happened to the black woman who could not be absorbed
into domestic service in the cities at the end of the nineteenth and
the beginning of the twentieth centuries? The only alternative
occupation which was easy to adjust to because of its nature and
demands was beer-brewing.

At this stage we need to remind ourselves that these black women
came from the country, where some of the accepted practices and
ways of living were seen as malpractices and unacceptable in urban
life. The brewing of beer – the nourishing traditional drink which
for several generations was unfortunately known by the derogatory
name 'kaffir beer' – was an accepted family practice in the rural
setting. It was one of the tasks black mothers and other women of
that community excelled in. It is therefore not really surprising that
brewing became one of the major occupations of many black
women who could not be placed in regular employment in the cities.
I cannot help but marvel today at the negative criticism which was
levelled at the brewers in those years. They were seen as immoral
and debased. As I look back, these questions come to my mind:

To what extent did poor dwelling structures contribute to this
unfortunate image?

Did limited living room space and poor lighting give misleading
impressions?

Did lack of entertainment in black townships, and the desire to
seek out one's racial or tribal group, draw together people of
clashing cultures and educational background? With what effect?

Throughout this period, South African liquor laws banned the
selling of liquor to blacks, except through the special municipal
'beerhalls' – which were to be prime objectives for the young rebels
in the 1976 uprising.

Did prohibition in the black community create the desire for
strong types of beer? Did this in turn make room for more harmful
brews which persisted even after the abolition of prohibition in the
1970s?

Did the inability of black men to bring their families to the mines encourage wives and other women to move unaccompanied to cities? With what effects?

Did the coming of such women alone to the cities make room for deterioration of moral standards in the black urban communities? A deterioration which finally affected even the steady life in the rural setting.

Was this deterioration peculiar to black people? Could this have happened to people of other racial groups, if they had lived under similar conditions?

These questions can be answered fully only if they are dealt with in relation to what happened in the more privileged community, the white community of South Africa.

Let me put my final questions: If the mining industry and the Crown Colony government's municipal corporations had placed human rights before economic gain in amassing their wealth at the peril and detriment of the black population, would that have facilitated better human and race relations in this country? Is there anything that can be done to correct this glaring inhuman error even at this late hour?

The fact of the matter is that liquor sales – often referred to as 'illicit' liquor selling – is still a widespread industry in this community. The types sold range from the regular wines and beer to other more intoxicating drinks like brandy and gin. The people in the lower income group who traded with liquor in the early days had a clientele who preferred home-made beer to any other. It is unfortunate that in their effort to provide their customers with something 'hot' to suit their taste and pocket, the owners of the shebeens after these early days had to use ingredients which gave a real kick to the drink, but which rendered it dangerous and unwholesome. The old *bojaloa*, *joala*, *mqombothi* was, and still is, the best beer, health-wise. The demand for something strong with a kick, however, compelled the brewers to explore other methods of producing the quality of beer wanted by their customers. Many different names have been used for all the types which have been produced over the years. Most of the names of this hot-stuff type of drink are very descriptive, and themselves tell a story.

There was the *Skokian* of old which gave its name to its producers – women called 'Skokian Queens', very successful in their business. To this day I have not been able to determine the meaning of the word *Skokian*. *Machuruchuru*, on the other hand, has the connotation of something which fries quickly. The literal interpretation of *sebapa le masenke* is something 'side by side with corrugated iron'. It is difficult to grasp the meaning here. It could perhaps mean a drink which affects you so much that you have to lean against zinc or corrugated iron. Most of the early dwellings for blacks round the industrial places were shacks, erected with old corrugated iron which was relatively cheap in those years.

Mbamba is a very deadly drink brewed with yeast. Men who have taken this drink over six to twelve months begin to grow very thin hair on the face; the colour of their skin turns dirty grey, and later the skin cracks and peels off. The victims of *mbamba* soon develop swollen feet, and end up with distended abdomens. More often than not, after that stage they do not live long.

Names like *gavini* and *macontsana* are given to some of the brews in Natal. *Mokoko o nchebileng?* is another. The assumption is that after drinking this, the imbibers have queer visions, the most common and constant being a cock which seems to be staring at the intoxicated drinker. Hence the question, *mokoko o nchebileng?*, which means: 'Cock, why are you gazing at me?'

The last one I am going to discuss is *O hamba no bani?*, which means, literally, 'With whom do you go?' The real question is, 'In whose company are you?' The brewers of this drink, I understand, are reluctant to supply it to anyone who is not accompanied. They fear that she or he will have a blackout and will need help to find her or his way home.

There is no doubt that these concoctions have detrimental affects on both the physical and psychological well-being of those who use them. Not for a moment would anyone with the interest and well-being of her or his community at heart defend wholeheartedly those who promote these deadly and undesirable brews. Yet, on the other hand, I find it necessary to try to understand without prejudice what prompted some black women to brew such noxious concoctions. What prompted them to depart from brewing the regular, healthy *mqombothi* or *bojaloa*, which was accepted as a wholesome, refreshing drink?

To arrive at some satisfactory explanation for the change to dangerously strong liquor, we need to look at some of the possible contributing factors of that time. The first among these is prohibition. Black men were not allowed to enter a bottle-store to buy the drink they wanted, be it beer, wine, brandy, gin or any other drink for that matter. The result would be the arrival of the police who would arrest them and put them in jail. This would cost them their jobs as well as earn them criminal records which would tarnish their reputation in the eyes of the law and of prospective employers. Since the open buying of liquor was illegal, with the passing of time the 'illicit' liquor trade thrived and became the lucrative occupation of black women who, as we have seen, had no opportunity earlier in their lives to prepare themselves to enter the open labour market in urban areas.

These women gradually explored new methods of producing what to them and their customers constituted acceptable, stimulating type(s) of beer. It became common practice for them to stock their home-made brewed beer along with regular drinks bought from the bottle stores. However, they did this at the risk of being arrested and fined large sums of money or sentenced to long terms of imprisonment. Persistent arrests created a core of hardened women who in the process, developed their business of 'illicit' trade and gained experience both in brewing and in standing up to the wrath of the police, using defiance, concealment or downright cheating or bribery of the police. Some of the women became experts in this game over the years. Several attained notoriety as 'Skokian Queens' (a title later changed to 'Shebeen Queens' as the trade gained sophistication).

My father's house was 1092 Merafe Street in Pimville, Johannesburg. About two to three houses away lived several of these 'Skokian Queens' who carried out a lucrative beer-brewing business They were also generally seen as immoral and undesirable members of the community. But it was amazing to see the other side of their lives once you came to know them as residents, individuals and ordinary people. Their faces pass through my mind as I write this.

I recall particularly one lady named Motena. She was a lovely person, warm and very orderly in her life as a mother and housewife. Her house was the only shebeen I ever ventured to enter. Except for a few benches for her customers and other guests, there was no other furniture. At the far end of the room was a pile of blankets, which clearly marked the corner used as the bedroom. The blankets were clean and fresh, because they were washed every week, a habit very common among the Basotho people. A piece of string fastened across the corner near the pile of blankets served as a wardrobe, where skirts, trousers and other clothing were hung. At the other end of the room were all the household utensils, which included a number of enamel plates and mugs, a few cups and saucers, a number of shiny spoons and a few different sizes of

three-legged pots, some used for cooking meals, others for boiling
the water used for brewing. There were also a number of empty
shiny jam tins for serving beer to customers or guests. There were
two to three well-built *stoeps* inside the house, like steps, measuring
about one by one-and-a-half yards in size. These served as
cupboards or dressers for the kitchen utensils. The air in this
one-roomed shack was very fresh, from constantly smearing the
smoothly-prepared floor with fresh cow dung. Within the constraints of that one-roomed house, in a yard congested with similar
houses, spilling on to an untarred street which also carried all the
dirty water from all the homes, I have every reason to credit Mama
Motena (Mother Motena – a term of respect for addressing adults in
the black community) with great qualities of cleanliness and
tidiness. She showed great ability in maintaining the clearly defined
boundaries of various room services in that one room. Many black
women in congested urban accommodation share that quality.

As a little girl on a farm, I had lived very closely with Basotho
mothers and fathers who were labourers and handymen on my
maternal grandparents' farm. I had gone to primary school with
some of their children. I had played, quarrelled and even fought
with some of them as youngsters, and had exchanged visits with
them during that period. I had seen similar simple but very clean
homes on the farm, very like Motena's except for the size. The
major difference between the country and urban homes was that
beer was commonly accepted as free food in the former, that is, as
nourishment, whilst in the latter it was regarded more as an
income-generating commodity.

I accepted refreshment in such homes with an open heart,
because of the ever clean and tidy surroundings. My favourite dish
there was a special type of very soft fermented porridge like the
popular *mageu*, the equivalent of offering wine by today's standards
and practice. *Seqhaqhabola* was Motena's most popular dish, which
I enjoyed as much as I used to enjoy it in the homes of those
countryfolk. Occasionally I went to her home at her invitation to
have a mug of fresh *seqhaqhabola*, at other times I asked for it
without apologising. She was a lovely respectable mother who sold
liquor for survival.

Perhaps my father and my step-mother never quite understood
my interest in Motena, although they never questioned it. They
rarely questioned any of my decisions unless it was really necessary.
In such cases, Father raised the issue, while my step-mother kept in

the background. The likelihood is that they recognised Motena's qualities and integrity, and stopped there; while I expressed my appreciation and admiration of her by my visits.

But make no mistake, she was also a very successful liquor seller.

The homes of the beer-brewers were also places of entertainment, particularly for the group of Basotho miners, who were regular weekend visitors. These were the times that I cursed the beer-brewers, Motena included. About sunset on Saturdays we knew that gangs of Basothos would be arriving at Pimville. They were generally seen alighting from the train, and emerging from the station, or sometimes arriving in a taxi. They were easily identifiable by their dress and strange habits. They always went around in groups of four or five, or more, wearing their traditional blankets, which were red with different coloured patterns and motifs. The different designs, as well as the texture and quality, placed them in different categories. To an outsider, black or white, the different names of these designs made no sense, as all the blankets looked the same to them; but to Basotho ba Moshoeshoe they signified important distinctions of wealth and status. The few I remember include *lesolanka, rope sa motsoetse, mo hodu,* and *qhibi* – but there were many others.

On hot days the blankets were thrown over their shoulders in a very casual manner. Many wore grass hats called *modianyeo*, and several wore vests instead of shirts, with their trousers invariably left hanging loose over the waist line, without a belt, or at best a loosely tied one. Some wore *diferehla*, a sort of napkin, instead of trousers. They always carried sticks varying in size and shape according to individual taste. Their favourite musical instrument was the concertina while one or two members of the group had flutes or one might have a simple, traditional guitar. Each one had a whistle, used as an alarm in times of need, or for entertainment at other times. Although these people came from Lesotho (then Basutoland, a British Crown Colony), the absence of passports in those years made the idea of Lesotho as a foreign state very remote and far-fetched.

Saturday nights were marked for entertainment and celebrations. *Timitis* were occasions of great and special interest, resembling the 'marabi dance' familiar in the cosmopolitan communities of Sophiatown and Doornfontein in the late 1920s and 1930s.

The afternoon arrivals congregated at the home where the timitis was due. Their group singing, *mokorotlo*, and the ululating by the womenfolk which punctuated the singing by the men, sent a vibration through the air, and also warned the neighbouring homes of their presence and of things to come. Even my loved Mama Motena took her turn when it came and joined in the events in a communal manner accepted as the natural way of life among that section of the black people of South Africa.

From about eight o'clock in the evening, the concertina player would join forces with the rest of the 'orchestra' to accompany a male soloist. Some of the musicians shook tins filled with stones, others beat drums, the singer meanwhile ably described some incident or person. And all the time there arose from the audience a dancing, deafening rhythm as men and women constantly stamped their feet in time to the music. This merry-making continued from mid-evening to daybreak.

All types of intoxicating drinks, sold by the woman of the house, together with a meat stew made with tomato and onions and served with mealie-meal pap (maize porridge) were the main money-making dishes. The limited space in the room allowed no privacy for any children to rest; whilst their mother was preoccupied and too busy making money to care for them. It was indeed everyone for herself and himself and God for us all.

Those who have watched the *famo* dance have not one good word for it. I never saw it, for the rigid class distinctions of those days would have stopped me even from peeping. It is said to be a most ungodly, wild type of dance, where women dress in such a way that, as they dance and spin, their dresses fly up, leaving them exposed from the waist downwards. The behaviour between males and females, from hearsay, leaves much to be desired during such sessions. My own experience involved spending sleepless nights from the noise of the *timiti* sessions during my stay at Pimville with my father and his family.

It was a common occurrence to hear a woman's shriek in the middle of the night, pleading for help, whilst the sound of either a stick or *sjambok* (a rhinocerous-hide whip) rhythmically landed on her body. Then a male voice would hurl insults at the punished woman: '*Ke re na o tsoa kae?*' (Where have you been, I ask?) or '*O no o na le mang? o etsang?*' ('Who were you with? What were you doing?') All the time the poor woman would be weeping and wailing in an effort to explain her absence and to convince the man of her innocence. This punishment would be administered by a husband or lover.

This was one of the most disturbing and frustrating features of township life in the 1940s and 1950s: the *timiti*, an event which was both an entertainment and a living for many women of the community, compelled to participate for their survival. There is no doubt that on their return to their rural homes, such women found themselves misfits and out of place where they were once cherished and loved; but it is equally true to say that they coped as best they could in a very challenging situation in an effort to care for themselves and their families.

Many of these women left loved ones behind when they first came to the cities. Some came in search of their husbands, but never found them; some came as a result of the deaths of their husbands in the mines, or because they had become invalids from a mine disease. They were drawn to the cities by the hope of better opportunities and were pushed out of the country by white legislation and control. In the end, they shared whatever profit they made, in cash or kind, with those they left behind. The emotional deprivation of those left behind was compensated for by material gain brought back from the cities by their dear mothers, grannies, aunts or sisters; a contribution which could never be clearly measured in any way but which made a positive impact, no matter how limited, on the lives of those who benefited from it. Most of them have passed on, leaving their followers to improve on their efforts and humble, limited contribution.

Their reaction to the 'liquor squads' was another interesting feature. Over the years, the women developed such thick skin that they seemed immune to the fear of being arrested.

In those years, offenders were locked up in police vehicles, commonly known as *khwela-khwela* (pick-up vans). *Khwela-khwela* means 'get in, get in' in Zulu or Xhosa and is what the police said, in their fury, arrogance and agitation when arresting people. Women climbed into these vehicles full of giggles and laughter; at times even throwing insults at the police and using abusive language from sheer frustration, or perhaps in response to the abusive mood of the police. Some incidents were worse than others. It was common for the offenders to relay messages to their relatives through the 'burglar-proof' (grill) of the van as it started to move away: '*Bolella Dineo a tlise leshome la diponto*', meaning 'Tell Dineo to bring ten pounds' ('to court' was understood – it didn't need to be said). Such messages were given amidst shouting, singing, sometimes stamping, laughter and very carefree behaviour by the so-called offenders.

The brewers' homes were well known to the police. One of the most effective ways of escaping arrest was deserting one's home after locking it, once the warning of the presence of the police was passed round the neighbourhood. The brewers developed a strong bond of loyalty to protect themselves against the perpetual, malicious wrath of the police. It was as good as a union. They devised various methods of concealing their brew from the police, and they carried out some of their practices under very trying conditions in their struggle for survival.

As I shall stress time and time again in this book, the majority of black women for too long have been discriminated against as women and as blacks. This state of affairs has created for them untold hardships. They have been challenged to the point where they have developed in some areas ingenious defence mechanisms and a very subtle sensitivity in handling some of the hideous and humiliating situations to which they have been subjected in their daily living in the foreign town life. This has been interpreted as dishonesty in some quarters.

Take the discredited underground 'liquor cellars' of the 1940s and 1950s. These were devised to evade the notorious sporadic police raids pouncing on the so-called 'illicit' liquor traders, to arrest them. Illicit liquor brewing was common among women from Lesotho. After brewing what they regarded as their best product, according to their standards and values, these women earmarked areas where they dug deep holes to hold the large containers of their brew. There was nothing special about the choice of ground: in most cases, the holes were dug on common streets or on street corners to avoid detection by the police. The women took great pains to prepare the holes to make sure that they were large and deep enough to hold the container. To avoid the slightest possibility of the soil contaminating the brew, the containers were fitted with air-tight lids. A smooth, flat piece of iron was then placed on top of the lid; and the iron made firm and secure by smearing a mixture of soil and cow-dung on it to conceal it and render it immovable. In this way, the hoard was detectable by the owner, but not by the police.

It was common practice for the brewers to work on their individual 'liquor cellars' either during the very early hours of the morning, when the rest of the township was still asleep, or sometimes after sunset when it was not easy to be detected or identified. Street 'liquor cellars' replaced house 'liquor cellars' after the police discovered the practice and hounded out the brewers.

It was very interesting to witness the agility with which the women carried out their task of concealing the liquor underground, and how they dug out the holes when under pressure, from the police or from the demands of their customers. Some had large bosoms and were well-developed to the point of being hefty. In addition, they wore full, gathered skirts over several flannelette petticoats of different lengths, to emphasise the thin waist in contrast to the wide heavy bottom. From the waist downwards, they resembled garden umbrellas. According to the fashion in their culture, those who excelled in that style of dress were 'with it'.

In the course of time, the police developed methods of really pouncing on these brewers. It pained one to watch the police punch several holes in the underground 'cellar's' containers; sometimes they would take the drums out and spill the contents over the streets which were left muddy and slippery and the air filled with the intoxicating aroma for several hours. The flies in summer under these conditions were a real menace.

The women, on the other hand, developed other tactics to counteract the police practices. They coined certain calls to warn one another of the arrival and wrath of the police once they were spotted in the vicinity. The most common and popular one of this 'trade union' I remember to this day was 'khu – khu-u-u – khu'. The sound is still vivid in my mind as I sit and write this. 'A ra rae' was another, second in importance to the first. That sound, coming from one quarter in the township, would set all the brewers into action one way or another.

These were the 'Skokian Queens' of the 1940s, who in the course of their trade and determined involvement qualified as professional brewers and sellers of their various products, ranging from ordinary African beer to some really noxious drinks. 'Skokian' was, as we have seen, a notoriously strong home-brewed liquor. With the passing of time the Skokian Queens earned themselves the more respectful title of Shebeen Queens. The principal difference was in their social standing. The Skokian Queen of the 1920s and 1930s, and into the early 1940s, practised in the crowded shacks of the notorious Dipolateng and Masenkeng – the names given to the shanty towns provided by the City Council of Johannesburg, or erected with their permission. In Dipolateng the shacks were single-storey, two-roomed houses made of mud bricks, and roofed with zinc; squatter dwellings stretched between the Canada and

Kliptown railway lines. Masenkeng ran west from the river which separates the present Orlando East from Orlando West. This was a real shanty town, built from bits and pieces of zinc, iron, cardboard, sacking, mud bricks – indeed, anything its residents could lay their hands on. I can recall vividly the endless rows of tin huts in Dipolateng. Both these quarters have now been replaced by the comparatively better houses of present-day Soweto.

Murder, rape, theft and many other crimes thrived in these two communities.

The 'Skokian Queen' catered for her customers in her one-roomed home in one of these districts. As her major concern was to bring in money, she disregarded her personal appearance which was often clumsy and untidy, with women who were fat. Because of the limited space she had no choice but to cater for the customers in the same room, to the point of even using the same calabash (a gourd used as a mug) to be passed from one customer's lips to another.

The title, 'Shebeen Queen', on the other hand, conveys a different image. It relates to the queen of the joint, the shebeen. The sprightly dressed Shebeen Queen of the 1960s was, and is still, very conscious of her appearance and selective about where she places which customer. She makes no bones about separating her customers into two district categories according to their educational standard, general appearance and social standing in the community and, above all, according to their choice of drink and the price they are willing to pay for it. To this day, a seasoned Shebeen Queen does not hesitate to place the customer who drinks the regular 'carton' in the kitchen, or outside on the benches in the back yard, whilst those who drink brandy, gin, beer or whisky receive the special treatment of being served in an exclusive lounge.

Some women have made a lucrative business in this way. In recent years, several Shebeen Queens have become selective about their customers just as they are selective about the products they supply. Today these very successful women drive expensive cars. They live very comfortably in well-built and well-furnished homes. To protect their children from ending up running shebeens, some have put their children through schools from which they have emerged as teachers, nurses or business people of some standing in industry and commerce and other professional fields. It is equally true that some familes have ended up with casualties, their children becoming loafers or, in some cases, criminals.

In the late 1970s and early 1980s men began to enter the liquor business, and tried to give it a better image. Many of the women in this trade have stood side by side with the menfolk in a new and up-and-coming organisation known as the Soweto Tavern Association where they are campaigning for legal recognition by the state; a very overdue development in this field as in many others. Sixty to seventy percent of the dealers in this field are women.

Whilst I don't condone or approve of some of the overall evils and drawbacks which go hand in hand with the consumption of liquor, I cannot for one moment pretend that women have not suffered and struggled against great odds to justify their right to be accepted on the same basis as any other regular bottle-store licensed dealer in this country. The arrests and the confiscation of their liquor – as well as the removal of the vehicles which convey it – have not deterred and will not deter them from this practice and their standing demand: to be recognised as legitimate licensed dealers. Being registered, of course, would render their individual and collective businesses far more wholesome, since the management would be obliged to conform to regulations stipulated in the industry for all dealers.

The present state of affairs will never be eradicated through arrests. It could be made worse. The harm it does in the community, its effect on the dealers and their families, the hazard of exposing the officials who work in this field to corruption, are all factors which make necessary the relaxation of restrictions against the issuing of licences to those who have shown 'progressive and orderly' management within the present constraints. Refusal by the authorities to grant licences can come across to onlookers only as promoting their own monopoly (i.e. the municipal beer halls) at the expense of the black masses.

As Chapter 16 will discuss in greater depth, black women in South Africa have had to fight very hard indeed to make a living for themselves and their families. There are few fields of employment which they have not now explored. In some cases, they have struggled to gain entry and they have achieved their results against great odds. To add insult to injury, their earnings after such struggles have usually been miserably low. Rather than starve with their families, or beg or steal, they have often taken what they could get and have made the best out of the poorest of jobs. By the same effort, they have sometimes achieved higher recognition and employment.

From their meagre earnings, they have provided food, clothing, transport, rent, fuel, light – all the essentials needed in a home. They have kept body and soul together only through great effort. The amazing thing is the number of children who have emerged with the minimum of blemish through heart-breaking family experiences in their struggle for survival. Some of these children seem to have been made even stronger by those experiences. Again, the so-called 'minors' have emerged as heroines and stalwarts, fighting against the odds on all sides, driven always by concern and love for their dependants.

Unemployment and meagre wages have been torments in the lives of black women. In addition to the apathy and despair these create, they also gave birth to several roles which ran counter to the laws of the country. These included shop-lifting among the younger women of the community. This became apparent in the 1950s when detected thefts and the arrest of the culprits raised the eyebrows of onlookers and left a stigma on the offenders within their communities. The whole community spoke in whispers as they judged and condemned the offenders. In those years, suspects were arrested at their homes after the searching of the home had already attracted neighbours and passers-by in large crowds. The suspect was then driven to the police station in the side-car of the policeman's motorbike. Curious eyes gazed inquisitively as the motor bike went by, while the arrested person looked down in an effort to conceal the face.

The shop-lifters and burglars of that era were driven too by the effects of the pass laws. Until the early 1950s, passes were a burden on black men alone. The close of the 1950s and the early 1960s saw women join the ranks of shop-lifting in large numbers as the pass laws started to make influx control regulations effective on black women's employment. Both opportunities for employment and the level of wages worsened as a result of the change.

Many of the girls who attended youth club programmes at Ballandene Hall in Pimville at the close of the 1950s, when I had completed my Junior Diploma in Social Work and was in charge of that club, for reasons at the time beyond my understanding, drifted into shop-lifting. Others went to weekend parties which had as one of their features drinking sprees of 'hot lines' – brandy, gin, whisky and others; some of the girls made no apology for drinking 'Barberton', a drink which has yeast as one of its major ingredients. When consumed in large quantities in this particular drink, yeast is condemned for its far-reaching effects on the drinker's health.

As a budding social worker, and a leader of this youth club, these unhealthy developments disturbed me a great deal. All attempts at counselling seemed to fall on deaf ears. My concern grew more and more when I saw some of the youth club girls who were very intelligent and had possible bright futures before them get wasted to the point of ruin. My long-standing commitment to women's welfare surged inside me. I felt hurt and helpless.

It was during this period that, as an employee of the Non-European Affairs Department (NEAD) in Johannesburg, I made a formidable effort to launch an office or department for finding employment for young people from our youth clubs. That effort was doomed to failure for several reasons. First, the attitudes of white employers in those years; second, the long distances between the establishments which were seen as possible employing agencies and my office; third, lack of telephones or private transport to contact those agencies; and, finally, lack of support and encouragement from my seniors at work who I feel did not attach importance to this undertaking. Sometimes I felt that they sabotaged my effort; they recognised that it was worthwhile, but they could not accept it because the initiator was a black woman, junior in her position. All the senior staff were white women, and not trained social workers, and it would have been very unusual if they had not felt threatened by the move I made. But after I left the Recreation Department of NEAD did create a department for placing unemployed young people in jobs.

But at that time, many young people found a living outside the law. Many girls went into the city's department stores where they pretended to be regular, respectable customers. They were conspicuous by their wide dresses and long warm coats even on hot mid-summer days. The wide dresses were used to accommodate and conceal stolen goods of any size or type. A number of the girls were arrested and sentenced to long terms of imprisonment; some went back to jail several times for this crime. Others, however, carried on their shoplifting without being detected, ending up as real professionals. I know of girls who abandoned this practice after getting married. Stealing of this kind is another indication of what happens when one is driven to the point of despair in the search for survival. Indeed, even some of the people with the best intentions in the world would end up as criminals if they were pushed for existence and survival.

Shoplifting in this era thrived side by side with soliciting, a practice which is gradually embracing more and more young women from the black community. Black women, and in recent years black girls too, have explored some of the seemingly negative vices when everything wholesome and positive fails to come their way. Some of them have got away with it; others have gone through the hardships of imprisonment, isolation, fear of loss of friends, and degradation in the eyes of those who once held them in high esteem. Some young women who could have had a bright future have degenerated into drunkenness and regular law-breaking.

Later in the book I shall pay my full tribute to the many, many black women, old and young, who emerged uncorrupted regardless of the obstacles which blocked their way in an effort to make ends meet; the women who have made both humble and outstanding marks in education, industry, commerce, social commitments, trade, sport, and in day-to-day family life. These are the women who impress me beyond all telling. But in the present chapter I have been anxious to show how circumstances conspired to drive women in the townships to illegal and underground activities. If there was weakness, then that weakness is shared by all members of the human race; my point is that there was virtually no choice for these women in how they came to conduct their lives.

Let me end this chapter by giving an example of the difficulty found by the women in earning a living and at the same time keeping strictly to the law. (In Soweto one cannot say, living under the 'protection' of the law.)

It is common in Soweto to see women in the afternoons on the street corners with vegetable-stalls selling their goods to women who are returning from work. I have criticised this in the past as a non-profitmaking effort; but in recent years I have come to realise that my criticism was unfounded. After some investigation, I have discovered that many mothers are making a reasonably good living out of the venture.

Round about 1978 to 1979 there was a move by some well-meaning people with money. Out of the blue they offered to build stalls with shelters for the women and men who sold vegetables. I thought this was a good idea. However, I arranged with the would-be philanthropists that, before any initial steps to build the shelters were taken, I should carry out some form of investigation into the acceptability of this scheme to potential consumers. I rounded up as many of these vegetable vendors as possible, within a radius of about 200 yards in Soweto, to ask them to attend a meeting at an acceptable time and day in a nearby church used for welfare programmes for old people. On the day of the meeting, no fewer than 30 elderly and sickly young women came along. Only one or two men attended – and they came because they thought the aged were going to receive food parcels.

Never before have I heard elderly women so very articulate about an issue; and the meeting came to a unanimous conclusion. The ladies informed me that for years they had been applying for permits to allow them to sell as they were selling at present, and to protect them from police raids. I heard this for the first time. They emphatically expressed the desire to be left to sell on the street corners unsheltered, and so risk the vicious winter weather as they had always done. Their reasons for this were as follows: first, they felt strongly that the 'philanthropists' would never have sufficient funds to build shelters to accommodate all the approximately 5000 vegetable-sellers operating in Soweto; and if they really did have the money, they would not be able to obtain sufficient land to erect shelters for all the sellers. Second, the meeting felt that the vegetable-sellers would certainly be obliged to pay rent for use of the stalls, and that their takings were too meagre to allow for such an expenditure, at least at that stage. Third, the women expressed their fear and concern for those who either could not afford to rent a stall if the scheme was accepted, or who would not get one because there was none available. They felt that those who failed to find a stall at the proposed complex would fall prey to victimisation, exploitation and outright harassment by the police.

One very able speaker stood up and said, 'Mrs Kuzwayo, go and thank your "friends" on our behalf and tell them we appreciate their generous gesture but that, at this point, it will not do us any good.' The scheme ended at that point. The women still make their living through selling vegetables in the open on the street corners. On the surface, these ladies appear very scattered and unorganised, but they have a strong bond of solidarity.

References

1.Average monthly wages for female domestic servants in May 1941, according to the *Handbook on Race Relations in South Africa*, were £3.5sh in Johannesburg, £4.7.6d in Cape Town. South African Institute of Race Relations, 1942.

3
Violence in the Community

In the previous chapter I talked about 'institutionalised crime' and its effects on our people who have no say in the making of laws or the running of their country. In this chapter I want to show how in South Africa 'institutionalised crime' combines with 'institutionalised violence' to provoke in the black community bitterness, fear, hatred, despair and, at times, retaliatory violence.

During the unrest of 1976 I saw with my own eyes a terrifying incident involving an unmarked police car – a nightmare vision in Soweto in those days. There were several passengers in the car; and I was near enough to note that they were all men. As they passed through the streets in White City, an impoverished township in Soweto, they fired shots from the windows indiscriminately. Mercifully, these shots missed any human targets. But on another occasion the bullets found their mark. In front of our clergyman's gate a group of youngsters were playing marbles with his son. Another police car passed, with the passengers taking pleasure in their usual shooting pranks. A so-called 'stray' bullet hit the clergyman's son, a boy of eight, and was lodged in his skull. He spent months in hospital before eventually recovering.

Whenever these heartless and cold-blooded men were confronted by the press or in the courts with their evil deeds, they always claimed to be acting in self-defence. Adult men themselves, they fired at youngsters of eight to twelve years of age and left them seriously maimed or, in some cases, stone dead. How on earth they could live with their conscience and thoughts is still a great mystery to me this day.

Let me go back a little further to what happened in Soweto on 16 June 1976 – a date which events have marked as a national day of mourning for the black community of South Africa. That day saw the beginning of a massacre of black people, old and young – but especially of the young.

The 1976 unrest should never have been allowed to build up to its disastrous climax. What other government would meet with bullets the grievances of schoolchildren? And what were these grievances? The main source of unhappiness for the schoolchildren of Soweto was that the introduction of Afrikaans, in place of English, as a medium of instruction for almost all school subjects meant that they could neither understand nor learn since this language was quite foreign to them. Suddenly, they found themselves going to school day after day and returning home bored, frustrated, having learned nothing. Their only chance of an education had been cruelly snatched from them.

Exercising commendable patience, the children knocked at all possible doors in an appeal to the authorities to reconsider this new practice. Why should they not be allowed to learn with the minimum of difficulty and frustration?

In a very reasonable manner, the children shared their growing frustration with their parents. Some parents failed to react because their own lack of education prevented them from understanding their children's problem. Others dismissed the problem casually, because they saw it as an unnecessary fuss when they were under great stress themselves. I can well understand the strain and tension suffered by these scholars, when some of their parents – perhaps a very large percentage of them – could not grasp the seriousness and scale of the problem facing them at school.

It was at that point that pupils from neighbouring schools came together to share the problem. Their major concern at that point was to find a way of presenting their case in a manner which would make the authorities, and their parents, face the problem. First, the children approached the authorities in Bantu Education. Instead of listening and responding with understanding, the authorities dismissed with contempt and disregard the concerns expressed by the pupils. It was then that the children decided to march to the Bantu Education office in the city centre in order to present their case and, hopefully, to get redress.

Before anyone could assess what was really happening, the whole situation got out of hand, with students marching along the streets of Soweto, determined to do the 10 miles on foot. Alas! They did not only meet opposition; they came face-to-face with armed police. Instead of encouraging those in authority to communicate with the students, the insensitive 'lawkeepers' decided to display the power of their guns. One bullet shot dead a ten-year-old boy, Hector

Petersen, while many other children were arrested with great brutality. This started a long period of intensive struggle which ended with scores of children being shot dead, whilst others were reported missing and have not been accounted for to this day.

I was in Johannesburg that day, along with some colleagues from the township. As soon as we returned to Soweto, we were met with rumours that we were running the risk of being arrested. Although we did not know where the rumours originated, none of us had any doubts that they were true.

Before entering Soweto, just after passing the West Rand Administration offices (the Soweto local authority), in New Canada, the ground rises and you get a bird's eye view of Soweto. It was at this point that we were greeted by the sight of the local authority offices in flames. Smoke could be seen as far as the eye could go. It was a fearful sight. Most of my passengers got out in Orlando, before we reached the police station. The area looked like a battle-field, full of police foot patrols, and military riding in 'hippos' (armoured vehicles) each armed with a gun. The atmosphere was electric.

After dropping off my last passenger, I drove past every check-point, telling myself that I would stop only when I was stopped, and not before. I was terrified, and drove straight home under great pressure.

Once home, I left behind everything I didn't need with me then drove to a friend nearby, to get the story from her. Matilda Papo, a nursing sister, had been brought up close to me as a member of the YWCA. With her eyes wide open, her voice charged with fear and shock, she related the events of the day as she knew them, describing the scene of the battle at Dube, near Maponya's shop.

Her story made me increasingly impatient to see for myself what was happening, and we agreed to drive down to the centre of action. As we neared the area we came across buses and cars in different states of destruction – some were well alight, others smouldering, while others, though still in flames, were being stoned by the crowd, to satisfy their wrath. It was a terrifying spectacle.

Still shocked by this sight, we saw black youths – both boys and girls – seized with anger, running amok, stoning, burning, shouting, yelling, crying. Suddenly, a car approached and charged us. Matilda shot her arm out of the car in the sign of the clenched fist and shouted 'Amandla!' [Power!], urging me to do the same. I obeyed without question, and the car missed us by inches. I have never been so shocked.

We drove back to Matilda's house, left the car, and returned on foot joined now by those who were returning from work. We pressed on, undeterred by the fear of imminent danger, using the clenched fist as our password. Every concerned person defied the wintry weather to lend their moral support, and to share the agony of the day.

Buses and cars were not the only targets of the students' anger. Beer-halls and bottle-stores were burned down too. The young people had long expressed their frustration and rage at the fact that liquor robbed families, particularly mothers and children, of the fathers' wages, the money frequently being spent in shebeens and at bottle-stores. When the children burned down the stores, they believed that they were destroying a symbol of apartheid and oppression. Apart from the waste of money, they saw, along with many black leaders, that excessive drinking contributed greatly to the breakdown of family life and the endless brutality experienced at weekends and festive seasons, when the huge hospital in Soweto, Baragwanath Hospital, becomes a centre of great horror and deep misery.

The name of Hector Petersen was on everyone's lips; and the many other boys and girls who followed him to his death were given the burial of heroes and heroines; they were seen as martyrs of the black nation of South Africa. This was the era which introduced the practice of carrying coffins on the shoulders of boys and men, sometimes even of women and girls, to the cemetry, an era when modern hearses were discarded for donkey-carts. This was the era which preceded the tragic deaths of the Bikos, Mapetlas, Mdlulis, Mbathas, Bothas, and many others whose names will never be known, as they have never been identified as dead. To all of them, may their souls rest in peace.

Many children died during the uprising itself; others ended up in prison and died there. Some left their homes, never to return, leaving behind in some cases parents who to this day do not know their children's fate. In their efforts to trace their children, many mothers lost their jobs, since they failed to report for work for a number of days. A staggering number of women became unemployed during this period, some of whom have never got their jobs back or found new ones.

Many mothers wept their hearts out for their loved ones. They recalled the days when they had cherished hopes for their children; days of joy and high expectations; days which had given not the slightest warning of the sufferings and tribulations to come – the sufferings that are today's realities. Hundreds of black mothers can now tell their tales of woe, each with its unique emphasis. Yet in the end, in every one's story, there will be an underlying bitterness and fury at the injustice, expressing their emotional torture. In some cases, this feeling leads to a sense of total helplessness. Amazingly, though, some mothers have emerged as heroines, championing the course of the national struggle for liberation of their people – even if this means the sacrifice of their own well-being and freedom, and that of their children and families too.

16 June, then, has become a day of mourning in Soweto. It is a day when we remain at home to lick our wounds and comfort one another. Words cannot really convey what we continue to feel years after that dreadful day. Our hearts still bleed for our boys and girls who lost their lives, who were tormented and tortured in detention, who disappeared without trace, who have become wanderers and beggars in foreign countries – and all this, all this, triggered by conflict over the language the children were to learn in school.

On a recent visit to England, I could not help noticing young black girls walking proud and erect along the streets of London. I turned to my companion saying, 'Look at her. Who knows, she could be one of our "lost" girls from Soweto.' In a voice full of sadness and pity, but devoid of conviction, the response came back, 'It could well be, Ellen.' Let those young people who still walk the surface of the earth, anywhere in the world, know that wherever they are in their sufferings, in their efforts, in their failures, in their humble and big achievements, we still think of them, at the going-down and the coming-up of the sun. Our love will be with them always. May God help them. On behalf of all mothers of the black children in South Africa.

June 1976 is a month marked forever because it brought so much anguish to so many people. But before and since that month many, many families suffered, and still suffer, their individual torments.

How could the black community ever believe some of the explanations given about the blacks who died in detention? Take the case of Dumisane Mbatha, a sixteen-year-old student arrested in Johannesburg on 16 September 1976 with a group of students after the Soweto riots. He was reported to have been detained at Modder B prison on 23 September. Within two days of his detention it is alleged that he complained of feeling ill, and was taken to the East Rand Hospital, where he died that same day. And this is only one of many cases reported between January 1976 and March 1977 by the research department of the South African Institute of Race Relations.

Many other have died in detention. Joseph Mdluli, for example, was detained on 19 March 1976 and was reported dead the next day. Dr Barnard Van Straaten, a pathologist at the South African police laboratory in Durban, gave the following evidence: 'Mdluli died as a result of force to the neck which could not have been caused by his falling over a chair as claimed by the security police during the culpable homicide trial.'

Then there was the case of Mohapi Mapetla, detained on 16 July 1976 under Section 6 of the Terrorism Act. He was interrogated five times and died the same day at 6.30 pm at Kingwilliamstown police station. Dr H.B. Hawkes, who examined the body and conducted a post-mortem the day after Mapetla's death, said he was satisfied from what he had seen that 'broad-based force applied to the neck had caused Mohapi's death.'

Luke Mazwembe, 32 years old, and a member of the Western Province Workers' Advice Bureau, was detained in the morning of 2 September 1976 at Caledon Square police station, Cape Town. He was reported dead in his cell later that day, about two hours after his detention.

The list is long.[1] I could go on and on describing the gruesome details. But let me turn to examine the explanations for the deaths given by the authorities.

What about the claims made by the police and Prisons Department that some of the detainees took their own lives? If there is the faintest scrap of truth in these statements – that the detainees had either hanged themselves, or jumped out of the window – my first question is 'What drives a man to take such a desperate decision?' The only rational answer to this important question is that he must have been under intense suffering from torture of one kind or another. Taking one's life is not an easy thing to do for the bravest or most despairing person: it calls for extreme circumstances and immense courage.

All these men and boys were very dearly loved by their families –

some were husbands and fathers; they were also sons, brothers and uncles and precious to their close ones. Stop for one moment and put yourself in their position. Imagine someone you love meeting such a tragic death. Think of the pain, anger, disgust, hatred and bitterness that accompany such a tragedy – enough to send the mourners to an asylum, or their own grave. It is astounding and highly commendable that so many women have survived mentally, emotionally and physically.

The only consolation in the cases I have described is that these relatives are able to say so-and-so died on such-and-such a day under these circumstances and his remains are in his grave – number X at cemetry Y. The mothers who carry an unending pain are those whose daughters and sons were mowed down by the police and have disappeared from the surface of the earth. There are mothers in Soweto who would give anything just to know whether their children died in the 1976 schools unrest, whether they died in jail, or whether they left the country.

Many have died in detention and they are all remembered. In some cases the memories are vivid only within family circles. In other cases their lives still radiate light throughout the black community. Steve Biko was one of these.

Steve was my second son's peer, colleague and confidant. To this day I have dear, yet sad, memories of a familiar threesome: Steve Biko, Barney Pityana and Justice Moloto, the last my son. They would walk into the house without announcing where they came from or where they were bound for. 'Good morning', or 'Evening, Mom'; 'We know you are fine. We need a good meal, Mom – is it possible?'

What mother could refuse three charming young men such a dear request? On the contrary, I often felt privileged to do anything for them. At the end of their meal they would leave as casually as they had arrived. There were also occasions when Steve arrived without Justice, either with Barney or alone, or perhaps with another friend. It was always a pleasure to serve them.

I have shared a platform with this son of Africa at a number of SASO (South African Students Organisation) workshops when an aspect of black consciousness was under review. Then, I saw another side of Steve. I saw in him a clear-thinking researcher, a hardliner in language, and in action a planner, and above all a leader and soldier of great courage. Sometimes, I felt that he and his colleagues put black consciousness before idealism, but at the end of the workshop, without any effort or discussion, we assumed our roles of adult and youth, of mother and son or daughter.

Steve's involvement, commitment and charisma had earned him international recognition when he met his untimely death. And it is true to say of him that within this country, most especially among his own people, Steve was a model of black consciousness – a concept which has created awareness among blacks about who they are and were, and helped to build up the determination to regain their strength and personality as a nation – for young and old alike. He was respected, loved and highly valued and will always be remembered for his outstanding leadership. He told his mother, when trying to help her understand his commitment, 'I have a special mission to work with my people.'

In that young man, Matthew and Alice Biko gave the black nation of this country – and possibly of the whole of Southern Africa – a gift no money could buy. If anyone is responsible for Steve's death, he alone must know what he was face to face with before he overpowered that gentle, stable, Christian young man. He alone knows whether he is proud of what he did.

Yes, Steve Biko is dead; but his spirit will live for ever.

According to the *Daily Dispatch*, Steve Bantu Biko, in the company of his friend Peter Jones, left his mother at 7.00 pm on 17 August 1977, his jacket hung casually over his shoulders. His last words to her were, 'Mom, I'm coming back.' Two days later both young men were detained in Grahamstown. His mother first knew of his detention on 20 August. When Alice Biko learnt that her son was detained at Port Elizabeth, as any natural mother would, she sent him a change of clothes. All attempts by his family and lawyers to see him were refused by the security police. Imagine the mental torture of being denied permission to see your son, when you know he needs you most. This is the experience and suffering of many black mothers.

Before 8.00 am on 13 September, Alice Biko received a telephone call from Major R. Hansen, head of the Kingwilliams-town security police. He wanted to speak to Steve's wife. At that time Ntsiki Biko, born Mashalaba, a trained nursing sister, was at work at the All Saints Hospital at Engcobo.

Having listened to what Major Hansen had to say, like any concerned mother, Alice asked this official about the well-being of her son. He assured her that Steve was fine, and added that he would come over in person to pass on the message for Steve's wife.

There is no doubt that her hopes were raised by this official's remarks, because of his senior rank. As she said, 'At that time I never ever suspected anything was wrong with my son and the message I was given by Major Hansen came as a surprise to me.' It is only natural when someone very close to you is in a serious predicament to drive out your worst fears and hope against hope.

The normal practice in African communities, whether urban or rural, is for one of the women of the house to clean and clear up both the inside and outside of their home in the morning. Alice Biko would not have departed from this practice. I want to believe that when Major Hansen, head of the security police in Kingwilliamstown, arrived in the morning he would have found Alice sweeping her yard.

On his arrival he gave her this message: 'Steve was detained in Port Elizabeth where he fell ill, he was transferred to Pretoria where he died on 12 September.'

How very strange to bring such sad tidings about a son and announce them in such a way. This is the behaviour of someone devoid of compassion for humanity, of someone cold and insensitive to human feelings. Is this not a sort of violence too? It is hardly surprising that Steve's mother 'collapsed with shock and was still unable to recall the sequence of events from that moment'. Her road of pain, mockery and humiliation has been walked by many black mothers.

The announcement of Steve's death over the air and in the press shocked the nation and the world. A leader, a hero, a soldier, a man of integrity and repute had left this world, that message was loud and clear. Every quarter of the black community now prepared itself to lay to rest the remains of their young hero. Soweto was especially moved. Thousands of youths and adults converged at the YWCA's Dube Centre on that memorable Friday evening which preceded Steve's funeral. They were angry and bitter, and felt helpless, lost and dejected, their spirits only lifted occasionally as old friends met after a long separation. All were preparing for the long journey to Transkei to participate in Steve's burial.

With buses waiting and the crowd swelling as cars brought an endless stream of mourners, suddenly a fleet of very different vans arrived. These disgorged a host of police armed with batons, *sjamboks* [hide whips] and guns, and reinforced by vicious police dogs. Before the crowd realised what was happening, they were charged and indiscriminately set on by the dogs. Their screams and shrieks could be heard from far off as they scattered in all directions, leaving all their valuables behind. Purses, money, important papers were all abandoned as the people ran helter-skelter in an effort to save themselves from the ruthless attack. Many received injuries, some very serious. Others lost shoes and clothing. Their shock and the damage was so severe that many mourners cancelled their journey for which they had prepared so carefully, emotionally, spiritually and physically.

The whole area was littered with cases ripped open, clothing, unpaired shoes, food hampers and provisions. It was just like a battlefield after a considerable skirmish. On this day, the South African police confirmed the long-held belief amongst black people that the Nationalist government does not see them as human beings, and that it sees the South African blacks posing a real threat. The only clear thing, however, is that there is something about blacks in this country which unsettles the government and the majority of the white population. It now seems certain that the buses booked to convey the mourners to the Transkei added to the police's fury and their calculated and uncalled-for harassment of the crowd.

It is astonishing that their actions did not deter many of the mourners who escaped injury that night.

Thirteen buses had been booked for the mourners; in the end, only six left carrying about half the original gathering. One bus was occupied by members of the Soweto Students' Representative Council and the South African Students Movement. The others carried the youths and adults who had gathered both to mourn their tragic loss and express their solidarity with Steve's family and the black people as a whole.

Word had gone round like wild-fire among members of the YWCA about the aftermath of the police attack at the Centre. The appalling state in which the first staff member to arrive there found it sent her out as quickly as she had come in to work that morning. She broke the news to another member, and like bush-fire news spread. Within 30 minutes the members in the leadership had started to move into the yard although it was still manned by police. Without showing any sign of fear or expressing apology or doubt they went past the police patrol and into the Centre. There they discovered a mass of broken glass, filing cabinets and desks overturned, and food, clothing, bottles and papers littered all over the floors. Water had been spilt everywhere, and last but not least, blood was on the walls and floors to tell the story of the night's horror.

The police did not take kindly to the women's arrival. Present that day were Joyce Seroke, National General Secretary, Noniah Ramphomane, a member of the Management Committee, and the local President, Matilda Papo, as well as other active YWCA members and their relatives. The police moved forward aggressively, threatening to baton-charge and set the dogs on the women. Little did they know what they had let themselves in for. All hell was let loose from the women's side. Disregarding the police, their batons, their *sjamboks* and their vicious dogs, the women told them in no uncertain terms to get out of their premises, which they had built with the sweat of their brow. They were fearless before all that surrounded them; the police, their dogs, their guns, did not shake them one bit. On the contrary, they told the police off, and ordered them out. To protect their image the police tried in vain to resist the women. One white policeman tried to use his car and gun to scare them by driving irresponsibly at them, brandishing his weapon. The desired results were not achieved. The women were too mad with anger to be scared by anyone or anything. The police had no choice but to march out of the Centre; it had become too hot for them to remain there any longer.

The repairing of all the damage became the responsibility of the YWCA members. They have never forgotten the number of women's panties found lying around – evidence of the rapes which occurred that night.

Whilst all the West Rand Board Administration buildings, offices and halls were burnt down by black youths as a symbol of the *status quo*, the YWCA Centre was damaged by the *status quo* itself, in retaliation, I suppose. I ask, where is the maturity within the circles of the men of the law?

For as long as the damage remained, so were the sad memories of Steve's death fresh in the minds of Soweto residents.

Violence, then, is the ever-present background to life in Soweto. The institutionalised violence of white against black is not made easier to bear – or, more to the point, to resist – by the high level of violence within the black community itself. Rage, frustration, despair and recklessness are encouraged by the conditions under which black people live; and these feelings, inflamed by liquor, too often find expression in bloodshed.

Women somehow seem to cope with the pressures more successfully than men. Take, for example, the case of one woman who drives a taxi for a living. I met Mrs Esther Seokelo by chance one day, having not seen her for several years. I was amazed and horrified when I heard about her occupation. 'You are not serious, Esther,' I said. 'How safe are you?' Cool, collected and very dignified, Esther smiled and replied, 'Why not, Ellen? I am very safe.'

She went on to explain that there is a great need for women to penetrate every occupation, trade, industry or any other undertaking operated by men. I chipped in and pointed out the great dangers in the taxi trade, bearing in mind the almost daily killings involved. It was at that point that Esther shared with me the role she plays as a member of the Taxi Association. She referred to the violence which male members resort to at times of crisis, when they need to settle differences amongst themselves.

'You are aware of the number of killings in this Association at certain periods?', she asked. I agreed that there were frightening murders at certain times in the Taxi Association.

'Those are the times when women's presence is needed most. Time and again I have appealed to the men that we solve nothing by killing one another; that it is important and imperative at times of crisis to collect oneself and to be calm and composed. Time and again I have told these men that to achieve that calmness, you need to focus your mind on something more serene and within – in short, you need to pray about your anger, impatience, arrogance and display of power, and to pause before you put your feelings into action. At the beginning they thought I was a square and old-fashioned. I persisted with my deep-felt convictions. Soon, a few men agreed with my suggestions. Without boasting, Ellen Kuzwayo, I can proudly say that has stopped the misery of the numerous murders we had in this Association.' She ended with a wry smile and added, 'At least for a while.'

After speaking with this great, humble, dignified and self-confident black woman, I realised there were many things I did not know about my community and which I needed to know. I stopped and said within me: 'What a woman and oh! what courage.' It was indeed a revelation to me to discover there were some women who made a living by running a taxi service in Soweto. But that they went beyond that, to intervene in such delicate, dangerous feuds which often ended up in violence and killings, this was beyond all comprehension. This is an unusual but significant example of the invaluable contribution made by black women towards the development of their community and country.

References

1. For one list see the paper 'Administration of Security Legislation' produced by the South African Institute of Race Relations research department, March 1977. It is from this paper that the above examples are taken.

PART TWO

My Road to Soweto

4
My Lost Birthright

I was born on 29 June 1914, the only child of Phillip Serasengwe and Emma Mutsi Merafe, born Makgothi. My place of birth was the farm of my maternal grandfather, Jeremiah Makoloi Makgothi, in Thaba Patchoa in the district of Thaba'Nchu in the Orange Free State.

My parents named me Ellen Kate. My mother's favourite name was however Cholofelo, which means Hope. Later in life when I met my father and his family, I was introduced by yet another name, unknown to me, Nnoseng, the literal meaning being 'Give me water'. Among my mother's people I was popularly known as Motlalepule, meaning 'The one who arrives on a rainy day'.

Ellen Kate Cholofelo Nnoseng Motlalepule are all names I answer to. Please do not ask me why so many. I can only guess that both my paternal and maternal grandparents wanted to have a share in giving me a name to make their mark. At one time Mother told me that she gave me the name Cholofelo because I arrived (I want to believe that she meant conceived) long after I was expected. '*Cholofelo ga e tlhabise ditlhong*', was one of her favourite statements. ('Hope does not put one to shame.') Nnoseng is my father's paternal aunt's name. It is a common traditional practice to give children names of some members of the family, although this practice is gradually losing favour.

I am the author of this book.

When I became aware of myself at the age of six or seven years in the early 1920s, I learned that I was one of four grandchildren of Jeremiah Makoloi and Magdeline Segogoane Makgothi, born Masisi. They owned a large fertile farm through which flowed the Leeuw River. It was approximately 2560 morgen (60,000 acres) judging by the size of the farm my sister and I inherited in 1970. This was about 1400 acres, a quarter of the farm inherited by my grandfather's four children.

The farm was situated about 50 miles south of a small village, Tweespruit, about 35 miles west of Ladybrand, 20 miles north of Hobhouse and some 30 miles east of Thaba'Nchu. Yes it was a beautifully cultivated farm, with plenty of rich grazing pasture as well as cultivated land which yielded abundant corn and maize in winter and equally abundant wheat in summer. It was also a very prosperous dairy farm. This is the farm which was wrenched from my family as recently as 1974. In that year, without any thought for human feeling, the authorities declared the area a 'black spot' – meaning not that black people should live there, but the very opposite. A stroke of the pen made it illegal for black people to own land in that area; white farmers were to take over. My maternal grandparents owned the farm in the 1880s; it was home to my parents and to us children. There had been close to 100 years of legitimate freehold ownership; it had been earned and maintained with hard work and toil by our elders for the benefit and welfare of their children and their families. Through iniquitous and inhuman legislation, my family was rendered homeless and wanderers in the land of our birth.

It had been a farm anyone could be proud of. There were all types of farm animals in large numbers: cattle, sheep, goats, pigs, horses and rabbits, as well as a variety of domestic fowl such as turkeys, ducks and chickens. About 25 yards from the homestead, there were two dams irrigating a large orchard which had a variety of fruit trees which yielded plentiful crops. It was surrounded on the eastern and southern sides by a thick hedge of quince trees, which are still there to this day.

Until I was about seven or ten years old, we ate, drank, roamed, played and went to school together as old man Jeremiah's grandchildren, moving as freely on the farm as the birds in the air. It was common practice for we children each to carry a mug and walk single-file to the barn where they milked the cows, in order to get our morning ration of fresh milk direct from the udder. We were not allowed to drink any other beverage, except cocoa occasionally. Adults always alleged that we children would grow filth in the tummy if we drank anything else. For the same reason girls of a particular age were forbidden to eat eggs or the kidneys of slaughtered animals. For a long time I believed all those stories though with some reservation.

As recently as February 1984, a friend and I took a flying business visit to Thaba Patchoa. I was moved to see the main buildings of that once dear homestead, erected with white stones and cement and given corrugated iron roofing, still withstanding the harsh weather with dignity. The ceiling and floors, finished with wood, are strong and intact after approximately 100 years. Other houses around that living monument sadly are beginning gradually to fall apart. At the homestead patches of hard earth floor are sagging under the fast growing reeds, where once our little feet moved swiftly. How sad. All these tell a story of a people who left footprints where they moved.

The church building was about three minutes' walk from the homestead. It was built with the same materials as the main buildings of the homestead; however, it had an earth floor and no ceiling. This building was used as a classroom from Monday to Friday. From an early age we took turns to clean the church on Saturdays to have it ready for the service on Sundays. During the week the students were allocated turns to clean it. As youngsters we enjoyed collecting cow dung and preparing it to smear the floor of the church in readiness for the service. It was in that church building that I started my schooling from Sub A to Standard 4.

Treasured memories come back to me now of the early lessons in the three 'Rs' which I received there, as well as the Bible classes and the catechism lessons – which often bored me. The highlights of the programme of those early schooldays were action songs and physical exercises which I was good at and loved. I recall the faces of some of my classmates, the playtime games and the meals we shared and so often exchanged. My cousins and I looked forward to the tasty sour porridge dishes brought by our schoolmates from the village; they in turn just loved the butter and jam sandwiches which we exchanged for their porridge. But treasured memories can never replace our fast-fading past.

I remember vividly the petty childish quarrels we often had; some ended with a fight on the sandy river bank not far from the school but certainly out of sight of any possible intrusion from adults. Once I got a good hiding from one of my classmates. She was a bully and a bull-fighter all right. I lacked skill in fighting. Perhaps I had been 'tamed' by the Christian teachings of unending forgiveness and 'turn the other cheek' I received from home, in school, and from the pulpit.

Some very dear moments come back to my mind. I see the faces of the teachers who taught me in those years; and I hear the beautiful tunes we sang in that farm school in the late 1920s.

Teachers Jacob Thepe, Michael Mokae and Julius Valtein all taught at different periods in this school. I recall a particular hymn we often sang at early morning prayers during teacher Valtein's time, 'Trust and Obey'. Yes, it was this hymn we sang to bid him farewell the day he left the school. We cried our eyes and our little hearts out. Now that I come to think of it, he must have been the favourite of the three because there was a song composed about his achievements by one of the pupils. There were great composers in that school in those years in the 1920s; they could easily match the young black composers of the present day – perhaps even their age-group from other race groups as well.

This is the song about teacher Julius:

Tichere e na ea rona
E tsoang koana Thaba'Nchu School
(E tlilo ruta x 3) taba tsa Modimo
Taba tse Molemo.

It means:

This our teacher
Trained at Thaba'Nchu School
Has come to teach the word of God
The good word.

It is very simple in music and words, but great in meaning to his pupils. Perhaps it was even so for our teacher.

Julius Valtein came later than the other two, who were his senior in age. Teacher Mokae was a jubilant chap, an entertainer and a disciplinarian. He insisted on quality performance in schoolwork and in recreational activities. Some of the favourite songs he taught were 'Swanee, How I Love You', 'The Wild Wild Women' and many others, which made our school concerts bright, popular, enjoyable and up to the mark.

Teacher Jacob Thepe, an older man who taught at the school earlier than the other two, had a great sense of humour and was very fond of teasing, particularly those of us whom he didn't consider to have distinctive good looks. I was pleasantly surprised some years ago to meet his daughter, Judith Matee, a nursing sister with the Cripple Care Association and a devout member of the Young Women's Christian Association here in Soweto where she has lived for many years. The surprise was greater when it dawned on me that Meriam Mothale, a typist I had interviewed and recommended to be employed by my office in November 1978, turned out to be Judith's daughter. This discovery after three months of working together with Meriam meant a great deal to me. I often taunted her about her ever-teasing, pleasant grandfather. She was more than taken aback to hear me tell her how well I knew him. Indeed this is a small world.

As a youngster, I looked forward to weekends, when I had two days without accounting for homework to my teacher. Homework was a real nightmare in those days. Sundays and Christmas Day were the times most welcomed. These were good days to display my homemade dresses to my friends; to relax and talk while we fetched water from the spring about 50 yards from the homestead.

It was one of our duties to ring the bell for the church service and to make sure that the chairs, benches and tables were well dusted and placed in their proper positions before the service. My grandfather conducted most church services on Sundays. His favourite hymn, 'Itsose Moea Wa Me', ('Awake My Soul' in English) is very dear to me. As I grew up, I realised more and more what a remarkable and impressive man Jeremiah Makgothi was, both inside and outside the church. Indeed, it is only within comparatively recent years that I have acquired any kind of a full picture of his life and I have been taken aback to realise the degree of respect and affection accorded him by many different people in all communities.

He was a graduate of Lovedale College near Alice in the Cape Province and very near to Fort Hare. In those years, Lovedale was one of the most renowned boarding schools in the country. It was run by the Church of Scotland Missionary Society for the black community. We got to know later in life from his only surviving child, my aunt Blanche Dinaane Tsimatsima, the youngest of his four children and now 83 years of age, that as a student, Grandfather travelled to college by ox-wagon over a distance of more than 500 miles with all his provisions and belongings packed on the wagon. At the Orange River, the wagon crossed over to the Cape side and continued the journey to Queenstown. There Jeremiah transferred his belongings to a post carriage drawn by horses or oxen to Lovedale. He remained at Lovedale for the duration of his training from 1875 to 1883. At the end of his school career, Grandfather obtained the Junior and Teachers' Certificates. On graduation he returned to Thaba'Nchu, his home.

All these facts have been confirmed by Grandfather's own reports in a notebook I discovered in Blanche's bookcase, during one of my efforts to compile some authentic data on this stalwart of his age. In addition, I found a few of his textbooks. They include among others, *South African History and Geography* by George N. Theal, *First Latin Reading Book* by William Smith DCL, LLD, *English Accidence* by Rev. Richard Morris IID, *Plain Geometry* by W. & R. Chambers, *Plain Trigonometry* by I. Todhunter NAFRS, and several others. Some of these books are dated 1879.

He became the headmaster of the first boarding school in Thaba'Nchu for African boys. In addition to this post, Grandfather taught in a day school attended by both black and white children. Among some of the students who attended school at that time from the white community were the children of the local Methodist pastor, Rev. Daniels, and one of his children became our family doctor when I was about eight or nine years old. Dr Daniels was commonly known as 'moroa monare', meaning 'son of monare', I cannot say why Dr Daniels was called so. My only guess is that Rev. Daniels must have made a lasting impact as a pastor on that community, to deserve the Setswana name 'monare' in recognition of his service.

During his years of teaching in Thaba'Nchu, Grandfather played a major role in the translation of the New Testament into Serolong, working on this project with Canon Crisp of the Church of England Missionary Society.

The archives at Lovedale contain the following entry on my grandfather, dated 1885:

Jeremiah Makoloi was born at Thaba'Nchu, Orange Free State in March 1860. Both of his parents are church members, his father being a class leader in the Wesleyan Society. He was taught at the school there by David Goronyane, under whom he also acted for a year or two as monitor. He came here in November 1875, with fair attainments and attended the second and third years and student classes and, in 1878, he obtained a Government Teachers' Certificate of Competency, standing thirty-fourth in the list.

Whi'e carrying on his studies he assisted in the evening preparation classes and in the office. He gained by competitive examination the Eckhardt Bursary for three years. On his return home in 1883, he was engaged in general work for some time, but latterly assisted in the translation of the New Testament into his own language (Serolong) by the Church of England Missionary, Canon Crisp.

The following is an extract from *The Friend*, the still surviving daily English newspaper in the Orange Free State, regarding Grandfather's work:

We have been shown a copy of a new version of the New Testament in Serolong, which has been issued from the Church Mission Press at Thaba'Nchu, during the past week. Nearly forty years have passed since Dr Moffat published his translation in the Setlhapi dialect. Since then much progress has been made in the knowledge of the language, especially with the assistance of the educated native helpers. The new translation is in the Serolong dialect of Sechuana and is issued tentatively, with the hope of obtaining as much criticism as possible before undertaking a stereotyped edition. Canon Crisp has been assisted in the work by Jeremiah Makoloi, who was educated at Lovedale Institution and of whose assiduity and ability the Canon speaks with much respect.

Grandfather was very active in the political life of his community at the turn of the century. He was the Secretary of the Native National Congress (later the African National Congress) and his brother-in-law, Moses Masisi, was the Treasurer. With several others, they worked closely with Sol. T. Plaatje, the great challenger of the 1913 Land Act in the black community, and author of *Native Life in South Africa*, a book which powerfully denounced the new legislation. It is in this book that Grandfather is mentioned as an interpreter at the Dower Meeting held at Thaba'Nchu racecourse on Friday, 12 September 1913. There Barolong men and women had gathered to receive clarification on this traumatic legislation whose lamentable effects included the early up-rooting and dispossession of the black people. The meeting showed no way forward for the people and sent home those who attended feeling completely hopeless and thoroughly frustrated.

It should be noted, however, that early in this century in Natal, the Cape Colony, Transvaal, and the Orange Free State, there were already scores of men of Jeremiah's calibre in the Native National Congress, fighting on an intellectual and political battlefield to stop the colonists' iniquitous law-making. They laid the foundation for the unending struggle against these callous laws.

My grandfather subsequently became a court interpreter in the magistrates' court, working with the presiding officer and the black

offenders, most of whom had not had the opportunity to go to
school or to learn English. He became a very committed Christian,
local preacher and church steward in the Wesleyan Methodist
Church as well as a prosperous farmer. He died on 23 May 1920 at
the age of 60.

Unlike my grandfather, who was a gentle person, my grandmother was outspoken and direct in her speech and dealings, to the
point of being blunt. She had very fine features and was a woman
with her own values and standards. I can never forget how on one of
our many trips in the family Cape carriage (a covered four-wheeler)
to Thaba'Nchu, she monitored and commented on Grandfather's
driving for the whole of the journey. The bone of contention was
that she felt Grandfather was giving too much space to any white
farmer's cart, car or carriage travelling in the opposite direction.
She repeatedly told him: 'Jeremiah, you must not go more out of
the way for the other traffic than is necessary. You are entitled to
your portion of the road as much as they are.' In a gentle way,
Grandpa would reply: 'It is all right, Segogoane, do not worry!' He
was unruffled by her remarks throughout the 30-mile journey. To
use the modern expression, he kept his cool, and always with a
slightly remote smile.

The climax of the journey came when we reached town and
stopped while my grandparents did some shopping. As the couple
were discussing their plans, and deciding what to do, a white lady,
close to Grandma's age, approached the carriage and addressed
herself to Grandma in Afrikaans, saying something like 'Ek soek 'n
meid wat in my kombuis kan werk' ['I am looking for a maid to
work in my kitchen']. My grandma gave her one look and without a
moment's hesitation, replied: 'I am also looking for that type of
person – can you help?' No one will ever know whether the
Afrikaner woman simply expected my grandma to help her find a
maid, or whether she was indirectly insulting her by asking her to go
and work for her; your guess is as good as mine. If that was what she
meant, she received an appropriate response. The white lady turned
her back and left without a word. Grandpa was more embarrassed
than hurt. He spoke firmly but softly to Grandma as if objecting to
her reply. That incident shows just how straightforward Grandma
was in her talk. It left a lasting impression on my mind.

Her housekeeping could not be faulted. She demanded the best
from those responsible for household chores in the home. In short,
she was a disciplinarian. She expected us to be clean at all times,

even when we were out playing on our own. She insisted we returned promptly for meals, and that we sat down to a meal and finished it. She adhered to evening prayers and all children had to go early to bed. By bedtime Grandma *meant* bedtime. She accepted no giggles, silly or pretentious coughs or whispers after we were put to bed.

It was when she insisted we do something that we found it very difficult to suppress our playful tactics. We often ended up being spanked, and in tears. Despite her strictness, we loved our granny very dearly; she meant a lot to us, full of mischief as we were. It was common practice for us during the day to make fun of her prohibitions from the night before. We always ended up laughing our lungs out after going through the happenings of the night.

It was somehow an accepted fact that every time she went to Thaba'Nchu, we children went along with her. We invariably travelled in the Cape carriage, drawn by four beautiful stallions. The workers in the house took pains to prepare for that trip. Among the tasks to be accomplished was the sorting out of our attire, this included bonnets called by the Afrikaans word 'kappies'. These bonnets had two or three frills, starched and ironed smooth without a single crease. Our dresses were worn without a sash or belt. They had a high yoke and a well-gathered, full, knee-length skirt. All our dresses were made from the same pattern and were made from the same quality and colour material; only the sizes were different. We were really not thrilled with either the pattern or the uniform colour when we grew older. Our coats were white, made out of long silk – like mohair. Our whole costume made us look painfully different from the neighbourhood children. According to their standards and judgement (and ours) we looked odd, and we stuck out like sore thumbs. With my grandmother, however, there was no nonsense about clothes. We wore what we were told to wear.

On the long 30-mile journey between the farm and Thaba'Nchu we spoke very little or not at all, except to answer a remark or question from Granny. Like all children of that era, we were more seen than heard, and we accepted that state of affairs as law.

As I have said, although Granny was so strict we loved her very dearly. Proof of this was when we were on our own and playing, when we would relive the experience we went through under her care and drive away any hurt by imitating her and laughing at it all. Now, as I look back, I find it rather unusual that during that period in our lives we were more attached to her than we were to our own mothers. We addressed her as Mother and Grandpa as Papa. Only one of my cousins, Serekego, a little girl about three years younger than me, right through her life addressed Granny as Segogoane, never as Granny or Mother. As children we felt Granny was particularly fond of this little girl (indeed she was lovable). Apart from allowing her to use the name Segogoane, Granny always responded in a very intimate way to this little girl: she used to say to Serekego 'O no o reng Rakgadi'a mme?' ('What do you want, my mothers' aunt?') Serekego was named after my grandmother's aunt and she thus enjoyed the respect we did not. To this day, children named after an old person in the family are accorded respect and recognition. We often felt Serekego got away with what some of us would have received a spanking for.

As in any other family, we children played, ate and went to school together, and often even shared our clothes and food. We teased each other constantly, sometimes even to the point of telling tales to our elders, or fighting it out amongst ourselves. We roamed these beautiful hills over-looking the homestead; crossed the dongas (gulleys), from which we practised jumping; collected wild fruits we were forbidden to eat from the veld (open country); drank forbidden water from the dams; plucked fruit from the orchard, often before it was ready to eat; and occasionally went horseriding, to fetch the post from the local store. We became real experts in recognising the calls of different birds and in imitating them. It was easy to tell owls, wagtails, doves, and sparrows by their song without setting eyes on them. Our favourite pastime was playing 'house-house' and dolls.

We got a real thrill out of using mother's sewing-machine without her permission. We did this as often as there was need to make clothes for our dolls. The 'dress-maker', Aunt Elizabeth, (my mother's much younger sister), would shake her finger at those of us who were notorious for tale-telling as she strongly warned us: 'Any one who tells Ausi Mutsi (meaning Mother) that I have been using the machine will get it from me and, what is more, I will never again make clothes for her dolls.'

These were the enjoyable days when we children grew up as one family at Thaba Patchoa Farm. Even after the death of our grandparents (they died within three months of each other in 1920), and we each went to our own parents' homes, we still exchanged visits during our school holidays. To this day when there is a happy or sad occasion in one of the families, it is always a very happy reunion for those present, regardless of the circumstances. This is how strong the bond of family ties was in that home.

It is amazing that despite differences of kinship within the family, none of those grandchildren born of Jeremiah's daughters addressed their own mothers' sisters as Aunt – we all called both our mothers and aunts 'Mma' meaning 'Mother', and this is how all Blanche's sisters' children address her to this day when they speak to her directly, myself included. To that extent, therefore, my cousins on the farm in those years were as good as sisters and brothers to me. Yet, like children everywhere in the world, we would pick arguments with each other, and sometimes I was clearly the odd one out. One of my cousins would count her sisters and brother . . . 'One, two, three Setlogelos' . . . and would go on to count the Makgothi adults. When it came to me, however, I was alone. I was 'One Merafe'. They would laugh, leaving me alone staring into empty space, with no defence or explanation. This was repeated on several occasions in the blunt, unkind way peculiar to child behaviour. But in a split-second the initiator of the unpleasant division would turn to me and shower me with love and kindness, saying, 'Ngoanyana oa ga Mme Mmutsi, eo montlenyane, tlo re tshameke' ('Lovely little girl of Mama Mmutsi, come let us play'). Somehow the feelings of unpleasantness and shock would vanish in me as fast as they had come. We would then resume our normal play, as if nothing had happened.

I don't remember any days when I actually shed tears over such experiences, but it is also true that I was puzzled, perplexed and confused by their behaviour and perhaps hurt more than words could tell. It was a problem which occurred and ended where and when we played, and I suffered in silence, never sharing it with anyone, as it was difficult to talk about. Yet, left to myself, I tried in vain to understand why I was the only child with the name Merafe. Why were there no other adults with that name? These questions often crossed my mind, but I never shared them with anyone, not even my mother.

Time and again, Mother would call me 'Moradi Merafe' ('daughter of Merafe') although she never explained why I alone had this name. Nevertheless, she always communicated an unspoken support and sympathetic understanding for me. As if to appease me, Mother's family turned my clan name into a personal one and called me – and still do to this day – 'Mokoena' ('of the crocodile clan'), which was added to the long string of names I have already mentioned. I answered to Mokoena too.

Fifty years have now passed, but I can still recall instances when Mother paid particular attention to me – times when she gave me instructions about a simple household chore such as sweeping and cleaning a room thoroughly, or making and serving tea correctly and on time. She often spoke to me about personal hygiene, too, and the importance of correct conduct in public in speech and manners. She emphasised the importance of correct behaviour for girls in particular. A few years before she died I remember her saying just once, 'Cholofelo (the name only Mother and her sister Fanny used), remember you are a Merafe child. No one should ever prevail over you to change that name. If some day you meet someone wishing to know your origin, do not hesitate to tell him you are a Merafe.' This lodged in my mind. Much later I learnt that my parents had divorced when I was an infant, the knowledge coming to me in an indirect and unpleasant way which hurt me deeply. After all, I was not responsible: if anything I was a victim, a sufferer from their divorce.

Until I was about seven or eight years old three men who meant something to me had registered in my mind. My grandfather, Jeremiah Makoloi, who took the role of a father to me, despite our different surname; my Uncle Ephraim Setlogelo, my mother's younger sister's husband, who was kind and loving, often bringing home sweets for us from work. I was aware that he had the same name as my cousins and that, perhaps, he was their father; and my maternal uncle, Peter Makgothi, Mother's only brother, who oozed with love for us all. We all called him 'Malome', which simply means maternal uncle.

Then, when I was about seven, in 1921, another male figure came into my life. This was Abel Phogane Tsimatsima, who became my step-father. His integration into our family was so smooth that I cannot recall a single detail about the change. His pleasant nature earned him the admiration of the whole family. He was a gentle person, yet alert, sensitive and calm at all times. He always called my mother Chum. I never saw him agitated for any reason in the 17 years I lived with him, when he took the role of father of the family.

My parents' marriage was blessed with a daughter, Maria Dikeledi. Mother always called her Maid. Her arrival opened a new chapter in my life, and I became very attached to her. She filled me with new hope, joy, satisfaction and love. It was as if she completed an unfulfilled mission in my life. Although our family names were not the same, she became a part of me in the same way I had seen amongst my cousins. I felt we belonged to each other. This relationship has been maintained to this day throughout our life's challenges.

For the first time I felt I had a companion, a sister, someone I could share my life with. Perhaps the baby came unconsciously across to me as a link between me and Mother, first and foremost. I have heard people talk of half-sisters. No, not Maria, she has never at any time been anything else to me but a full sister.

In 1939, long before I ever considered marriage as a worthy proposition, my sister married Thari Pilane, son of Chief Ofentse Pilane of Saulspoort in the district of Rustenburg in the western Transvaal near the Botswana border. When signs of ill-health surfaced in Thari's life, for reasons best known to him, he hurriedly made arrangements to move his family, lock, stock and barrel to Mochudi in Botswana, where he eventually died. To this day my sister lives there with her children and some of her grandchildren. The fact that she is a mother with four sons and four daughters and lives in Botswana, none of this, has in any way taken away from our close-knit relationship.

My step-father never displayed any signs of preference for one child over the other. He treated me as Maria's elder sister, and he supported and encouraged me in my schooling at all times. As a great reader, he was never without *The Friend*, magazines and other periodicals such as *The South African Outlook*, *The Farmers Weekly*, *The Government Gazette*, *The Homestead*, and others. In these, he always marked out what he saw as important and actively encouraged me to read and try to understand the gist of some of the articles, although at that time, when I was in Standard 4, it was not easy to grasp the meaning of abstract subjects and topics. He patiently coaxed me into reading, even if it was just for reading's sake. He often sat on the veranda in the middle grass-thatched main house, in his special chair he used on his return from the fields, when it became unbearably hot.

When my grandfather's estate was finally wound up, my mother was allocated the old homestead and the land around it. It was renamed 'Tshiamelo' ('Place of Goodness'). My step-father maintained the same standard of excellence established by his father-in-law on the farm.

Not far from the homestead – about 50 to 60 yards away – across a channel which led water from the two dams to the orchard and vegetable garden, stood a cluster of houses on a hill top. This comprised the homes of the families who worked on the farm, some of them as labourers or handymen. The name of the settlement remains today even though its inhabitants and their dwellings have disappeared. It is 'Mocweding', ('fountain' or 'spring'), as we drew water there from the nearby spring. Most of these families built and owned their homes and reared cattle, and flocks of sheep and goats, each family according to its means. In addition, each family owned a piece of land which they cultivated to grow whatever crop they pleased, depending on the season. Amongst my grandfather's papers, I found a notebook which had the name of all the families on the farm in 1911 with details of their assets in terms of livestock – sheep, cattle, goats, horses, pigs – and cultivated land and grain. All these details are recorded in Grandfather Jeremiah's own handwriting: a clear record of a conscientious and well organised farmer.

In those days it was common practice for families to organise work-camps, known as *matsema*, for major duties, such as ploughing, reaping and threshing. Much time and planning went into arranging and carrying out those work-camps. Word would go round to announce a work-camp for whatever purpose at least a fortnight before the actual event. All work-camps had certain features: for example, the camp organiser had to ensure that there would be enough food for those who came to work.

The men brought their own equipment and tools for the day – a plough and span of oxen, or hoe, rake and long fork, whatever was appropriate for the job. If the camp had been arranged for corn threshing, the men brought 'knobkerries', short sticks with a round head about the size of a clenched fist. The women brought their *maselo*, which are grass woven utensils for separating the chaff from the grain, and grass brooms for keeping the threshing area clean.

Some families lent a hand by bringing dishes to supplement the food and refreshment supplied by the camp organiser. This was the responsibility of the village women. Dishes which were invariably provided were *bojaloa* (home-made beer), some sort of meat, a staple – either *samp* (a sort of stiff porridge) or dumplings – milk, when available, and *motogo* (sour porridge) which was also known as *seqhaqhabola* when used as a cold drink. The quality and quantity of food would differ from family to family depending on their means and status. But every family, including my grandfather's, the landlord's, made an effort to be represented, even if this meant seconding someone. Joining in the camp was both hard work and a celebration.

The most popular camps were those organised for threshing and hoeing. They were always accompanied by some form of entertainment – by singing beautiful, descriptive, traditional songs punctuated by the piercing ululating of the women; whilst the hoeing and threshing itself was carried out in a rhythmic movement which together gave great pleasure to both the eye and ear, and made what could have been a tedious task much easier and more enjoyable.

As youngsters, our main duties were to run errands of various kinds between the home of the family organising the event and the scene of action. Such errands included fetching drinking water, bringing needed tools and carrying food to where the work was taking place. We offered our services with joy, keenness and willingness. This aspect of country life held great attraction for me, and I anticipated the work-camps with great joy and expectation, even when I was away at college – these were the events I genuinely looked forward to on my arrival home.

The main meal, including plenty of beer, was kept as the last event of the day. Everybody participated in this meal – men, women and children, but it was accepted in those days that *bojaloa* was for the adults only. Children were forbidden to take any form of intoxicating drink, and accepted the ruling without question, as a way of life. The climax of the day was highlighted by dancing and singing after the day's hard work. This was a well-earned relaxation and entertainment. Womenfolk excelled in the dance 'Mokhibo'. 'Mohobelo' and 'Mokorotlo' are two corresponding dances for Basotho men. In both, men sing in unison, one of them sticking his knobkerrie (a short stick used for threshing corn, and sometimes as a weapon) up in the air. The music is sombre and the mood of the men is subdued. In some instances one man will lead as a soloist and the others respond in harmony. It was both beautiful to watch and listen to.

On the other hand, 'Mokhibo' can be performed by individual women or in pairs. The participants kneel upright facing each other. The movement is concentrated on the breasts and shoulders, extending to the arms, with an occasional neck movement. If it is done by those with experience, it becomes a real joy to watch.

'Moqoqopelo', by contrast, is a free-for-all. Those who provide music and clapping of hands stand in a circle round the main dancers. Generally, the dance is by partners, male and female. While the women are dancing gracefully, the men jump up and down and, rubbing their legs together, dance around the women. Any other man can enter the circle and join any couple. The man who has been dancing is expected to relinquish the circle to the newcomer. It was a great joy to participate in 'Moqoqopelo' as a young girl. In this fashion, every work-camp was brought to a close with great joy and excitement which lingered in one's mind for weeks or months after the event.

The success of the individual work-camps depended on the joint efforts of the father and mother in that particular family. After deciding on the date for the camp, the father planned its announcement. He informed other families and made sure that there would be manpower and sufficient equipment to carry out the job to be done. The mother, on the other hand, was responsible for providing sufficient meals for the day. The variety, quality and quantity of the provisions for the day were all her responsibility. The support the family received depended very much on what support they gave at the work-camps of other families. It was on such occasions that the community support-system was demonstrated at its highest level.

The part played by wives on such occasions was outstanding. The actual performance of the day, including the work and the celebrations, during the work camp and at the end of the day, depended very much on the atmosphere created through the quality and quantity of the food provided. This was the responsibility of the wives in their individual capacity and as a group.

As a teenager I participated in all chores designated for my peer group, regardless of whether or not the work-camp was at home. Any adult could instruct any child and, as youngsters, we carried out instructions or errands without question. Respect for age was the order of the day.

Some of the mothers in the community ended up as instructors and supervisors at the girls' *Lebollo*, that is the circumcision or initiation schools which are run for both boys and girls among Basotho. There was always a strong warning when the boys' session was in operation not to dare and go in the direction where the ceremony was taking place. We were told they would tear any girl or woman to pieces if she went anywhere near their *Lebollo*.

The girls, on the other hand, were peaceful and harmless. On their return they assumed an air of superiority, and openly looked down on those who had not been through this process. In addition to this, they refused to share their experience of the *Lebollo* or give any information related to it with anyone of their age group who had not been there. As youngsters we were very curious, and keen to know more about what happened. The little information I ever received was from someone who had received it second-hand herself. As little girls we got to know that the main concern was to teach girls about adulthood and womanhood. The fact that there was so much secrecy about matters of circumcision from those who were directly connected with it, added to the fact that my parents had such strong feelings against it, meant that for me this situation left much room for suspicion, speculation, gossip and assumptions which were never checked or corrected.

All the same I got to know that for the two to three months that the girls were there they had female tutors who were themselves graduates of that school; further, that sex education was one of the areas given attention. Looking back, I recall some very strong remarks made about children born out of wedlock, a happening which was very much despised and shunned in those years, and indeed very rare. The tutors in the *Lebollo* – who were commonly known as 'basue' – played a very important role in building up the moral standards and personal stability of young girls of that time; a very important role, regardless of the low opinion educated Christian people had about *Lebollo*.

Besides learning about adulthood and womanhood, the girls were also trained in the beautiful dances designed for their *Lebollo*. Their bodies were covered with white ochre, from the face to the arms and legs. It was during this period that these girls – known as 'bale' in Sesotho – displayed the spirit of youth by being jubilant, full of fun and adventure, and participating in singing and dancing which were all enjoyable to watch and listen to. On their return home the girls appeared in completely different attire of ox-skin skirts and were smeared with red ochre, which covered their hair and body. They adopted a sombre, reserved mood and appeared mature and dignified. They were called 'ditsoejane' at that stage.

Let me briefly give you a picture of some of the involvement of these girls during their stay at the school. From this it will be realised that, besides some of the difficult lessons of adulthood and womanhood, these girls had fun, entertainment and some pleasure in between some of the hard tasks they performed.

The beauty and grace of their dancing was accentuated by their unusually impressive traditional attire. On their heads they wore a frill of reeds, beautifully made, covering their faces and tied around their heads. Their faces, arms and legs were smeared with whiteish clay or soil called *phepa*. Around their loins they wore seemingly pleated skirts made of a type of grass. Their trunks were bare, displaying their beautiful, round, small breasts which were regarded as a symbol of virginity.

As a child from a Christian home, I was strictly forbidden to associate in any way with the girls who had accepted *Lebollo* as part of their lives. This restriction from my family did not dampen my burning desire and curiosity about what transpired at the school. I secretly and carefully planned a visit to see for myself the beautiful performance by *bale* so often described to us by *Lebollo* graduates or villagers who had watched their performance. I managed to watch them dance for about 15 to 20 minutes. It could have been more, because I stood there spell-bound by the harmony of the music, so common but striking in this country among blacks, their rhythm and graceful poise, their agile movement, all this accompanied by the joy and perpetual smile on each face. Perhaps in the final analysis the less sophisticated people with little or no education, who make no fuss about their religious affiliations, derive far more satisfaction and happiness out of their supposed primitive simple life. Their lives have far fewer 'don'ts' than the lives of professed Christians. They are, by and large, more open and they readily accept other people.

At the end of that beautiful performance, I quickly trotted home, an innocent, respectable little girl, keeping to myself this rare enjoyable experience, for fear of remonstration by my parents.

I had planned my visit well. It was on a day when I was sent to the village shop, which was about one-and-half to two miles away from the homestead. I timed myself well to depart from home at about mid-day, knowing that the shop closed for an hour at lunchtime. When I left home, all by myself to conceal my movements, I made straight for the initiation ceremony. My feet swiftly carried me in that direction. As I approached the group of white-ochred young girls, I slowed down from fear of how they would accept me. My first reaction was to turn back and run away from them. What if they chased me and beat me up? As this thought crossed my mind, a voice from the group pierced the air shouting in my direction: 'Tshoeli'. It was echoed by a few others, 'Tshoeli', 'Tshoeli'. I had been forewarned to throw a gift down once this word was hailed. I was armed with about eight to ten safety-pins which I had collected from the house with the full intention of presenting these to the *bale*. With my fingers trembling from fear, I made loose two or three pins and threw them down in quick succession to appease the girls.

As they rushed to collect them, I threw down a few more in a different direction in order to scatter them. and, hopefully, to help me run away from them if they attempted to charge me. My mind was full of many ideas at that point. What if they beat me up? What explanation would I give back home for coming here? I could see in my mind the wrath of my family and how they would pounce on me for going to witness the ceremony of 'heathens', as families which still adhered to traditional, cultural practices were often described.

As I threw the last of the safety pins down, the girls were already in the process of re-grouping with a song. Their hands clapped in rhythm as they formed a semi-circle and started dancing on tip-toe, with their necks and shoulders responding to the rhythmic music which penetrated the air and its surroundings. I stopped spellbound with admiration at the combination of beautiful songs and the agile movements of the dance.

I have never had any guilty feelings about pretending to my elders that, from the time I left home, I went straight to the shop and back, with the delay of lunchhour at the shop in-between.

It was this exposure, and others similar to it, which earned me envy and recognition in later years when I became engaged in youth programmes related to traditional drama, as an employee of the Non-European Affairs Department of the City Council of Johannesburg. I valued that opportunity which I stole for myself in my youth, and have never once regretted it.

Women and girls in rural communities have always played a significant role in the growth and development of their families and communities; this was so even among the employees on farms privately owned by blacks, who encouraged family bonds among their workers. I watched this happen from the time I became aware of my surroundings. It happens up to this day. The cultural influences from other racial groups, and some of the harsh legislation which has often disrupted family life in black rural communities, as well as the hideous migrant labour system, have not succeeded in destroying the commitment of women to fulfil their role as wives and mothers.

I have written earlier about women and girls preparing meals for work-camps; and they did so too at other feasts of joy and sorrow, carrying out these duties individually or as a group. Beyond preparing meals, fulfilling other household chores, and rearing their children, women and girls have stood side by side with the men herding flocks and working on the land. In some communities they have even built homes. However, I wish here to highlight the contribution of women to their individual family incomes as well as to the general economy of their communities in the country, as far back as the 1920s and 1930s. Black women inherited from their parents, families and their communities varied creative skills which enabled them to make noteworthy contributions to the well-being of their families in particular, and that of the community in general.

Pottery was one such skill. Many mothers over the years have been engaged in this craft. They chose the clay for the pots (big and small) with great care and made and maintained the condition and quality of the tools they used for shaping and cutting to finish their products. It fascinated me to watch them work on a clay pot from start to finish. The selection and working on the clay to be used seemed tedious to the onlookers; but to the one who made the pot it seemed a great joy. They sifted the clay carefully, and mixed and worked on it at length, testing it and remixing it if necessary.

Their skill was well displayed when they rolled the clay between their hands, taking care to put sufficient pressure on the clay to avoid it being uneven. They handled it with great dexterity, rendering the rolls supple, flexible and ready to take the shape and size of the planned pot. The coils of clay were piled evenly one on top of the other in a long continuous roll, working from the base upward. Then followed the swift, light fingerwork – gently smoothing the clay into one, even, solid creation, so taking the shape of the finished pot. At this stage, tools – such as a piece of sharp zinc – were used to level the edges of the mouth of the pot. The finished product was carefully protected from the weather with a light covering and left to dry – a long, delicate process. The women would carefully examine the pots for possible cracks. In the absence of these, the pots were prepared for firing and, finally, for cooling. It was a very involved process which produced clay pots of different shapes and sizes, for varied purposes, some as household utensils, others as ornaments. The finished product was of high quality.

Marketing the pots was no problem, as they were made to order for neighbours. The sales were on the barter system. There was no problem of delivery.

Another craft common on the farm was grasswork. Women specialised in grass mats which were used for sleeping on, or for spreading on the floor for guests to sit on. (It was mostly women who used them for sitting.) They also made baskets known as *ditlatla* or *ditlatlana* in Setswana and *diroto* in Sesotho. These were used for carrying harvested food in from the fields. The 'beer strainers' – *Metlhotlho* in Setswana – have no equivalent in English, but they were placed at the bottom of the grinding stone to collect the ground corn as it dropped from the stone. *Leselo* similarly has no equivalent in English. This was an implement used for separating the grain from the chaff after threshing or stamping.

All these were important household utensils of great value in every home in those days. Today they are used as ornaments in many homes, in memory of past times. The products penetrated all communities, defying the social, racial and political barriers.

During those tender years of my life, my world went just as far as my eyes could see. The mothers I saw and lived with in Thaba Patchoa, their involvement in their daily chores at home and outside in the fields and elsewhere, modelled the image I had of the black woman in rural areas. After I left that world, I never expected to find again a community with similar customs and practices to those experienced in Thaba Patchoa. Some 25 years later, however, as I shall describe in Chapter 9, I was to find such a community approximately 100 miles away from that dear home.

My childhood had been a happy time, full of the warmth and security of a traditional country life. At the age of fourteen I passed Standard 4 and moved to Thaba'Nchu to continue my education.

5
Unfolding Horizons

When I moved from the Lower Primary School on the farm to St Paul's Higher Primary School in Thaba'Nchu, in 1927, I went to live with my mother's youngest sister, Aunt Blanche.

The big yard where the homestead stood accommodated a large stable with doors on both sides and divided by an inside wall into two halves: one for stabling the horses, and fitted with a long manger for their fodder, whilst the other end was for the carriage, the cart and trap, as well as saddles, harnesses, tools and garden equipment. There was a *rondavel* (a circular thatched building, used as a guest house) in front of which stood a well furnished house, with five large rooms – three bedrooms, a living-room and a kitchen. Photos of our grandparents, great-grandparents and other members of the family decorated the walls. Like the farmhouse at Thaba Patchoa, it had a corrugated iron roof, and was finished with a wooden ceiling. For two years this was home for me during the school term – during the holidays I was expected to go back to the farm, much against my will.

This was indeed a new era in my life. Being a pupil in a town school in Thaba'Nchu, I felt different – important and elevated. I was no longer a lower primary pupil but a higher primary student. I was a town girl and no longer a country girl.

I was able to assert myself at St Paul's. I formed a girls' singing group, which I trained – and they sang and acted very well: I was very happy with their performance. One day I had the idea of taking the group to perform at the farm, and shared my thoughts with Mother when she came to visit us. (She was still living on the farm at this time, but she would come and stay in town because of ill-health.) With her consent, I went ahead with planning the trip to the farm, and asked Van der Merwe, a young coloured man who owned a car, to drive the six of us there. He said the charge for the return trip would be £1.10s, (we used pounds and shillings then, not rands and cents). I told him we would pay him from the takings of the concert. The sense of adventure now had complete hold of me. Mother knew nothing about these arrangements, and I made no allowance for any mishap.

As fate would have it, the Friday we left for the farm it just poured down. But we were determined to go and we did just that. The roads in those days were not tarred, so when it rained you travelled on mud, right through. As we emerged from a long pass, thick forest on one side and a high Thaba'Nchu mountain on the other, the car skidded and spun to face in the direction we had come from. Needless to say, we were all shaken – except for the driver. He quickly took out chains which he fitted to the wheels of the car, and assured us that we would be very safe. We arrived at sunset, and I prepared supper for the group.

But the concert itself was a financial flop and panic started when the driver damanded his pay. I managed to raise ten shillings and promised him the balance on arrival in Thaba'Nchu, which he accepted. The trip back to Thaba'Nchu was less hilarious, as the leader of the group was now very concerned about the balance of one pound. In those days owing anybody a pound was a real burden as that amount was like a fortune – more so for a schoolgirl.

Mother was furious with me when she found out what had transpired. Before she paid the balance for me, she gave me a good spanking and told me never to do that again. I learnt my lesson and gave up that particular kind of enterprise.

The first school holidays in Thaba'Nchu presented Mother with a problem as I was reluctant to go back to the farm after my first taste of town life. In the end, she had to bundle me bodily into the cart to take me home to the farm. Back there I convinced myself I was a different girl, better than the others I had grown up with. I was in standard 5 and, as far as I was concerned, I had nothing in common with them, as they were a class below me. I got it into my head, too, that the church youth group classes which Mother was in charge of were below my dignity, and that I had in fact gone past the stage of attending such classes. In short, I became too big for my boots.

In no time, Mother took me to task for this behaviour. She insisted that I join the church youth singing group rehearsals for a concert. I was very reluctant and dragged my feet, though without expressing any verbal resentment. But Mother had put her foot down, and not only put me in the group, but saw to it that I actively participated in some events – leading the march, or holding the banners. She disciplined me into action, and in anger and exasperation I excelled in my performance, judging by the number of requests for encores. The audience paid tickeys (a silver threepenny coin), sixpences, shillings or pennies for different performances.

My first year at St Paul's higher primary was a new chapter in my life. There I came into contact with a number of my classmates who gave me enough competition to show me up as not so very intelligent as I had believed myself to be at the farm school. There were men and women teachers there with outstanding personalities, talents and qualities who left a lasting impact on me. I was particularly impressed by the teachers' choir, with its twelve to fifteen members: their performances were impressive, to say the least. They would sing set pieces for competitions – including, on one occasion, Handel's famous 'Hallelujah Chorus'; as well as Setswana choral songs, such as 'Mangaung', composed by the Tswana composer Ishmael Booker (whose family name was Leepile Mompati, my Aunt Blanche's first husband, who met an untimely death while still a young teacher and husband). Aunt Blanche was herself a contralto of considerable ability, and sang in that choir during her teaching career.

I did well at school, and at the end of two years I had passed standards 5 and 6. In 1929 Mother began making arrangements for me to go to boarding school at St Francis' College, Mariannhill, in Natal. By this time, Mother had become bed-ridden so that, side by side with the arrangements for my schooling, were other preparations for her to go to the coast at East London for a change of air.

Preparations for my departure to college excited me. From the time the list of my college requirements was compiled, I was caught up in a mixture of joy, sadness and fear: joy for the love of adventure; sadness because of Mother's deteriorating health; and fear of the unknown about college life. This is a very difficult state of mind to describe.

Most of my clothes were bought in sets of six. They included six pairs of black cotton stockings, six vests, six panties, six shirts (half of these in khaki and the rest white), a twin set of jerseys, two gym dresses and two black skirts as school uniform, two pairs of school shoes and one swanky pair of shoes which Mother said I should wear on special occasions when uniform was not required. A lovely dress was also provided for such special events. In addition, I had a few casual garments to wear outside school, too.

Bedding included two pairs of sheets, two pillow cases and a pillow, two blankets and a beautiful blue-grey rug which I loved. One day Mother asked me to cover her with that rug as she lay in bed. I must have delayed doing so, for she had to remind me to cover her with it. As she repeated her request, she looked at me and said, 'Are you afraid I will pass my illness to you if I use your new rug on top of my clean sheets?' I looked at her in puzzlement at this suggestion. I always loved fulfilling her requests, but I realised then that I needed to be quick. As I turned to her to apologise for my delay, I saw her face communicating such a gentle, loving look, and as I placed the rug over her, she simply said, 'Thank you'. A couple of hours later she told me to air the rug on the line and then pack it. This incident slipped from my mind as many others have before and since. I never attached any importance to it until very recently. Perhaps it was another way of Mother expressing her love and concern for me, or maybe a way of saying goodbye. I can only guess. Did she have the faintest notion that we would never see each other alive again? If so, I can only imagine the emotional torture she was going through, when she realised she was about to leave behind two young girls of fifteen and seven years.

The day of my departure in February 1930 arrived amidst great excitement and anxiety about my new life at college. The stories told me some months earlier by my cousins who had already been, had unnerved me beyond description: I did not know what to expect. I had heard about harsh, taunting comments and unkind nicknames like Msila which means 'bushy-tail'. The thought of the one-and-a-half days' journey by train from Thaba'Nchu to Pine-town left me with really mixed feelings. On the one hand, I looked forward to my first long train journey; and yet I was scared to death, wondering if I would arrive at St Francis' College in one piece!

At last my trunk was packed, locked, labelled and ready to be railed to school. The horse-cart stood ready outside the house to take me to the station. I sat on Mother's bed to bid her farewell, little realising it was the last time I would say those words of parting to her. Shortly after, Mother left for East London.

She was on my mind from time to time while I was at boarding school. However, the new life there just swallowed me up for the first three to six months. There was the adjustment to the routine of classes, scheduled meals and study times; there was the competive rush by students to establish their ability in sports events during recreation periods. I was quite overwhelmed by this new and foreign atmosphere. The few times I wrote to my step-father I enquired about Mother's health. In his replies, he reassured me, saying that she was improving, so I was quite certain that I would see her in June when I went home on holiday. I cherished that thought and longed for the moment when I could hold Mother and kiss her and share my learning and new experiences with her.

Above all, I wanted to speak Zulu to her as she had fervently requested me to learn that language so that I could teach it to her. She firmly believed she was a Zulu by birth and a Motswana only by adoption. I had been brought up speaking Setswana. But if my memory serves me, some members of my family were in the habit of speaking English among themselves. I really do not remember any special effort among us children to speak English to each other, though. We did read English in our school textbooks, on the lines of: 'A cat sat on a mat'; 'It is a fat cat', and 'I see the cat and the mat'.

As I grew older, and moved into higher classes, my step-father gave me newspapers, magazines and other periodicals to read, but I still read English with very little understanding. We were discouraged by the older children on the farm, who made humiliating comments whenever we younger ones tried to speak English: 'Listen to a Jakwa speaking English!' (Jakwa was the term used for those who had not started at boarding school). Or, at other times, they would shout 'Krobo! You're killing the King's English!' and roar with laughter. But in the end, my step-father's insistence that I read instilled the habit in me and I also developed the strength to stand up to ridicule when I made mistakes. By then, too, I was learning English grammar at school.

Since the imposition of Bantu Education in 1953, black students have had to learn in their mother-tongue and English. And now the government wants the blacks to become as proficient in Afrikaans as they are in English. Since 1976 there has been an effort to impose this third language as a medium of instruction at high school, and it was resistance to this that was an important factor in the uprising of the Soweto schoolchildren in that year.

I now speak, read and write Setswana, Southern Sesotho and English, and can read and write Zulu and Xhosa with some proficiency and speak both these languages with ability. Although my Afrikaans is limited at all levels, I am not at a loss in the midst of an Afrikaans-speaking group. I could have been more fluent in this language too if there were fewer political and social undertones associated with it. In my own home we speak Zulu, Xhosa, Setswana, sometimes Sesotho, and occasionally Afrikaans. English is the accepted language for communication, and is used with little effort.

On my arrival at St Francis' College I was surprised by the number of nuns in every teaching department. We lived with them, they taught us and supervised our manual work sessions, and we worshipped with them. They were all white. Everywhere I moved, I felt shadowed by a nun. I found them rigid, cold and strict, dominating and disciplinarian. They wore heavy, ankle-length, black cassock-like habits, with pure white hoods with long black frills, and similarly spotless white bibs or collars. Their costume complemented their domineering characters. Their English was unfamiliar to the point of being amusing to us and created a barrier to communication. Later, I discovered that they were of German origin. Some were young and beautiful, and it puzzled me why they had chosen this seemingly harsh life; others were old and not charming at all.

This was one aspect of college life I had not bargained for. Not one of the older students I travelled with from home had ever mentioned the presence of the nuns. The image of the nuns was made more complex for me by the Catholic way of worship. The rosary was a mystery to me: during prayers its unfamiliar black beads were not related to God in any way – at least, not in my mind. The many statues in the church struck me as idols, a feeling generated I suppose by my Christian upbringing in the Methodist Church. Reference to Mary, Mother of Jesus, conflicted with my faith in God the Father, God the Son and God the Holy Ghost; the observance of the Way of the Cross at Easter was both a punishment and drudgery.

The nun who lived with us in the residence was old and dogmatic about her Catholicism. For every small mistake a student made, she told us we would burn in Hell and that the offender was Satan's child. It was at St Francis' College that I first heard the word purgatory, which I perceived as a waiting 'trail station' for small-time sinners. Time and again the non-Catholic students were told they would end up in Hell.

Confession was another puzzle to me. The belief that if the priest pardoned you your sins, God would pardon you too conflicted with my Christian teaching and orientation, and I could not accept it.

The ethics of my faith ran contrary to the teachings of the Catholic Church; at least, that was my feeling at that time.

During the first two or three months at St Francis' College I had some very upsetting experiences. Perhaps, as I reflect on them today, they may seem very minor. However, at that time, as a new teenage student, they weighed heavily on me. One Sunday morning we were going to mass at the chapel, which was in the grounds of the boys' school. We used to march there in a crocodile, an accepted routine in all institutions. The nun in charge that day was doing her inspection. She called me out of the line, took out a razor-like instrument from one of her pockets, and told me that my dress was too short, and that it could create problems for the male students. Puzzled, bewildered, hurt and humiliated, I walked towards her. In no time she had ripped open the hem of my dress and ordered me back to the line. The bottom of the dress, with its unpressed, ripped-out hem, and threads of cotton hanging at all angles, left me a pitiable sight. Some girls giggled, some sympathised, others looked at me and shrugged their shoulders as if indifferent – but at the same time were passing remarks that I could not hear.

Another time I was reprimanded for wearing my smart shoes regularly to school. The next opportunity I got, I shared my frustrations with my class teacher – a nun – who, unlike all the others, showed care, concern and regard for her students. Although I never got any feedback, I am certain that she intervened, because embarrassment about my attire ended that day. The fact that most of my classmates and age group wore their best shoes only occasionally might have singled me out as wanting to appear different and better.

These regular and uncalled-for incidents left a scar on my mind – not so much about St Francis' College, but about nuns in general. I lost respect for them at that time; and similarly, my opinion of the Catholic Church has been clouded to the present day.

There were no organised sports at Mariannhill. The few games that were available were enjoyed by senior students only. No nun participated in sports and as there was no one to supervise the junior students, we had no recreational activities, except with the senior students. We went to class, came back for meals, attended church or benediction, but had no organised recreation. The motto of the school was aptly Ora et Labora ('Pray and Work').

The need for someone to look up to in this strange atmosphere grew by the day, and as time passed, I found myself drawn to a group of senior students, some of whom were my Aunt Elizabeth's friends. Aunt Elizabeth, Mother's first cousin, lived with us at home, and was very close to Mother. She went a year ahead of me to Mariannhill. She was younger than these senior students, but she was very close to them. I broke away from my own classmates and kept company with some of these more senior students, particularly at the students' residence. In this inner group there were two very senior students, who were doing the Higher Primary Teachers' Course – the highest level in teacher training in the black schools at that time.

One of these students, Phidelia Moshoeshoe, was a Catholic who later married the Reverend S.S. Tema of the Dutch Reformed Church: an unusual combination. Her closest friend and classmate was Henrietta Moalosi, who is now Mrs Sedikelo. These two senior students soon gained my admiration and respect, and became a source of inspiration for me. Their general appearance, their warm disposition towards junior students, their readiness to offer guidance or even reprimand such students when necessary, the way they applied themselves to their schoolwork and how they conducted themselves after school hours; all these aspects made a tremendous impact on my mind. They seemed to me to be ideal models of senior students and adults, and I knew that I would love to convey a similar image when I was in a senior position. They helped to reduce some of the bitterness and frustration I felt at the hands of some of the nuns.

Most of these up-and-coming senior students came from the Transvaal and Orange Free State, an area commonly referred to as up-country in Natal. Up-country was recognised as an area of marked progress and development in terms of urbanisation and adaptation to western standards and way of life, qualities which were highly valued then.

I have met Phidelia and Henrietta at different times and under different circumstances in recent years. Although ill-health has struck one of them, they both still maintain those ideals which they expressed in the 1930s. Indeed, it was because of my admiration for them, that I was inspired to return to St Francis' College to continue my studies.

My first journey home was filled with many thoughts: there was my determination to return to school and to follow in the footsteps of

my seniors; there were the exciting surprises I had to share with
Mother. Would she be back from East London? If not, would she
return in time for me to see her before my holiday was over? How
would she be? I pictured our reunion and felt very impatient for it.

I arrived home before her and waited anxiously for news of her
return. Instead, a telegram arrived to say that her condition had
deteriorated. This was followed by another, within two days,
reporting her death. Needless to say, my world just crumpled under
my feet. My step-father and Aunt Blanche had already left for East
London after receiving the first telegram. I was too shaken, grieved,
helpless and disappointed, to shed even a tear for her.

Instead of caressing and kissing her to welcome her home, I had to
join the crowd awaiting the arrival of the train bringing her remains
back to Thaba'Nchu, her home. Many people were there to mourn
with us and bid her a last farewell. She died very young, only 45
years old.

I often stop and wonder why did she not live just a little longer to
see some early rewards of her struggles. From the hands of this
warm, calm and loving woman I have got to know so many other
black women who have had an impact on my life and who have also
made a remarkable contribution towards the development of their
own families and community.

When I emerged from the dark cloud of shock and despair, one
thing was very clear in my mind. That was the conviction that one
thing Mother would have loved to see was my return to school.
Accordingly, at the end of the holidays, I returned to St Francis'
College and passed the teachers' preliminary examination at the
end of 1930. On my return home, in December, my hair was
gradually turning grey. Our family doctor, J.S. Moroka, spoke to
me very strongly about the importance of shedding tears of grief,
and after a few months' treatment, my hair colour became normal
again. My little sister, Maria, was too young to grasp that Mother
had died. She often wept and pleaded with me to go to East London
to fetch her home. This pained me so much.

On my return to college in 1931, I was fully aware that Phidelia
and Henrietta would be finishing their studies that year, and that
life without them at Mariannhill would be empty. I discussed this
with my step-father, who was very understanding, and he helped me
to apply to Adams College at Amanzimtoti. I started there in 1932,
continuing my studies for the teacher training course. On leaving

Mariannhill the only person I dearly missed was Sister Lucia, my class teacher. I have never looked back.

When I entered the gates of Adams College in Amanzimtoti, on the coast south of Durban in Natal, I entered a college which was part of the community which surrounded it.

The students' quarters in the college grounds comprised a male students' residence, popularly known as 'Jubilee', and a female students' residence, know as 'Esidlaveleni'. Jubilee was situated towards the west and Esidlaveleni towards the east of the college campus. In between stood three large buildings, used for the teacher training course classes and the high school classes and the administration offices. They were set amongst trees, which added to the beauty of the surroundings. A few yards away stood a chapel on the road leading out of college towards Durban. In addition, there were the homes of the management and administration personnel and married staff members; unmarried staff shared the students' residences.

The principal's house was high on a hill among the trees, its white painted facade and black roof making it visible from a distance. The other staffs' homes were scattered at the foot of the hill forming part of the college complex. Staff members came from both the white and black communities.

There were sports grounds on the college campus which both the staff and students used. There were tennis and tenniquoit courts – the latter is a game played with a rubber ring over a net, rather like volley ball – basketball, soccer and track games.

From the day I arrived, I felt accepted by the students and authorities and within six months I had established a group of friends including classmates, room-mates and members of the societies I had joined.

Discipline was quite strict, and the college rules were posted on a notice-board. As in all teaching institutions, we attended classes from Monday to Friday. There were also evening study periods supervised by a rota of staff. We were expected to attend all religious services, and mealtimes were stricly observed. Finally, we were expected to keep order at the college both as individuals and collectively.

Particular days and times were set aside for leisure-time activities including sport. The most popular sport was soccer, and the college team was known as the Stars. The team was popular with everyone, and the students supported them whenever the team played at college or an away fixture, to demonstrate their loyalty and love of the college. Shopping trips were organised on specific days under the supervision of a teacher or senior student.

Other important features of college life were the debating society, the fellowship groups and cultural activities. When I arrived at Adams a choir of senior students was rehearsing a cantata based on the bible story of Esther. The producer was Mrs Frieda Matthews, the wife of the late Professor Z.K. Matthews, later to be principal of Fort Hare, the first university for Africans in South Africa. The performance was outstanding, but was given only once.

There were regular organised debates either in our classes, or between different classes, and sometimes between the teacher training college and the High School. The high event of the college year was choosing the debating team to compete against Sastri College, an Indian school in Durban. When the society was scheduled to compete with another college, there would usually be several male students – and Ellen Merafe. The other girls did not seem to take an interest.

In 1933 I graduated as a lower primary school teacher, and over the next two years I studied and qualified as a higher primary school teacher – the highest grade that could be attained by blacks at teacher training college. In all, I was at Adams College for four years. In the course of my studies and from the different activities I have described, I came into contact with many students and teachers, many of whom I still hold fond memories of; and as I remember them, I remember too the contribution they made to that community, because above all, Adams College was a community.

I hold dear memories of Faith Caluza, now Mrs Namo. She was very musical, and sang and played the piano beautifully. I had formed a singing trio with two other students, Jabu Dube and Matilda Mpetsheni, and Faith Caluza was our accompanist.

As classmates, we formed study circles to improve our class performance and many of these students have impressed me since, not by attaining any particularly outstanding academic achievement, but by following their teaching profession and making a marked contribution in this field. The names of three sisters come to mind: Mattie, Regina and Frances Gumede, from the Inanda Seminary. They were the daughters of the American Board Mission priest. All three qualified as teachers, and have since accepted other jobs outside teaching, backed by their earlier training. Their only brother was a doctor.

Looking back, it seems that in the 1920s and 1930s boys had many more professional outlets than girls, who were restricted to teaching. Later, some went into nursing. In those early years girls seemed scared by the science subjects. The likelihood is that they were scared not because they were stupid but because they had been told over and over again that women students had no aptitude in this field.

Groups of friends offered a strong support-system in most areas of life. For example, we shared in depth some of the very sensitive issues of our age group: courtship and personal relations. Two of the friends in particular I shared my thoughts with were Norah Fries, now Mrs Manasse Moarane, and Epeinette Moarane, who married Govan Mbeki, one of the African National Congress leaders who later, in 1963, was to be sentenced at the Rivonia Trial to life imprisonment. We had a catch-phrase to express difficult decision-making: 'Learn to say no, even to some good things.'

As a group, we attended what we called fellowship sessions. These sessions came to a peak during the principalship of the late Dr Edgar Brookes, and were run at his own house. They took the form of bible study classes, because we used the bible as our reference, but in essence they were directed towards personal growth goals. No one was compelled to attend, you went out of choice because you felt they fulfilled a personal need.

Perhaps I remember Norah and Epeinette particularly well because I associate them with the time we started to live away from both parents and teachers for the first time, and turned for support to our earlier lessons at Adams College.

Several women teachers made a lasting impression on me while I was at Adams. First there was Sis Frieda – as we called her – the producer of 'Esther', which I mentioned earlier. She was a very good-looking woman, kind but firm, and very outspoken on the subject of courtship. Her approach was more on what girls should do than on what they should not. She was the first woman in my life to talk openly about sex. Perhaps I valued this informal education because I had lost a confidante in the person of my mother. Frieda provided a model of married life and motherhood for all of us. Hers was a family which embodied a life of deep love, respect, peaceful living and sincere love of children. It hurts me to know that this country lost citizens of great potential by failing to recognise in her husband and many of his colleagues great leadership potential simply because they were black. Z.K. Matthews was a great educationalist, but with others of his calibre, was taken to court in the notorious 1956 Treason Trial, simply because he was articulating some of the injustices and hardships suffered by blacks under apartheid.

The 1930s and 1940s saw the beginning of the disintegration of the moral coherence of the black community. Parents began to fail in their duty to discuss questions of relationships between boys and girls with their children. And there was very little written material we could turn to. So sex education was handled at school, either for boys and girls separately, or in mixed groups.

The main difference between the youth of that era and that of today is that whilst the former relied to a very great extent on what the adults told them, the latter believe much more in what they learn from books, and in some cases are suspicious or doubtful of what is passed by word of mouth. It is true to say that it can be rewarding for young people to find out the answers to their problems for themselves; but it is equally true that while experience is an effective teacher, it can be costly. Many young people – and especially young girls – in this country have ended up with severe physical and emotional scars for which a remedy is not easy to find.

It is imperative for the black community to encourage young people to use the information from whatever literature is available to them; but they must also be encouraged to leave the door open for the support of parents and other adults, who are qualified and willing to handle some of these crucial and sensitive topics freely. When firmly established in groups or communities, the sort of values conveyed to us by Mrs Matthews at Adams College sharpen critical faculties and the judgement of daily events and occurrences. For example, when carefully studied, some South African legislation makes a laughing stock of those who draft the laws. I am thinking particularly of the Immorality Act which was formulated to check or stop any possible sexual contact between men and women of different races. This means that if men and women of the same racial group commit adultery, the government is not perturbed. But the Scriptures make the unqualified statement, 'thou shalt not commit adultery'.

Many of the teachers at Adams College who lived at the girls' residence made a lasting impact on us. I have in mind particularly Ellen Ngozwane, who was popular and very much loved by all the students. She was also a great friend of Professor Matthews' family.

She was a charming and attractive woman, dark in complexion, and well-built, but certainly not stout. She had excellent taste in clothes and always looked very elegant. She was someone who could not escape the on-looker's eye. As young girls, we were not as innocent as the school authorities thought we were. When relaxing amongst ourselves, and up to our naughty pranks, we would start matchmaking the teachers. Every time we assessed Miss Ngozwane, we always found she had no match among the male staff – in our estimation, she was high above all the bachelor teachers. Our convictions were confirmed later when we learnt that she was married to an eminent Ugandan named Kisosonkole (the father of the Kabaka, king of Buganda).

Another teacher, Miss Mama, a friend of Miss Ngozwane, was a very withdrawn person, very quiet. She taught domestic science, but her teaching went beyond the classroom. In her quiet way she followed us up in our daily duties at Esidleveleni to see that bathrooms, bedrooms, the dining hall and the immediate surroundings of the residence were in good order. She took us to task on all these and on our own appearance, reminding us to mend our own clothes when necessary. There is no doubt that many girls benefited from Miss Mama's forthright manner. She was meticulous in all she did, and saw domestic science as a way of life, not simply as an examination subject.

About five miles from Adams is a famous village known as Umbumbulu. It is predominantly occupied by the Makhanya clan, one of whose members was a highly influential woman. This was Violet Sibusisiwe, who was born on 11 August 1894, the eldest of seven children.

Most rural black communities are based on the extended family. In some villages there may be as many as 100 to 200 families totalling perhaps 1000 to 2000 people in one clan. This was the case with the Makhanyas at Umbumbulu. In this sort of community, its members are bound by an unwritten common code of ethics, which is respected as the basis on which that community operates in its day-to-day activities. It was impressive to observe the stability, tranquility and security which permeated these villages before the introduction and enforcement of the relocation legislation.

Sibusisiwe came from a background like this. Her mother had been one of the first students at Inanda Seminary, when it was run by the principal, Miss Edwards, an American. Sibusisiwe received her primary education at Umbumbulu, her high school education at

Inanda Seminary, and trained as a teacher at Adams College. Her first teaching post was at Bizana in Pondoland in the Cape – even in those early years some black women worked very far from their homes – she later transferred nearer home, to Inanda. She was one of the first women to demonstrate that black women were capable of looking after themselves away from their parents and free from dependency on a man, either a male relative or husband. The pinnacle of her achievements came on 22 June 1927, when she left for the United States on a study visit sponsored by the American Board Mission. She remained for three years at Tuskegee University where she graduated as a social worker.

It was on her return from this trip that I met her. She was different from other women of her age; for example, in the way she dressed and her hair style. She left an indelible impression on my mind. Apart from telling us about her travels and educational achievements overseas, she also told us about her work in her community since her return from the United States. Her programme was directed towards the informal education of women and girls. She told us that she worked with women in her community on ways of extending the range of cookery. She specialised in using natural ingredients, found locally, preparing dishes from young green mealies and common green vegetables. Her father gave her a piece of land where she had erected a building to be used as a centre for women's and girls' programmes.

That building stands to this day – long after her death in 1971 at the age of 77 years. A large sign over the building reads: Umbumbulu Community Centre. She never practised her social work through a registered welfare agency or voluntary organisation, nor was she employed by any organisation as we commonly expect today. No. Sibusisiwe worked among her people as a community worker.

As for how she managed to live, I can only guess that she might have received a salary from her church. I heard her speak on only a few occasions, but on each of these her conviction about the value of her work shone through.

In 1953 her community gave her recognition by naming a school built through her influence and efforts Sibusisiwe High School.

At the end of my training I began to feel that the academic side of my education was inadequate. I was confident about my ability to teach after five years' intensive training in teaching methods and principles of education, and teaching practice. But I now felt a growing need to return to college to study in greater depth the subjects I was expected to teach, including History, Geography, Biology, English, Sesotho, Physiology and Hygiene, and others. I felt I had put the cart before the horse. After turning the matter over in my mind, I decided to leave Adams and enrol at a college with a good academic reputation.

I therefore consulted my step-father, who recommended Lovedale. I was thrilled by his advice as Lovedale was the college where my maternal grandfather, father, step-father, aunt, cousins and other relatives had all studied. This underlines the point I have already made, that the black community had a long educational history by the time the Nationalist Party came to power in 1948, with educational institutions run by various churches all over the country. Even in the early nineteenth century, Natal, the Cape Colony and the Transvaal had a few colleges. The long list of graduates bears witness to the high standard and quality of education achieved by blacks.

What this government has succeeded in doing since 1953 to reduce our education to something far inferior to that provided for whites. As a result it has created a community of poorly educated and ill-trained blacks to maintain the relationship of master to servant between whites and blacks. But they forget that nothing lasts for ever. To this day Bantu Education is not accepted, merely tolerated – and then only because of the canings and shootings, the setting of dogs on people, and choking them with tear-gas every time they express their frustration and disgust with the laws of the country.

The story of my life, my education, you see, cannot be buried quietly and safely in the past. How can I remain quiet when I see the choices open to the younger generation constantly restricted, their hopes fading into dreams, and the dreams becoming nightmares?

This challenge has haunted me through my entire life.

6
Further Education and Growing Doubts

Lovedale Institution had established traditions, values and practices of its own, and a unique atmosphere. It stood in close proximity to Victoria Hospital to the north-east, where the first black nurse in South Africa was trained; and south-east of the Institution stood the oldest black university in this country: Fort Hare. (I was last at Lovedale forty-five years ago; in case my assessment of direction of all these places is not correct, please bear with me.) The Tshumi River runs between Lovedale and Fort Hare. I believe that the close presence of these other educational centres helped to give Lovedale the dignified atmosphere and fame it enjoyed.

On the south bank of the river is the small town of Alice where we students did our shopping: we had to cross the river by a swing bridge. The first time I crossed it, I prayed I would get across and back safely. With experience over the months I accepted it as a normal happening, and it became real fun in the long run.

If my memory serves me well, the grounds of Lovedale were covered with lovely tall oak trees, which added beauty to the towering buildings of the college. As well as the girls' and boys' schools, which were known as 'Umzana' and 'Umzimkulu' respectively, there were also high school and teacher training departments. The large hall was a popular meeting place, where students assembled for services and other events such as concerts. The chairs in this hall were arranged in such a way that they left a central aisle with male students seated one side and female students on the other. The aisle was popularly used by female students who arrived late and wanted to attract attention; it was accordingly known as 'Smiling Avenue'. The passage between the female students' chairs and the wall was known, in contrast, as 'Sad Avenue', and was used by timid students arriving late because of circumstances beyond their control. Strange to say, those of us who were not brave enough to use 'Smiling Avenue', admired those who did and saw them as sophisticated and brave. It may be too that we envied them more than we admired them.

Sundays were special at Lovedale. It was on this day that we assembled under the oak trees for the religious service, and all looked forward to Sunday worship. It was a great source of pride and joy to be 'under the oaks'. The breeze together with the beautiful green vegetation elevated our spirits. The college had a large organ with many pipes, played on Sundays by Miss Parker. The harmony of the organ, blending with the students' voices, transmitted to the air music which enhanced the beauty of the surroundings and was both soothing to the ear and elevating to the inner self. In those years Miss Parker was held in high esteem by the students because of her great musical ability.

Some of the sermons I listened to in those days rang with a note of truth and sincerity. Those who delivered them showed commitment, concern and dedication. We believed and trusted those in authority. What we were told fifty years ago still has value for us today. If I were asked, 'How certain are you that they were not just putting on an act?' my answer to that would immediately be, 'Indeed, I would not put my head on the block for one. But, if they were just pretending, I would certainly not pass them off as actors, but as confirmed hypocrites. It is from some of those teachings that most black children of my age group grew emotionally, physically and mentally.'

The surroundings and amenities at Lovedale reflected the ideals of the college. The dormitories, the dining-room, the classrooms – all were well equipped and orderly. Being a student in this college influenced your outlook, values and way of life. Whilst the classroom provided our formal education we were all thoroughly aware of the surroundings in which our education was taking place. The inspection of our premises, a practice which did not appeal to many of us, turned out to be an informal way of learning in the long run.

The students at Lovedale were committed to their studies. I was immediately taken into a group of three girls who were ranked as the cream of the class. Dineo Mamokopu Mofolo was the daughter of a Mosotho author, Mr Thomas Mofolo, who wrote *Pitseng*. She often ceded top position in class tests to Petronella Sikhweza, from the Transkei. Petronella was very conscientious about her schoolwork. The third member of the group, who always came third in class, was Betrina Mrwetjana. They invited me to join them in their study group provided I was prepared to adhere to the standards they set themselves. Among these were: to be on time for the study period the group set itself and to sit right through the time set down for that period; to do one's best during tests or examinations; to make sure that we fell within the first four positions in class. As a new student at this college and in this class, I found all this a really tall order, but as I was determined to do my best, I counted myself very fortunate to be invited into a group of students with this rare approach towards their work, and I accepted the challenging invitation.

For the nine months we were classmates in 1936 we kept our pact. When results were announced in class, we always held the first four positions. The fifth position went to a male student. We naturally felt very good about this. When the first four names were announced, we would simultaneously exclaim after each of the names, 'Obvious!'

Those girls, two of them the same age as me, one slightly younger, set themselves strict tasks which they adhered to. They developed their potential to the fullest, and demonstrated their determination to study and to challenge male students. They had great potential and their future appeared to be bright. It was with great sadness that I learned that two of them died young. Dineo I know got married and had two children. Petronella died unmarried. I have not heard anything about Betrina since we parted at Lovedale.

Lovedale was certainly an ideal example of the type of school provided by the missions for the black community in South Africa. The detested Bantu Education (and its successors) introduced by the Nationalist government in 1953, in contrast, provides no education at all; it seeks only to suppress talent, to lower morale, and to produce obedient servants to carry out instructions without question, even when urgently needed. When I see the quality of teachers produced by Bantu Education and training, I bow my head in shame; that an Act like this can come from a so-called 'Christian' government! The truth is, it is reinforcing and maintaining the *status quo* servant:master relationship between blacks and whites in South Africa.

It was at Lovedale that I received direct coaching in public speaking. Miss Schindler, my English teacher, was our coach. We were assigned specific tasks with a time-limit set for each: either impromptu speeches, or speeches carefully prepared in advance.

Leisure-time activities at Lovedale centred on athletics. Both male and female students participated in these. The highlight of the year was the inter-school competitions between Lovedale and Healdtown. All we students, whether athletes or not, prepared ourselves for this big day, and accompanied our school team to the venue of the competition. The star of 1936 at Lovedale was a young man named Smith from Ladysmith in Natal. If my memory serves well, he was a miler. Once he got into the arena, there would be a loud roar as the students shouted S-M-I-T-H until he reached the winning-post.

I did well during that school year, keeping my number four position in all school tests and obtaining a second class pass in the examinations for the junior Certificate. My teachers, study group and the tone of the college helped me. But, for some reason or another, my eagerness to continue my studies waned. Perhaps it was because of my initial disappointment at failing to get into the matriculation class; perhaps it was the result of the exhaustion induced by cramming a three-year syllabus into one year.

Even after forty-seven years, since I left Lovedale, the pleas of my step-father, Papa Abel Phogane Tsimatsima, are still very fresh in my mind. I hear his gentle yet firm voice, accompanied by his peaceful countenance, pleading with me in vain to continue my studies – up to university junior degree level at least. I took in all he said, and valued it, together with the genuine moral support he gave me. Deep down, though, something was just not right, although I could not put my finger on what was amiss. I finally turned down that option, without any clear explanation for doing so, but very certain that it was the right thing to do.

Although I ended my schooling at Lovedale much against his will, my step-father remained the same father to me. He never turned away from me at any stage. Even when there were relationship problems in the family, he always reassured me of his support, though he often expressed his regret that I left school rather than go on to university. Now that I reflect back on this situation, perhaps he wanted to carry out the promise he made to Mother.

Before I left Lovedale, I received an invitation from Inanda Seminary near Durban to teach there, which I accepted. But before taking my new post, I took a short holiday in December 1936. This was my first visit to Johannesburg and I stayed with my natural father and his new family. There was a major event that year in Johannesburg. I do not remember the exact name of the event, but it had something to do with the 'Empire Exhibition'. I enjoyed the outings during my four-weeks stay with my father and his family in the company of my maternal aunt, Elizabeth Makgothi. We spent most of our time in and out of the house, but we really never settled down for me to get to know the family at all, except on the superficial basis of 'Good morning, how are you?', 'We had a fine day', and so on. But my father happily chaperoned us around Johannesburg and to the exhibition, as strangers in that city, and entertained us to the best of his ability. However, there was an emotional gap which is bridged and cemented only by a stable, continuous, normal family relationship. I did not know my father as a parent. He expressed his appreciation for my school success; but he never really replaced my step-father.

During this visit I was able to confirm what I had heard: that my father was a progressive man in the leadership of civic and political affairs of the black community in Johannesburg; that he was a gifted man in many ways; and that he was running a lucrative business in Pimville. As a child these attributes made me feel curious about him as well as quite proud, but until I met him, I had completely failed to visualise him in my mind. Even when I did meet him, I had no longing to hug and kiss him, a feeling natural in a normal family setting.

At the end of the holiday I went back to Thaba'Nchu and got ready to pack my belongings to join the teaching staff at Inanda at the beginning of 1937.

7
Physical and Emotional Shocks

I have already mentioned in Chapter 5 some of the catchphrases my friends Epeinette and Norah, and I set ourselves at a time when all three of us were far away from our parents – Epeinette from Matatiele, Nora from Nigel and I from Thaba'Nchu. We closed ranks and became a threesome which offered mutual support. Among those slogans we followed were: 'First things first', 'Start as you mean to go on', 'Learn to say No! even to some of the good things at times'. It is amazing the strength we derived from these simple yet far-reaching truths. We internalised them and used them at those times when we were face-to-face with major individual or group decisions.

Within the first six months of joining the Inanda Seminary school staff, I was abruptly separated from those dear friends through ill-health. When I look back, years after that very unfortunate experience, I put it down to the mental strain I experienced at Lovedale resulting from the pact to keep within the first four positions in class. As I have explained, I had to work extra hard to cover in one year the schoolwork that my three classmates had covered in their first two years there, prior to my arrival. It was this effort, I think, that almost cost me my good health once I started teaching.

Just outside Inanda Seminary stood a small village of the black community. The majority of the inhabitants were congregants of the American Board Mission Church which had built the girls' school. The Rev. Gumede, the pastor of the local church, lived with his family in this village. If my memory serves me well, he had one son and about five or six daughters. Some of his daughters were with me at Adams College as my class- or school-mates. They were very outgoing girls in their outlook, at least those I was at school with. Among these I remember Mattie, Tosh and Geja. They were by all standards as good as any from the cities and towns of South Africa. My association with these girls meant that I knew that their brother, Innes Gumede, was a doctor. So, the moment I realised my health was failing, I called on him. Without any waste of time, he gave me what medication was necessary and recommended to the principal of the seminary that I be released to go back home. In addition to this he gave me a letter for my family doctor at home, Dr J.S. Moroka. I was naturally very anxious about my journey home, as I was unescorted. But it passed well: the medication from the doctor helped; and so did the complete overnight rest on the train. In those days, a journey by train was both very safe and peaceful.

On my arrival home, I saw Dr Moroka who gave me full medication and attention. The moment I entered his surgery, I knew that I was in very safe hands. I had known him as our family doctor since I was about nine or ten. By nature he was very direct and approachable, and apart from prescribing medication, he took the time to discuss with all his patients their problems and to offer advice on eating habits, exercise and general conduct. Some of his well-known remedies involved eating vegetables and using the local spinach – commonly known as *morogo* – as well as learning to be steady in whatever you did. I can never forget the number of times he emphasised by his own manner the importance of avoiding unnecessary stress in any duty I was to undertake. He would unhurriedly walk to the telephone when it rang, gently pick it up, answer it in a very composed, unruffled voice, and continue his conversation in the same tone. He attended me from childhood up to my mid-twenties and, from time to time, even up to my early fifties. At the age of 93 years he is no longer practising medicine, but to all Thaba'Nchu children he is still 'Papa Ngaka', meaning literally 'Father Doctor'.

At the end of three months' treatment, I had regained my full health and was ready to go back to work. During these months my aunt, Fanny Mutsinyane Setlogelo, also born Makgothi, had left her home farm at Lekoala (or Somerset), near Tweespruit to come and nurse me. For some reason or another this aunt, my mother's younger sister, had been very fond of me from childhood. She and Mother were the only two people who called 'Cholofelo' meaning 'Hope'. She was the mother of those three girls and one boy I grew up with at my grandparents' home in Thaba Patchoa. She was indeed a very dear mother. Her eldest and youngest daughters are still alive and, to this day, we still regard ourselves as sisters. I suppose it is for this reason that I have been particularly close to her youngest daughter, Bernice Motlagomang Setlogelo. Other racial groups may deride the extended family as being backward and outdated, but it is a pillar of strength to black people.

Towards the end of my period of recuperation, when I was still under medical treatment, Dr Moroka prepared me for going back to work. In his gentle, matter-of-fact way, he kept reminding me that I should get ready to return to teaching. Before the schools closed in 1937 I sent a letter of application to the principal of St Paul's School, where I passed standards 5 and 6; and in January 1938 I started there under Mr Paul Ramotshoane Mosaka, the headmaster, one of the greatest educationalists of the black community.

For the first three or four months of my return from Inanda Seminary, I had spent the greater part of my time on the farm, only coming into town to see the doctor. However, once I was accepted on to the staff at St Paul's Higher Primary School, I had to move to Thaba'Nchu and could only visit the farm at weekends and during school vacations.

At the beginning of the year, everything was pleasant. I adjusted very well to my work, and life at home was, by and large, as it had been in the past. To begin with my thoughts were of Inanda Seminary, and I longed for my close friends, Norah and Epeinette. However, in the course of time this longing gradually waned and I renewed my old childhood friendships with some of the girls and boys who had qualified as school teachers at different teacher training institutions and were now employed at St Paul's. I have very dear memories of Ellen Sisinyane Fenyang, Winnie Motlalepule Monyatsi, Keneiloe Mojanaga, Stephen Gopane and Johnnie Nyokong, all members of the staff team I worked with.

Except for Keneiloe Mojanaga, who never married but continued to teach, all these girlfriends later found their life-partners and settled into family life in different places. Ellen Fenyang married Paul Mahabane, another teacher of repute; sadly, her life ended before she reached a great age. Winnie Monyatsi married William Kgware, who became the first black to head a university in this country – the late Professor William Kgware, rector of the University of the North. Winnie was to show great courage during this marriage. Her husband was seen by the community in Pietersburg as a collaborator in the government policies which ruled this tribal university. Winnie herself both challenged certain procedures affecting the students' welfare and security and took part in some of the black youth programmes which were seen by the government of the country as a threat to national security. She stood her ground steadfastly to the point of sacrificing the security and peace of her own home. To this day her image stands untarnished in the University of the North. She now lives at Mmabatho in Bophuthatswana. With regard to my Inanda Seminary friends, Epeinette married Govan Mbeki, as I have already said, and Norah became Epeinette's sister-in-law when she married her brother Manasse, another notable educationalist of the 1940s and 1950s.

In addition to my teaching work, I found myself at this time increasingly attracted to and involved in some of the community and national issues in my neighbourhood. In the summer of 1937 I attended the historic All African Convention which was held in Bloemfontein. The All African Convention was created as an umbrella body for all the groups and organisations existing in the black community, in the areas of education, commerce, health, politics, social welfare, employment, religion and sports. People came from all over South Africa for this event. There were considerably more men than women. There I met the men and women leaders in the black community, as well as those at grass-roots level. Among those in executive positions were Professor D.D.T. Jabavu, Professor Z.K. Matthews, Dr A.S. Xuma, Dr J.S. Moroka, Mr Selby Msimanga, Mr R. V. Selope Thema, and others. They came from all over South Africa. These men were chosen on merit by their community, not on ethnicity, to direct the affairs of the black people. There was peace, order, concerted effort and shared leadership in those days.

One group which left a very vivid impression on my mind were some of the old gentlemen from the Cape. Their spirit of participation in the discussions singled them out, as did their grey hair and dress. The majority of them wore military coats and carried walking sticks for support. But there was nothing sophisticated about them. They wore stout boots, which did not seem to handicap them in their movements. They smoked long pipes. They made a valid contribution to the discussions of the conference. It was when I met them that I first heard the word 'Bunga' which was frequently mentioned during the discussions. Bunga is a Xhosa word meaning 'coming together to consult on an issue'. At the turn of the century a black political body had been formed in the Transkei called 'Bunga'.

It was at this meeting too that I first met Miss Minah Tembeka Soga who was outstanding in her contribution when the constitution and policy of the Convention were drafted. This great daughter of Africa was born on 5 June 1895, near Queenstown, and qualified at Emgwali Training School as a teacher, where she first taught. She had insight and initiative. Amongst many other achievements, she founded a school for adult education in Queenstown. She travelled widely, visiting among other countries, India, America and Great Britain. She was outspoken about how she saw the role of women in the struggle for black liberation. I admired this gracious, tall, very fluent, dignified lady. She had a very strong personality and displayed integrity and intelligence. Minah Soga's leadership emerged when the menfolk were faced with very challenging issues and were geared for making major decisions over a very difficult period in the political life of the African community. Under Minah's leadership, the women hurriedly drafted a resolution for submission stating their desire to get black women all over the Union organised into councils. With the full approval of the Convention, the women organised themselves to stand side by side with their menfolk in the struggle for the advancement and liberation of the African nation in South Africa.

Except for the women's church groups, this was the first formidable black women's organisation in South Africa, and it demonstrated their determination and strength. They pledged themselves to serve their race and to liberate themselves from the shackles of humiliation, discrimination and systematic psychological suppression by their own menfolk as well as by the state through its legislation and administrative regulations. At the first national conference of the National Council of African Women (NCAW) held in Bloemfontein on 17 December 1937, Minah Soga, the founder, was elected General Secretary. She was National President of NCAW for fiteen years and is now Life President of the Council. A great leader, a great woman of Africa. She gave her full life for the service of her people and her immediate community as well as for the advancement of the black women in South Africa. NCAW was the first women's organisation that I joined; and I joined because of the image portrayed by Minah and some other women in the leadership of the organisation. The motto of this organisation, which has stood over 44 years is: 'Do unto others as they would do unto you.' It sums up her life.

I myself attended the first NCAW conference. The greatest

moment for me was when, at that conference, I met the legendary Mrs Charlotte Manye Maxeke.

Charlotte Manye Maxeke was a household name in the Transvaal during that period. She had played a prominent part in establishing the American Methodist Episcopal Church in South Africa, a church started by the blacks for the blacks and with the blacks. She had also travelled to the USA, obtaining a degree from Wilberforce University; in 1902 she was thus the first black woman graduate in South Africa. I learned recently that the African National Congress has named a creche in Tanzania after her.

When I first encountered her, her bearing, her upright head and clear eyes, proclaimed her as a woman of character and principles. She appeared firm and composed; a woman of values and standards. She gave me the impression of being conscientious and very business-like in her dealings but, above all, a woman very clear about the purpose and direction of her church and her community involvement. I did not find her easy to approach – unlike Minah Soga. I longed to get near her and talk to her; but except for hearing her address the conference, I never had an opportunity to speak to her. Now that I look back, perhaps the disparity in our ages was a barrier to my reaching her.

My membership in the Council at that time was nominal because of my youth. There was no active participation on my part, either through paying registration fees or playing an active role in the programme. I was attracted to the organisation, I suppose, partly because of a sensitivity to community issues brought about by my early childhood learning to accept people as people. I was also deeply affected by my early exposure at the All African Convention, which brought me in direct contact with individuals and groups who made a lasting impact, to surface later in life as distinct, personal guidelines. And then there was my attraction to the personality and image of Minah Soga and Charlotte Maxeke, who fired my imagination. However, I was too young and too immature to make a useful contribution.

The influence and insight of these women should never be underestimated. As first National President of the National Council of African Women, Charlotte Maxeke, for example, said, in her Presidential Address to the second conference, held in Bloemfontein on 8 December 1938:

I want to thank you very much and congratulate you on your

excellent deliberations. This work is not for yourselves – kill that spirit of 'self' and do not live above your people, but live with them. If you can rise, bring someone with you. Do away with that fearful animal of jealousy – kill that spirit, and love one another as brothers and sisters. The other animal that will tear us to pieces is *tribalism*; I saw the shadow of it and it should cease to be. Stand by your motto – 'The golden rule'.

This was the Charlotte Maxeke of the 1930s.

Even in those early years, 'tribalism' was recognised as a danger by the black community. It was no coincidence that the leadership of the black people in those days was consciously chosen on the basis of merit and not ethnicity, an evil which has come with the Nationalist government regime. I suppose it is used as an instrument to divide and rule blacks. These were the warnings given by one of the leading black women in South Africa as long ago as 1938. Even at this minute, I feel most justified in saying to Charlotte: '*Hamba Kahle! O dule o re gopola moradia Manye.*' ('Go well and think of us always, daughter of Manye.')

That period was enriched by a number of highly talented women in the black community. They worked together and with their menfolk on issues of national importance for liberation and also claimed recognition as black women fighting their own battles. Mrs Magdeline Sesedi was such a woman in the forefront of the struggle. Magdeline trained as a teacher in the Cape Rheinish Training School, the only professional avenue open for black women in those years. She was one of the founder members of the National Council of African Women and was elected its first Vice-President, an office she held for twelve consecutive years. She became National President in 1956. Through her zeal and effort, several branches of the Council were established in the Northern Cape and Eastern Transvaal. She was an active member of the Anglican Church and of the Mothers' Union. Later in life she became director of a general dealer's business and she encouraged other women to take an active interest in this field. She was a perfect model of womanhood, full of charm, beauty and dignity.

In 1938, I was elected secretary of the local branch of the NCAW, in Thaba'Nchu. Mrs Maggie Moroka, the wife of Dr J.S. Moroka, was the local chairperson. The Home Improvement Club became the major programme, involving members at all levels, particularly at the grass-roots, in cookery, sewing, first aid, knitting, crocheting and sport for the younger members. The involvement with a club of

that nature indirectly trained us in the basic principles of administration. As committee members, we developed the skills needed by
different office-bearers, such as minute-taking, preparing agenda
for meetings, collecting, receipting and keeping funds. We all
developed simple management and administration skills without
realising our personal and intellectual growth and development in
that field.

I was making progress, then, outside home. But at home, quite
unexpectedly, things were to change for the worse. At this point, I
ought to explain that Aunt Blanche, Mother's youngest sister, had
married my step-father in about 1932 or 33, and so was now my
step-mother. This change was smooth because, as young children,
all grandfather's grandchildren had been taught to address all three
sisters as 'Mother'. At first, this had a positive influence on my
relationship with Aunt Blanche. When Aunt Blanche married my
step-father, she was a widow and a mother of two daughters from
her previous marriage. Round about 1933, a daughter from her
marriage with my step-father was born. At the time, I accepted
these additions to the family as quite normal. My own half-sister,
who had started at Lovedale Institution in 1935, was also living at
home.

For the duration of my illness, as I have said, I lived on the farm
at Tshiamelo. This was home. When I recovered, Aunt Fanny went
back to her own home in Thaba'Nchu. As children of the family, we
sometimes lived in Thaba'Nchu and sometimes at the farm. Over
the years, it had become an open secret that the homestead in
Thaba'Nchu had been bequeathed to Aunt Blanche in my
grandfather's will. As a child, this had no significance for me. I still
regarded the homestead as home, in the same way that I thought of
the farm itself; and I lived there when I took my first teaching post
in Thaba'Nchu early in 1938.

It was during that year though that I first sensed some
unpleasantness in the atmosphere when I returned from the farm. I
never took Aunt Blanche's casual but stinging remarks as directed
at me personally. My aunt was a very forthright, outspoken,
temperamental, irritable person by nature. I had known and
accepted her as such for as long as I had lived with her. It was
halfway through 1938, when I was teaching in Thaba'Nchu, that my
aunt's attitude seemed to change drastically. She became aggressive
and resentful. Even then, I did not take this as directed personally
at me.

One summer day I was going about my household chores. It could have been a Saturday or during the school holidays, or it could have been in the afternoon after school. It is so very long ago. This one thing I do remember vividly: she was watering the flower garden in front of the main house with an old lady we had known for years as Mama Nnyelele. My aunt called me over: 'Motlalepule,' she said, and I replied, 'Mme Mma' and presented myself – as was expected. Her temperament had changed though – she appeared charged with emotion. I stood there surprised, puzzled, bewildered. She looked straight at me and said something to this effect: 'There is no home for you any more here. You should go and look for your father and your people in Johannesburg. You must go now or as soon as possible. I don't want to see the sight of you any more here.'

Truth can be stranger than fiction in life sometimes. For a split second, I thought I was dreaming. Yet, there I was, alive, aware. I was shocked and numbed to the marrow. I shall never remember how I moved from where I stood. As I glanced at Mama Nnyelele for support or protection, I soon realised she was party to the whole plot.

When I recovered from this sudden, unexpected shock, I went to my step-father to break the devastating news to him. I saw embarrassment on his face, and perhaps shock too. Even from him, Aunt Blanche's husband, I hoped for protection and some support, but he appeared completely lost and helpless. His look was empty and distant for a while and then, as if coming face-to-face with reality, he turned to me and said: 'I am sorry about this. Your "Mother" wants it this way and I cannot do anything about it.' I realised then that I was up against an insuperable problem. I now felt lost and hurt as well as uttlerly helpless. Yet I pitied him. I continued in this vein; 'I will write to Johannesburg and request Father to send me money to buy the rail ticket to Johannesburg. I will inform you of the outcome.'

For the first time in a very long while I missed Mother, missed her voice and her gentle smile. Quickly, though, I realised that weeping and moaning would not help me. So, I composed myself and wrote to my father. Thank God! I knew his address.

Then followed a long period of anxiety, waiting for his reply. Many questions drifted through my mind. Would he reply? After how long? Would he send me money? Would I be accepted by his family? What if they rejected me too? I felt utterly rejected and an outcast.

I now drew on my early Christian teaching and the beliefs this teaching had instilled in me. I remembered the early Sunday school teachings from my mother and from others – 'Christ loves us all.' I clung to that belief and told myself that he would never reject me even if the whole world does. With this thought in my mind, I started to collect my belongings together and to wash and pack in preparation for another journey.

The days and weeks which followed dragged. I visited the post office regularly, but came back empty-handed yet heavily loaded inside. If a letter and money failed to arrive, what would I do next? Another concern was to find a *job*. I dreaded the prospect of being both homeless and jobless!

Life in Ellen Kuzwayo's family at the turn of the 19th century. Seated is Mrs Moses Masisi, carrying her eldest daughter. Standing behind her, traditionally dressed, are the servants.

Jeremiah Makgothi, Ellen's maternal grandfather: the only layman to sit on Dr Moffat's Committee translating the Bible into Setswana in 1857; farmer; teacher in a multi-racial school in Thaba 'Nchu at the turn of the century; Court interpreter; Secretary of the first South African Native Congress in 1909; interpreter at the historic Dower meeting in Thaba 'Nchu in 1913.

Abel and Emma Tsimatsima, Ellen's mother and stepfather, on their marriage in 1921.

Ellen Kuzwayo, when a school teacher in Heilbron, holding her half-sister Maria's son. Taken in Thaba 'Nchu in 1939.

Opposite page, above: Lovedale Institution, run by the London Missionary Society, founded in 1820. Jeremiah trained there, as a teacher from 1874-1879. In his copy book written in 1874 Jeremiah describes his journey to Lovedale by oxwagon. Ellen Kuzwayo went there in 1936. *Photo: Cape Archives, ref. AG5885.*

Below: Lovedale girls' dining hall. The Missionaries unfortunately graded their students at table according to their financial background! Parents of the girls at table No. 1 paid £22, and those of the girls at Table 2 paid £14 a term! *Photo: Cape Archives, ref. AG5870.*

Left: Tshiamelo (A Place Of Goodness), the farm inherited by Ellen from her mother in 1930. It was declared a 'Black Spot' in 1974 and stripped from her. It was 600 morgen (1500 acres). *Photo Paul Alberts.*

Below: Tshiamelo: the homestead is in the background. The building in the foreground right was built by Ellen's grandfather at the turn of the century. It was used as a school during the week and as a church on Sundays. Ellen attended school there from 7-11 years old. Photograph taken from the film 'Tsiamelo. A Place of Goodness', made in 1983: Ellen in foreground.

Black women in Bloemfontein protesting against the carrying of passes by women, in 1913. Thousands of women within a hundred-mile radius of Thaba 'Nchu were imprisoned as a result of this demonstration. These nameless, faceless, courageous women staved off the carrying of passes by women for more than forty years. *Photo Cape Archives, ref VA3468.*

Opposite: Maria Pilane, Ellen's half-sister, daughter of Ellen's mother and her stepfather Abel Tsimatsima. Taken in 1939 in Thaba 'Nchu. Maria Pilane now lives in Botswana.

Senior students at St Francis College, Mariannhill, Natal. Ellen's aunt Elizabeth Makgothi is second left, seated (1930). Ellen was also attending this school in 1930.

Wedding photograph of Ellen's half sister (seated extreme left) in Thaba 'Nchu in 1938. Standing behind her is the groom, Thari, son of Chief Pilane of Saulspoort. Ellen is standing fourth from left and Ellen's stepfather is seated second from left.

Ellen Kuzwayo and Blanche Tsimatsima discussing their great heritage, before the shooting of their film 'Tsiamelo' in 1983. This film provided an opportunity for a reconciliation between Aunt Blanche and Ellen, after many years of estrangement. *Photo: Paul Alberts.*

1983. Aunt Blanche aged 83 years, taken during filming of 'Tsiamelo: A Place of Goodness'. *Photo: Cassandra Parker.*

Ellen and Aunt Blanche revisiting Segogoane's Valley farm, which was declared a 'Black Spot' in 1974. The farm was fully functioning when Aunt Blanche owned it. Now owned by the Government, it has been allowed to fall into decay. Photography taken during the shooting of the film 'Tsiamelo' in 1983. *Photo: Clare Goodman.*

Makeshift classroom in Dennilton resettlement area, built by the parents in desperation for their children's education.
Photo: Peter Chappell.

Soweto, a city within a city, with a population of over 2 million, stretching 32 square miles, south-west of Johannesburg. The grey 'matchbox' houses in no way reflect the strength and vibrancy of the majority of residents there. *Photo: Peter Chappell.*

Charlotte Maxeke, born
Manye, first black woman
graduate in South Africa. She
received a degree at Wilber-
force University in the United
States. First president,
National Council of African
Women, in 1937.

Phyllis Noluthando Mzaidume,
born Maseko, on left. First
black member on the staff of
the World-Affiliated Young
Women's Christian Association, as General Secretary
Transvaal region, in 1953. She
died in 1964.

Dr Mary Susan Xakana, born
Malahlela, first black woman
medical doctor in South Africa.
Graduated in 1947.

Mina Soga, founder of the
National Council of African
Women in 1937 and its
Secretary for 12 years.

Mrs Mamadikoe Manthata, courageous mother of Thomas Manthata, many times detained, founder member of Committee of 10.

Albertina Sisulu in 1981 at the Conference of the Federation of South African Women. At this time she had herself been living under a banning order for 17 years, while her husband Walter Sisulu served a life sentence on Robben Island for political offences.

Annie Silinga, heroic campaigner against passes for women. She died in 1981 without ever having carried a pass.

8
Farewell Thaba'Nchu

My whole childhood had tumbled away. The place which had been my dear home for all my life was now alien and empty. The people I had looked upon as my parents became strangers and remote. The household in which my daily chores had been undertaken with joy and pride, with laughter or the humming of a tune, seemed to reject me. It dawned on me for the first time that I was a stranger, an intruder, that I was imposing myself where I was unwanted and perhaps did not belong. In my confusion and misery, I wondered whether I should move out and go to Somerset farm to Aunt Fanny Setlogelo in Tweespruit district. But as this would create a rift within the family, I decided against it. Making a cup of tea or preparing a meal for the family, tasks which were my usual duties, became odious and nerve-wrecking to me. I wondered whether certain members of the family would accept that meal. For in our culture, acceptance of food is symbolic of acceptance in the home; and to refuse a meal is a symbol of rejection. It was much easier when the whole family sat at table; they would come or not after hearing the table bell. My problem lay in taking a tray to those members of the family who did not sit at table. It was now an ordeal to carry out this simple household duty. All the same, I carried out my duties to the last, and in spite of those uncertainties and hesitations, I survived the ordeal.

While I remained in Thaba'Nchu, I lost all sense of personal direction and identity, I felt so rejected by the people and surroundings I had once cherished as part of my very being. I was in a state of shock but had no one to share my hurt and shock with. Relatives and family friends who called at the homestead no longer seemed the same loving adults I knew. I began to see them in a new light. I gradually became suspicious of everyone around me and feared to share my feelings with them in any way. In short, I became paranoid. Time and again I told myself that I did not really belong to Thaba'Nchu; that I should have realised earlier that I was the only one with the family name 'Merafe'; that I should have searched for my father's family before I was made a stranger. But the answer to these thoughts quickly crossed my mind. Mother was there, she was everything to me, she had told me about my people but she had never suggested I should search for them.

Through all this emotional strain I tried to find out where I had really gone wrong, and who had really been hurt by me. Could this person not put me right, even punish me, and then forgive me so that I could remain at home? It was clear that Aunt Blanche was hostile, obdurate, and that she had just had enough of me. My step-father, on the other hand, showed none of this negative behaviour. He seemed hurt, embarrassed, ashamed and utterly helpless about my plight. The different reactions of these two most important people in the home and in my life left a very lasting impact on me; and; from that day my whole attitude towards them was altered.

Twenty-one years after my step-father's death, I still hold him in high esteem, and keep fond memories of him. I remember how he encouraged me to read; how he often explained very difficult passages to me, how he pleaded with me not to leave college before I had qualified to enter university. He was a dear, loving father who had no family favourites because of his blood relation with them. He loved all of us and supported each one of us when we needed his support. It came as a shock to many in the family – particularly to those who had believed themselves to be his favourites – that his will not only contained my name, but furthermore, that I was placed at the top of the list of heirs, as the eldest child in the family. That will was dated 1947; I first saw it towards the end of 1964, about three years after his death. It earned me extra hostility from certain quarters in the family, and it increased my admiration and respect for my step-father.

I finally heard from my natural father, but the last few days before I left for Johannesburg to join him were full of one conflict after another. He had not sent me the railway fare and this increased my anxiety in as much as it made my aunt even angrier. To this day I can never fathom out why my step-parents did not offer me the train fare themselves so that I could disappear from Thaba'Nchu. My only guess is that my step-father probably refused to participate in something he was not responsible for and which he was not in favour of. As far as Aunt Blanche is concerned, your guess is as good as mine. Perhaps she could not part with the cash.

Her hostility and rejection of me have remained with me over the years. It is only partly true that time mellows many things. I learned to reject someone, when I first responded to my aunt's rejection. I tried everything possible to appease her in my own child-like way but all that failed. I finally realised she had turned away from me and I accepted the challenge. She had expressly ordered me out of the home. She had further told me to look for Merafe's family, people I had never once seen. I was left with no alternative but to accept the challenge that was forced on me. And so I was driven out of Thaba'Nchu.

Strangely enough, the writing of this book 45 years later opened the first meaningful communication between me and Aunt Blanche since that painful rejection. In 1982 I returned to Thaba'Nchu to seek out material for my book. To my amazement I found Aunt Blanche had a priceless archive of rare documents, photographs and records in a suitcase under her wardrobe.

I felt honoured that she was able to share these with me. It had a bitter irony in that finally Aunt Blanche respected and trusted me to guard and publish all this material. She even gave me a document she had written about her own life which she asked me to guard and publish as her obituary. I was bowled over when I finished reading these papers; they suddenly disclosed the other side of Aunt Blanche, a natural historian who recognised the rich heritage of the Baralong and her own family.

Elizabeth Wolpert was one of the many friends I shared this discovery with. She asked to join me on my next trip to Thaba'Nchu to meet this remarkable woman of 83 years. It was on this visit that Aunt Blanche, Betty and I decided to make the film 'Tsiamelo: A Place of Goodness', which tells the story of our family, the dispossession of our land and the history of the great men and women who preceded us. Although the pain of that early rejection will always remain with me, working on this film with Aunt Blanche created a new opportunity for reconciliation, for sharing in family concerns and a new mutual respect.

My father's reply, enclosing the train fare, arrived after a long anxious wait. I completed my packing and locked my trunk, and at the same time tried in vain to wipe out all the fond memories about the people and surroundings which had been part of me for all my

life. My thoughts started to drift beyond my journey to Johannesburg, posing many questions, about the type of people I would live
with, the home I was going to, my father – would he accept me as
his child? What about his wife and the rest of the family? My
mother's teachings supported me at that time and I almost thought I
heard her say: 'One day when you go to your father, you will find a
mother there. If you are rude to her, you will be doing that to me
and if you respect her, you will be respecting me.' I felt better
prepared to meet my father's family after this.

As I stepped into the horse-drawn taxi which took me to the
railway station that afternoon, I felt a painful separation in my
heart. Tears filled my eyes, but I stopped them from falling. The
cart pulled away from the homestead which had been my fortress,
stronghold, security; from those I had accepted as my parents over a
long period; from the people I had known and accepted as my
people. I felt pushed out like pus from inflamed tissues. I felt
naked, helpless and forlorn. On my journey to Johannesburg, I
clutched my railway ticket as my only link with the unknown world I
had been forcibly thrown into, without warning or preparation.

Throughout that journey I searched my soul as to what could
have driven my aunt to treat me in that manner. I examined past
actions, speech and behaviour. Certainly, I had made many
mistakes in the home, mistakes of omission and commission, but in
my mind these were not different from errors made by the other
children in the family. I concluded that my aunt had never cared for
or loved me, and that the true feelings she had for me had finally
surfaced and could no longer be contained.

I had mixed feelings about reaching my destination. One moment
I would feel bored with this long journey and wish that I had some
magic to push the train to arrive; the next moment I would be filled
with foreboding, when the unknown crowded my mind with scores
of questions I had no answers for. Thank goodness for the night,
particularly the sleep, which gave my mind a break from the taxing
exercise of exploration and panic. When I woke, I had just enough
time to wash and gather my belongings before I reached Johannesburg.

The turmoil and conflict in me, coupled with the uncertainty of
my reception within my new home, heightened as the train pulled
into the station. Would my father be at the station to meet me?
Would he be on time? What if he wasn't there? I was torn inside
with the burden of uncertainty about so many things. The sight of

him on the platform as the train pulled into Johannesburg was indeed a great relief to me. I immediately felt protected and safe in the massive complex of Johannesburg station – very strange to me. I alighted from the train after I had passed all my luggage through the window to him. It is now a long, long time since this happened – forty-five years. Perhaps I delayed my actual getting out of the train in the hope of adjusting to meeting my father. As I walked towards him he met me halfway. We shook hands and kissed without embracing, both radiating an awkward joy and happiness – awkward because neither of us was acting naturally. We both lacked to a very large extent father/daughter natural love, longing and joy on our reunion.

I was bewildered by everything that was going on around me. There were crowds, some moving, some just waiting. There was the noise of the locomotives, the shuffling of feet and the voices of the commuters. A steep flight of steps led up to each platform, and huge pillars rose up around me. I found myself walking hand-in-hand with my father as we followed the porter who was wheeling my luggage to my unknown destination.

My father was keen to tell me how long he had been on the platform to avoid us missing each other. I was very grateful to be in his friendly company, whilst all the excitement and bustle around me certainly eased the tension and awkwardness which prevailed when we first met.

Finally we got into the train which was taking us to his home in Pimville. My father asked me many things about Thaba'Nchu: the people there, the climate, the weather. He asked me too about my journey, but he never referred to the cause of my departure from Thaba'Nchu. I did not offer any explanation either. Perhaps he was suffering his own guilt feelings, as he had never tried to contact me when I was in Thaba'Nchu, not even after my mother's death.

My father looked like a businessman and was very impressive. He was well dressed in a three-piece suit and highly polished shoes. I noticed that his tie matched the silk handkerchief in his jacket top pocket. I stealthily eyed him from time to time whenever he spoke to some of his friends he met in the train. Their casual discussions centred on civic issues. They exchanged thoughts on some articles which had appeared in the *Umteteleli wa Bantu*, a local newspaper which carried the black community news about Johannesburg. When his attention was taken away from me by his friends, my mind would drift back to Thaba'Nchu. I thought of my step-father and in a sense compared him with my father. I thought of Aunt Blanche, and wondered if she was now having second thoughts about chasing me away. Occasionally, my attention was caught up in my father's discussions – how they analysed very knowledgeably whatever they said. I was convinced that my step-father, with his steady, subdued nature, could have made a very valid contribution to their conversation in his own way, although he and my father differed much in temperament.

We arrived at a very lovely, spacious, scrupulously clean home. One look told me the type of person my step-mother was. I was correct in my assessment, because she maintained her standards and values for as long as I lived with her. Gradually I got to know my father and to learn to love him. Although the other children in the home used the Merafe name and sometimes Morake too, I soon found out that they were my step-mother's sister's children and that in fact my father and step-mother had no offspring of their own. I became part of this family to the best of my ability, but I never became fully integrated, perhaps because of my recent shock, or because there was something I could not fathom in the home or family, or the family itself could not reach in me. Adjustment was not easy. By tradition in any African home, urban or rural, the role of a girl is to assist with the household chores. We all know though that each home has its own way of running its affairs, so that much as I was experienced in household chores, I found myself compelled to observe the mode of operation in what was going to be my new home. The fact that I was trained in household work in Thaba'Nchu did not seem enough to give me confidence to adjust to my new surroundings. I was emotionally unstable. I needed someone to hold my hand and say 'Welcome home'. I expected this from my new mother. But she was neutral, and refused to commit herself.

There were days when things were not bright, without having any special incidents. I had moments of deep longing for Thaba'Nchu, and it was on such occasions that I remembered many past experiences. I was concerned about finding a job, because I realised that money had a different value in my new home. I thought of my step-father, and of the furniture I bought and left for him in Thaba'Nchu. I was grateful that I had managed to say thank you to him even if it was in a small, humble way. I recalled some nasty experiences with insurance companies, where I had taken out a policy which had lapsed because the rules and regulations written into it were in a language which did not encourage me to read with any understanding. Then and only then did I realise the amount of money I had lost. Many of us blacks, particularly women, have been caught up with insurance policies, losing lots of money, and not knowing what to do about it. Although I felt depressed and discouraged by such memories, I also accepted them as a process of learning. But to this day I still dread policies. I reflected on the days when I used my £6.0.0 a month salary as pocket money, buying clothes, or presents for friends; the days when I enjoyed my teaching career because it gave me status in my community. Now things had changed; I needed a job to give me an income just to make ends meet.

Although I was with my natural father, I found it difficult to look to him for help in the same way I had done with my step-father. I had to carry myself and stop seeking support from other people. However, this was easier said than done. Nostalgia for home led to fantasies about an escape from this sudden frightening experience.

Nevertheless, there were certain benefits which I derived from my new life. Prior to coming to Johannesburg, I had been inhibited from saying anything about the Merafes, my people. The only person who seemed to have some regard for them was Mother, who always spoke positively about my father in particular. She never shared any feelings of bitterness when she referred to him. Strangely, my father never said anything at all about Mother, either evil or good. Whilst Mother never directly praised him in any way, she never ruled out the possibility that I might meet him. Indeed, I think that she wished me to have this opportunity. My arrival in Johannesburg gave me this opportunity to know my people. I lived with my paternal grandmother and enjoyed her company very much. I saw my uncles and one aunt and my cousins, and realised they were as human as anybody. I met all the family members around Johannesburg and confirmed that they were relatives anybody could be proud of. I was even able to check on some of the false things which had been said about my father in particular. So this was worthwhile for me.

More than anything else, I saw my father in his role as the civic leader in Pimville. I saw him campaign for local Advisory Board – Advisory Boards were the nearest thing to local representation for blacks – elections for his political party. I saw him acting as chairman of the party and saw his unchallenged leadership because of his dedication to the service of his people. I often read the statements he prepared when he was making representations to the

Non-European Affairs Department run under the auspices of the City Council of Johannesburg. He was a brave man. He was an honest man. I saw him fight some of the most hopeless cases of influx control administration victims. I saw him save many men from being 'endorsed' out of Johannesburg where they had come in the hope of finding a job to maintain their families. He always prepared detailed written statements to present to the relevant office. It was from him that I learned the importance of keeping accurate records. I rarely ever heard him say he had failed in his representation. He was concerned about the security and well-being of black people in Pimville. This was my father.

Once or twice I attended the conference of the All African Convention with him and heard him make his contribution there. In later years, when I got to know him better, I realised he was much more of a civic than a political leader. In those years the distinction was very clear. Since the coming to power of the Nationalist government, there is absolutely no line of demarcation between civic, welfare and political programmes for blacks, with blacks, by blacks.

I have often told myself that I inherited my tendency to community involvement from my father. On the other hand, I can also say that my mother too showed concern for people. She often sent me to call from the open road which crossed through her father's farm, people in distress who moved from one farm to another seeking seasonal jobs. Much as I privately resented this, as a child in the family I carried out instructions. It was part of my duties to prepare meals for such people and to serve them. Perhaps that is why I was always reluctant to call the passers by from the highway.

Thinking always of others can be a burden when one grows older because it becomes second nature or second self. To this day, working with people, in particular with women and young people, is a concern I cannot divorce myself from. I believe that I inherited my concern for people, a concern which embraces social, political, civic, educational and all other aspects of life. But all these aspects are seen as political in South Africa if administered by blacks with blacks for blacks.

I value this heritage from my parents.

There I was then, living in a modern home with a talented, busy and sociable father. But I still felt lost and lonely and in need of support of some kind. I decided to look around me and see how I could improve my situation.

The answer came to me quite suddenly. I remembered my maternal aunt was in Heilbron not far from Johannesburg, Mrs Elizabeth Tlhapane, born Makgothi. She was someone I had grown up with in Thaba'Nchu, as she was my senior by only about three or four years. As a child, I had believed she was my elder sister and not my aunt, as she was very close to my mother. I immediately established contact with her and informed her of my desperate need for a job and my desire to teach in Heilbron near her and her husband, Solomon Makankane Tlhapane, a teacher of excellent reputation in that community. They helped me to get a teaching post there, and I looked forward to January 1939 with excitement, eagerness and great expectation. My relationship with Aunt Elizabeth Tlhapane was deep and profound from the many childhood years we had spent together and from the daily sharing we had at play and during household chores. The thought of going to live with her again filled me with new hope for the future. It was this same Aunt Elizabeth who had accompanied me on the trip to Johannesburg in 1936 to visit the Empire Exhibition.

I cannot now remember clearly my father's reaction to my decision to live and work in Heilbron. He did not actively encourage my departure, but I suspect that it came as a relief to him because of the underlying tensions in his own family. Although I do not remember the details of my departure, I know that I received some financial support to cover my train fare, and some pocket money. By that time my step-mother seemed to appreciate my cooking and baking skills, much as they were not perfect. I prepared my own provisions for my journey and had a reasonably warm and pleasant send-off, with my father coming with me to Park Station.

My adjustment to the Tlhapane family was very smooth. Uncle Solomon Tlhapane, who was intimately known to me as Uncle Bunky at that stage, was no stranger to me; I had met him several times when I visited my aunt in Kroonstad where she was teaching. I had watched with interest and excitement – though with discretion – the warm deep friendship which developed between them. The fact that I was the chief bridesmaid at their wedding is itself testimony of my closeness to that couple. I was thus welcomed at Heilbron by this very loving warm young couple, both in their home and in a sense in my working situation because of the recognition and influence they had in the community. This cushioned my stay at home and in my job, and immediately created an atmosphere full of security and support.

My time at Heilbron was a really helpful transitional period of weaning me away from my almost dependent situation in Pimville where my expectations would have been unfulfilled, ending up in utter frustration. My aunt became a very progressive model for me. From her I learnt some very basic needs for daily living; saving was one such practice; contributing towards family expenditure was another. She was a young wife, mother and housewife; she and her husband became very good companions to me as they were not old enough for generation-gap problems and yet mature enough to be exemplary in their family life. The two years I stayed in Heilbron helped me to get over my Thaba'Nchu shock, to adjust to a new life where I was called upon to mould both the material and moral side of my life, and to dismiss expectations I was starting to have about Pimville as my new home. That family saw me through some of the most traumatic experiences of my life. Their contribution to my whole personal growth was positive and supportive in that it was temporary and effective. It weaned me from dependency. I joined social circles in group-singing, ballroom dancing, debating societies and Home Improvement Women's Club programmes. The requests I received to serve as an office bearer or a committee member made me gain more and more self-confidence and self-reliance. It was at Heilbron that I learned the basics of decision-making in personal and group matters. This period also marked a turning-point in my life. The humble achievements that I registered in those years have gone a long way to influence some of the major events which have been highlights of my life. It is for these reasons that, with the passing of time, I have seen my imposed departure from Thaba'N-chu, painful as it was then, as a blessing in disguise.

Since then, I have visited Thaba'Nchu twenty or thirty times, or even more. My first return visit took place while I was still living in Heilbron. Although I felt inhibited about visiting my old home, when I received word that my sister was due to get married there, I defied all previous decisions, went to Thaba'Nchu and damned all the consequences.

I was upset to see Maria getting married at a young age. This was my beloved younger sister and the groom was Thari Pilane, son of Chief Ofentse Tlhabane Pilane of Saulspoort in the western Transvaal. But the thought that Maria had not gone far with her education troubled me. I found it difficult to prevail on her to continue her studies since, as a married woman, she would have many additional responsibilities. In addition, they were to live in Saulspoort, miles away from the nearest town. I also realised that there were many restrictions and taboos she would be compelled to adhere to in her new role as wife of the chief's son who was next in line to take his father's office. However, her husband's education had liberated him from some of the most restrictive taboos and practices. For that I was very grateful. I finally resigned myself to the inevitable, but made a secret pact with myself: that I would keep in contact with my sister as much as possible and to the best of my ability.

9
A Home of My Own

At the end of 1940, I accepted a new teaching post at Phokeng which lay about eight miles west of Rustenburg and about 25 miles south-east of Saulspoort. I joined a staff which consisted of two male teachers, Mr Grootboom and Mr Kekana. The three of us worked very hard as a team to launch the first High School in Phokeng, and together we laid the foundations for a level of education which has left its mark in the community.

Phokeng was a relatively primitive community compared with the other places where I had lived and worked. On the other hand, it was not difficult to recognise the slow but unquestionable development of the community, judging by the new houses which were being built – the size, quality and style were far superior in many ways to the houses already in existence there. The community also had a desire for a higher standard of education. The era of the catechism level of education undertaken by the German missionaries was being overtaken by the newly established High School education. The proportion of girls to boys in that school was comparatively high and there was a satisfying number of girls in our High School, the first in that community.

As a young lady teacher, with much more than book work to offer, I soon noticed the attraction I had for students, particularly female students. Alongside the Girl Guide sessions I organised for the girls, I introduced physical exercise classes for open-air displays. It was during one of these sessions that the local Chief spotted us while he was on his rounds, and stopped his car. As I did not know him, I continued with the girls' physical training undisturbed. As he walked nearer to watch the display, I sensed some restlessness, a subdued excitement, in the group. I didn't link this restlessness with the stranger; he looked just like an ordinary father, interested in our programme.

When he finally stopped and watched with interest, the attention of the girls became uncoordinated. Their eyes shifted between me and the stranger, and I stopped. The Chief then walked up and expressed his deep appreciation for the performance and, without disclosing his identity, he invited us all to come up to his house. As he was wearing overalls, as far as I was concerned he could have been a motor car mechanic. He did not wait for me to say 'Yes, we are coming', or 'No, I am on duty, we cannot come', he just walked away. I was both puzzled and stunned.

The group smiled and giggled. When I judged he was out of hearing, I asked the girls who this commanding gentleman was. One of the very excited girls turned to me and said, 'Don't you know him? He is the Chief of this place, Chief Manotshe Molotlegi, and we must go there because he has invited us!' I followed the girls with mixed feelings. 'Chief!', I pondered. A man so simple and unassuming. I decided to exercise a wait-and-see approach. Picking up our equipment we followed him.

By the time we arrived, there was beautiful music coming from the house. The tune was ideal for the rhythm of our exercises. The girls rushed into the *lelapa* (courtyard), a feature in every traditional African home, a space where the family relaxes and receives its guests. They fell into line and got ready for their display. I too was carried away by this unexpected accompaniment which inspired all of us. The girls excelled in their performance.

After a few repetitions of the exercises, the music ceased, and the performance ended. The 'stranger' now emerged from the house and formally introduced himself as Mr Manotshe Molotlegi and I, in turn, told him my name. He expressed his joy at seeing this performance and asked the group to perform again. He opened the door, left it ajar, sat in front of the piano and played the song which had thrown the group into action. I said to myself: 'So this mechanic is also a pianist of renown and a Chief as well. What talent!'

More than all his acquired abilities, I was particularly impressed by Mr Molotlegi's personality. I got to know that he wore overalls to attend to his tractors, ploughs, cars and any equipment which needed repair. Chief Manotshe Molotlegi was a humble, unassuming, approachable, industrious, progressive and supportive leader of his people – a rare mixture of downright simplicity, humility and royalty. I hate to make comparisons, but I can only say I still hope to meet another Chief as versatile and selfless.

Almost all the girls who were in that physical exercise group have become nursing sisters. It was great joy to meet some of them again at Baragwanath Hospital in Soweto in the late 1950s and to find that they had very responsible jobs there. They are now married and live in Soweto where they share in the leadership of that community in different spheres of life. They managed to beat the influx control regulations and became seasoned 'Sowetans'.

There was a regular bus service running between Rustenburg and Saulspoort via Phokeng, and I soon found that it was no problem to visit my sister at Saulspoort. However, the railway-bus in those years was slow and very uncomfortable: the seats were not upholstered, and although there were window panes, the bus collected so much dust that by the end of the journey the passengers were covered with a reddish powder, as most of the roads were still not tarred. This was the only regular transport service for commuters apart from the train which only went as far as Rustenburg town. There were no taxis in that era on that route, and very few families owned private cars.

My first trips to see my sister were made by this bus. In addition to all the inconveniences mentioned earlier, the bus was always overcrowded with passengers and their huge boxes of groceries, suitcases, or bundles of blankets and the like. In summer, all were sweating and sweltering in the intense heat; in winter, the cold was aggravated by the wind which rushed in through all the crevices and left the unheated vehicle freezing cold. Although seeing my sister was a pleasure, going there was really depressing and tedious.

The first time I visited her, I was unfamiliar with the conditions and I was not dressed properly for the journey – my clothes were a little too dainty for the trip I was taking. The trip was dull. It was not easy to read anything because of the loud conversations, the dust and the overcrowding, and I had no one to speak to. When we had travelled about a quarter of the journey, my eye was caught by someone who possibly had singled me out as a stranger. We exchanged smiles. The first chance this gentleman had, he moved towards me and introduced himself as Ernest Moloto. We chatted, and I told him I was visiting my sister at Saulspoort. When he realised who I was talking about, I saw his face radiate joy and excitement. He knew my sister and her husband very well. They were friends of his. It was a great relief to meet someone to talk to on that lonely, dreary long journey. On arrival at Saulspoort, he was not in a hurry to leave. On the contrary, he offered to walk with me to my sister's place, and for this I was very grateful, as a stranger in that community. For the duration of my stay in Saulspoort, my escort called every day and offered to show me around the place. He was the headmaster of a large local primary school. As well as the joy of being with my sister, his visits made my stay in Saulspoort exciting and interesting.

The reunion with my sister was fulfilling. It was such a joy to be with her again. At first, though, I felt very awkward because of the traditional manner in which they, as Batswana royalty, were given respect. I could not accept this as my sister's new way of life: men and women clapping hands and bowing to her when they should have simply greeted her. I was embarrassed. That way of life was not in accordance with the way we had been brought up. As a guest, I had to go along with it too. It was on this occasion that I realised that persuading my sister to resume her education would be creating problems for her. I never even raised the subject.

This first visit to Saulspoort gave me a superficial insight into life there. Saulspoort was a semi-rural place with a long history of the influence of Dutch Reformed missionaries. Not far from the village, to the south-west, stands the George Stegman Hospital, whilst the church and school are in the village itself. Much of the village is built on the mountain range running to the north-west, which towers over the village and bush land unfolding eastward, broken up by muddy ponds. Much of the village is covered by this thorn bush which grows all over the area. The Saulspoort of the 1940s was characterised by grass-thatched homes built in clusters of rondavels, and rectangular-shaped houses for each family homestead. The number and size of these structures told a great deal about the wealth of the owner. The Saulspoort of the 1980s is changing by the day, judging by the rapidly increasing modern homes built by the younger generation who work very hard to change the quality of life in their community. I was taken by surprise and great joy to see a few windmills erected in Saulspoort in recent years. Lack of water had been a scourge of that community for a very long time. In those earlier years, the Chief's house stood out above all other homes. Today, the homes of the commoners compare well with those of royalty.

At the end of my visit when I returned to Phokeng, my friendship with my escort was well developed.

In March 1941, I was approaching my twenty-seventh birthday, and like all women of my age who had spent their youth at school preparing for their future, I was going through a very exciting period of building castles in the air about my life of tomorrow and the next day. I was very much aware of myself and very conscious of my appearance; and yet I was haunted by my past. The undisputed truth that my parents had divorced, which was rare, despised and shameful in those years; the uncertainty about any place I could call home without hesitation for fear of being rejected; the trauma of a sudden severance from my roots and those I had known as parents and relatives; all these realities led to introspection – they were realities I would have to share with whoever I was destined to spend my married life with. I found it a challenging demand.

But life did not stop. I had my youth, with all its adventures and vain expectations. Looking back, I was a popular person. I made friends and kept them. I had more male friends than female at this time, a fact which caused my father great concern when I joined his family in Johannesburg. I soon realised that to him male friends were more than *just* friends. I had done my best to introduce a boyfriend of mine who was then at Fort Hare, who used to escort me to functions. When my father got to know that he was the son of his ex-teacher, Mr Moikangoa, at Lovedale, he openly told me that it was not in my interest to continue that relationship. I can never say how much his influence ended that courtship. However, I am also very mindful of other developments which militated against that particular friendship. I wish I had asked my father what had happened earlier between him and his teacher.

I became more and more aware of my admirers as I realised that the answer to my feelings of homelessness was to find myself a life partner – a desire to 'live happily ever after', a wish often cherished by young people.

The yearning for a stable home had grown in me. Certainly, my father was well established in Pimville by the values and standards of those years: he was a civic leader of reputation; he owned a shop; and judging by some obvious day-to-day living standards, he was prosperous. I stayed with him and his family during school holidays but for the greater part of the year I was not with them. It was during the time when I lived on my own that I missed a home my mind could turn to; a home I could look forward to going back to at the close of the school term; a home where I was expected and accepted as a member of the family. I yearned for a home where there was peace and love. A home where I would have a family I would love and care for. A home my friends and relatives would visit and relax in. A home which would help me forget some of the problems I had suffered as a child. This was my dream.

It was against this background that I considered the marriage proposal of my new boyfriend, the elegant, well spoken and seemingly very well groomed gentleman I had met on the bus when I first visited my sister at Saulspoort. He was the second young man in my life who had caught my admiration and to whom I had responded, like all normal young girls with, 'Yes, dear, I love you' – a very special moment for a young girl, a time when you feel fulfilment in your life. When I finally acepted his proposal of marriage, I believed fully that I would never come across a better man than him in the world. But I had judged him as an individual away from his surroundings and environment and, as a result, I had overlooked some very important factors in making a decision so vital in my life.

You may ask what I had based my decision on. My answer to that is very simple. He was a handsome, well built, rather tall man, with a husky voice. He was reading for a Bachelor of Arts degree. He spoke very good English, and was very fluent in Afrikaans. When I first met him, and right through our courtship, he was gentle and appeared very polished in his manner. He seemed a real gentleman, who wouldn't hurt a fly, as they say. When he visited me in Johannesburg, he stayed with Rev. Mpitso's family, a Wesleyan Methodist Church pastor. I looked forward to his visits. They filled me with joy, excitement and great expectations.

It was before the marriage registrar in Pretoria towards the end of 1941, that I said 'I do' to this good gentleman. Yes, no matter what happened later in life, at that moment he was my 'good gentleman'. I sincerely looked forward to a peaceful, loving, family life. To me, a young inexperienced woman, marriage was an end in itself. I told myself that I had arrived.

Once we were husband and wife in a home of our own at Saulspoort, where my husband was headmaster of the largest Higher Primary School in Pilanesburg District, I started to get to know him; and there is no doubt that he also began to know me better too. I had to face the reality that marriage did not mean the pinnacle of life, but was its stark beginning. It was a harsh, shocking discovery for me. In my mind I said to myself: No, Ellen, not again! There was no way out; I was in the middle of it all and I was compelled to see it to a finish, for better or for worse.

My first pregnancy engaged my thoughts and in a way sheltered me from some of the things which would otherwise have unsettled me: things which were happening under my nose in my own house. I either pretended I did not see them or I refused to believe what I saw. But they came as a rude shock, such a shock that I refrained from sharing them with my sister, at least at the beginning.

The birth of our first son on 26 June 1942 gave me the break I needed: I could keep my mind occupied with nursing and caring for him, and the new attitudes and relationships his birth caused changed the atmosphere in the home. On 26 July, exactly two years after the birth of our eldest child, we were blessed with the birth of our second son. They were lovely boys; they took most of my time and protected me, as it were, from the daily harsh and hurting experiences I was exposed to.

My image of married life was far removed from the torture I was exposed to. I went through both physical and mental sufferings. Day by day I realised I was being humiliated and degraded, an experience I have in recent years come to realise is suffered by many wives the world over, within different races, cultures and religions. At that time I believed I was being singled out as an individual, particularly since I was looked on as a stranger and foreigner in that community. In desperation I did spend some weeks away from Saulspoort with my Aunt Elizabeth and Uncle Solomon in Heilbron. They said very little but provided for my immediate needs with great warmth and caring. They were in no position, however, to provide a long-term solution.

Some time in 1946 I realised that I was expecting a third child. It took me the better part of eight weeks to inform anyone about my condition: I was filled with conflict and I was also afraid of what my husband's reaction would be. Although my hands were full with bringing up my two boys, the possibility of the third child being a girl filled me with new hope. A girl in the family. If my wishes were fulfilled, I would have a friend, a companion who might bring joy and new hope. She might even change the sour mood prevailing in the home. For weeks on end I pondered whether or not to share my news, and if I did, with whom. It is a great hardship to have your trust shaken in someone so very close to you. Even now, I find I cannot write in detail about it. My life was going from bad to worse. The values, standards and ideals that I had cherished about a home were strange and foreign to my immediate circle of contacts, and so I felt lost and isolated. Even a simple task like going to fetch water from the school yard nearby became emotionally traumatic.

My pregnancy ended at eight to ten weeks. It almost cost me my life. I remained unattended and without any medical check-up, and ended up bedridden and dazed by severe pains. I became weaker by the day as there was no one to give me food or water. I prayed for recovery, so that I could at least bring up my sons if nothing else. I finally found someone to send to the local hospital to inform them of my condition. The doctor called to see me. All efforts to convince her about the seriousness of my condition failed. She ended up telling me that there was nothing seriously wrong with me and that what I told her was more in my mind. In short, I understood her to say I was not giving a true account of my condition.

As I lay in bed, I pondered seriously about what my next move should be when I was fully recovered. My experiences left me no other choice but to return home to my father. That is when I decided to save myself for myself, and for my two sons. By that time the façade of putting on appearances had lost its meaning. It was replaced by hurt, humiliation and total frustration, but it did not kill my desire and determination to live my life to the fullest, given another opportunity.

It was at that stage that some of the past lessons from my mother and certain teachers came back to me. 'Cholofelo, even if I were to live for a long time, I would not always be with you everywhere', and 'Remember, unlike a beast, a human being is responsible for her actions at all times.' These were my mother's words to me before she died. Dr Edgar Brookes, on the other hand, had a very popular and meaningfull end-of-year message for us students: 'You are going into a harsh world, students; you will meet many obstacles, my provision to you on that long hard road is "Make your difficulties a stepping-stone to success".' These messages now came alive for me, and I fell back on the old practice and tradition of my family: prayer. I lived on it, and planned my future once more. My marriage was a thing of the past at that stage. I was determined to get away from Saulspoort.

My sons were a problem though. Their father was very fond of them and he would not let them go. On the other hand, I did not believe he could care for them at that age. I was in a serious conflict. If I go, what of my children? If I stay, my life is at stake. I concluded that to sort myself out and see my plans through, my next move, on recovery, was to go to Legkraal, to live with my mother-in-law in a community with close family ties. And if I was indeed compelled to do so, that would be the ideal place to leave the boys. By that time the idea of a peaceful, loving home had vanished before my eyes like vapour into air.

As I lay in bed, helpless and distressed, I heard a voice I recognised as that of Mr Philemon Lesejane, my husband's brother-in-law. He was a school teacher of long standing who commanded the respect of his family, community and colleagues. I was so happy to hear his voice that I prayed that he would come in and say 'Hello', although the air in my bedroom was by that time most unpleasant. I strained my ears to hear him request to see me. I forced a cough in between to announce my presence. It was with great relief that I heard him say from the front room, 'Let me say hello to Ella.' In that part of the country which has a strong Afrikaans influence I was commonly called Ella.

He walked in, calm and composed. I wanted him to stand away from the bed, as I had not been able to attend to myself for days. Yet he came near, shook my hand and told me he had come to take me to his home for his wife to nurse me. I was happy on the one hand, but puzzled on the other because I had heard his request to take me away emphatically refused. He looked at me, his eyes full of compassion, hurt and shock. He helped me to my feet, without showing any sign of disgust at the appalling condition I was in, and repeated his intention, saying 'Ella is going with me'. He wanted to know if I had seen the doctor. I told him I had, and that I had told her that I suspected I had a very serious injury, but that she had dismissed this and had said my condition was not that serious. He prepared warm water for me to wash with, and gave me something to eat before he took me to the car for the 40 mile journey to his home in Elandsdoring.

His wife, who had two years' training as a nurse, helped me as much as she could, but I had only been there for about three or four days when my condition deteriorated rapidly. Fortunately, on the day when things turned for the worse, the doctor was doing her district calls there, and the Lesejanes asked her to call at their home. As she walked in, our eyes met. She recognised me, and blushed and softly said in a shocked voice, 'Mrs Moloto'. I turned and said, 'You refused to accept my story at my house in Saulspoort when I told you what had befallen me.' Without any waste of time, she had her tray of instruments in the room. She asked for water and gave me all the attention due to a patient from her doctor. Then she took me back with her to George Stegman Hospital. After a week or two, I was transferred to Kruger Hospital in Rustenburg where I underwent a major operation.

As I lay in bed, my mind resigned to the pain I was experiencing,

I had a faint idea that I saw my husband walk into the ward. He looked grey and his lips appeared parched as he stealthily moved towards my bed. I don't remember him saying anything. He stood for some time, not very far from my bed, and left without a word. I was aware that I was in a public ward with other patients. I did not see him again for the rest of the four weeks I spent there. I was happy it happened that way.

As I sit here in this garden in London on Wednesday, 6 June 1984, my children are busy at home in South Africa preparing the funeral arrangements for the burial of their father. That happening – his death on 28 May – has brought back so many questions in my mind.

Now that he is dead, I feel he has missed reading in this book my considered assessment of what our six years of married life together were to me. The violence, arrogance, meanness and downright selfishness which prevailed in our home eclipsed all the positives of his intelligence, his well-built stature and handsome appearance, his financial acumen – even if this was at the expense of his family. The atmosphere in that house left me no alternative but to leave, and in that way to save myself for myself as well as for my two sons.

Time and again I reflected on the line of action by the lady doctor I had seen at George Stegman Hospital. Was she trying to cover something up? Or did she fail to pick up what I had told her in her diagnosis following the first examination? I shall never know the truth. My condition in the hospital records was described as an ectopic pregnancy; there is no mention of the circumstances which preceded my ill-health. I often wonder how many such diagnoses have been made and recorded without ever trying to check the history of the condition, or paying attention to the patient's own story.

On my discharge I went home to Saulspoort for a while, then moved to Legkraal to be with my mother-in-law. Legkraal had far more community spirit than Saulspoort did, which was known as Moruleng to its Bakgatla residents. For one thing, it was a smaller village, composed of related families. The Legkraal inhabitants were Batlhako, a clan whose roots were at Mabieskraal in the District of Rustenburg. The headquarters of the Bakgatla people, who made up the greater part of the population of Saulspoort, are at Mochudi in Botswana. The most common name in Saulspoort to this day, and which is associated with royalty, is Pilane: in Mochudi the names Lentswe and Pilane belong to the royal family. In

Legkraal two family names were shared by the greater part of the population and these were, and still are, Ntsime and Phiri.

To an outsider these names may sound very insignificant; but in fact it is these names which told, and still tell, the 'Who's Who' of these communities. As in every community, some families with one of these names were wealthier than others; but the very fact that someone was born a Lentswe, Pilane, Ntsime or Phiri meant that he or she enjoyed the status of that name and received the respect and recognition accorded to members of that family, regardless of the individual's personal standing in the community.

I was astonished to find that the black rural community at Legkraal had very similar habits and practices to those I had known so well as a child in Thaba Patchoa some 25 years earlier — and some 600 miles distant. Families were dependent on the tilling of land for their livelihood; and women took the leading role in hoeing the land and harvesting. Other household duties such as threshing corn, drawing water from the well and collecting wood were also seen as women's responsibilities in that community, just as they had been in Thaba Patchoa. The one thing I did miss in Legkraal though were the organised work-camps, which I described earlier.

In addition to all these duties, I was particularly struck by the fact that the Legkraal women used the manufacture of pottery to meet the daily needs and demands of their families. In Thaba Patchoa this had been the case too. When I moved to Legkraal, drought was a yearly scourge. The consequences of this — scarcity of food, low family income, and low living standards — resuscitated some of the old skills still familiar to the older women in the community. Pottery was one such skill.

Individuals proficient in this skill would make the clay pots in their own homes on the pattern of the 'cottage industry' in Europe prior to the industrial revolution. The size and shape of the clay pots were very similar to those made in the Orange Free State in the 1930s. The principal difference I observed was in the method of firing. Needless to say, the finished product was the same. The mothers took great pains to produce the best pots, and displayed very sophisticated, skilled workmanship in moulding and firing their products. The Free State potters fired the pots on the surface, using a lot of fuel in the form of dry cow dung, which covered the pots completely. The Rustenburg potters, on the other hand, dug large holes to accommodate their clay pots, then skilfully packed them in these holes, with plenty of dry cow dung placed around to cover them in readiness for firing. When the potters were satisfied that the pots were well baked, they carefully covered them up to allow for their regulated cooling. To test their quality, they would be filled with hot porridge. To an observer this all appeared to be a very taxing process, yet the potters seemed to enjoy every step of the process. The clay pots were finally checked to be passed as fit products for the market. Any pots which were in any way defective were put aside for use in the family.

Long before the products were ready for market, the potters came together to plan the journey to convey their clay pots to distant, potential buyers. Some arranged the transport, others supplied the packaging for the pots, some prepared provisions, others offered to look after the children of mothers making the trip. Potters were often away from home for weeks or months, selling their pots on a barter system for grain, the price of each pot determined by the amount of grain it held. They had to provide the sacks in which to bring their grain home. The journey was undoubtedly both time- and energy-consuming, but the reward came when the wagon returned home crammed with different types of grain from *majako* (trading). This grain swelled the family income to buy household needs, such as soap, clothing, paraffin, tea, sugar and blankets. It added to the family food in the home; and it met other needs in the area of education of the children such as school fees, and buying books and uniforms.

The community would rally round to give the *majako* party a happy send-off. The last messages from the departing potters were given amidst excitement, panic, joy, anxiety, laughter, with mothers reminding their children of the duties they were expected to carry out: '*Hela Pule o se lebale go fepa dikgogo,*' someone would call ('Pule, please do not forget to feed the fowls.')

It is difficult to say how the amount of grain brought in by these means compared in quantity with the grain collected during the harvest season. But, judging by the naked eye, the quantity of corn and maize heaped up in the returning ox wagons often seemed to exceed that collected during the harvest.

The Moloto family lived at Welgevaal, near Pilanesberg, and although I never got the chance to go there, I learned that it was a far more progressive community than either Saulspoort or Legkraal. From hearsay, the Moloto family in that community played a leading role in the affairs of the Dutch Reformed Church. The Rev. Stephen Moloto was a well known pastor in that area, and his children were the first to achieve a higher level of education in the whole of Pilanesberg. Mrs Madira Raphadu, née Moloto, the Rev. Stephen Moloto's daughter, was a trained nurse in the 1940s, and her brother, D. P. Moloto, and their cousin, Dr E. S. Moloto (Ernest, my husband) were among the first young men to hold a BA degree in that area. Ernest Moloto lectured at the University of Botswana at Gabornoef, before returning to South Africa where he died.

My mother-in-law, Tabitha Moloto, born Phiri, had a very strong, domineering personality. I got to know during my stay with her that she grew up with the missionaries of the Dutch Reformed Church, where she learned to read the High Dutch Bible. Afrikaans was a common language in her family. When I married in 1941, my father-in-law was no longer alive. However, I learned from talk in the village that he was a gracious gentleman, who accorded his wife the treatment and standard of living of royalty. They were a well-to-do family.

For obvious reasons, I enjoyed my stay at Legkraal rather more than I did that at Saulspoort, and it was with great relief and joy that I got a teaching post there. In addition to teaching, I also participated in community projects and I started an after-school programme for girls. This programme was received very warmly by the girls who previously had not had any organised activities outside the scheduled shool timetable. For me it was an outlet from frustration, loneliness and boredom. This programme also gave me the opportunity to get to know some of the senior girls better than I might have done from classes only. The names and faces of some of these girls come back vividly. Matato Ntsime became a nurse, Boïotolopo Ntsime married the headmaster of the local school, Mr Setshedi. Others, like Majo Phiri and Motebele Ntsime, did not achieve any noteworthy academic work, but did become accepted as responsible members of their community. I was thrilled in 1977 to meet Nkunyane and Seasebeng Ntsime, née Phiri, as husband and wife in Mafikeng and later for a short while at Saulspoort.

It was here in Legkraal that I was able to assess my marriage and family situation with a minimum of subjectivity. The longer I stayed at Legkraal, the more distant and strained the ties between my husband and myself became. Any effort to restore a cordial relationship between us went unrewarded, and the naked truth came forcefully through: if I returned to Saulspoort, my life might terminate without warning, and my boys would be motherless at an early age. Nevertheless, I had to return temporarily. I waited to recuperate and gain strength. Some time at the beginning of 1947 I resolved to leave Saulspoort. It was a very difficult decision to put into action but I had no choice. I would have to pretend that my children did not matter to me, or I would have to trust that an unknown, supernatural power would take charge of them in my absence. Taking them with me was out of the question, as they were too young to go on foot. Public transport was a risk as their father might check the bus and take them back. The only resort was to leave them behind. On several occasions I failed to leave, as I could not bear to tear myself away from them.

With only two pounds that I had received from my brother-in-law, Abraham Moloto, and after much contemplation and sincere prayer, I left for Johannesburg, starting my journey on foot to conceal my movements. Although our relationship was so strained, for some reason or another, my husband did not allow me to return to my father unimpeded. I left close on sunset, lingering in the forest nearby until dusk. I then took the first opportunity to call on my sister to say goodbye to her. In desperation she gave me one of her children's blankets to cover my shoulders. I disappeared into the veld where I spent the night. It was during that time that I watched a car moving between my house and the shopping centre where the bus terminus was. The lights of the car betrayed its movements which I watched for the greater part of the night. Reports of the attempts to track me down throughout the night came to me later; of how a night vigil was observed between my house and the bus terminus up to 4.00 a.m., the next day. All in vain — as I was not there! At about 4.45 a.m., I discovered that I had been sleeping in the graveyard. I was shaken all right; but I had to move on for my own safety.

For fear of being seen in the neighbourhood, I took shelter with a relative of my sister's husband. This family gave me food and shelter and arranged for a donkey-cart to take me to the bus route towards Pilanesberg, to avoid my possible interception. The owner of the donkey-cart offered to take me further than Pilanesberg so I would have enough cash to reach home. Not once did I shed a tear on that journey, as there was no time for self-pity. This time I was not being forced out of my 'home'; on the contrary, the decision was mine. All the same, and perhaps I am wrong, I was pushed out psychologically.

I arrived in Johannesburg early in February. When I got off the local train at Pimville station, I dropped my head to avoid being recognised by neighbours or friends. For the first time, I was conscious of my shabby appearance; yet at the same time, I was grateful to find myself walking into my father's house. As I did, strange feelings took possession of me, which to this day I can't describe. I wanted to cry but had no tears to shed: my eyes were dry, I could not sob or scream. I was mute. Even at that hour of great stress, I refused to let go and give in. I walked in and greeted my father, who for a split second did not recognise me.

When my shock abated, and I found myself face to face with the reality of everyday living, my thoughts drifted back to my two sons. I was haunted by their innocent, tender voices. I imagined them helpless and in distress, sometimes whimpering and sobbing for a mother who had vanished like vapour before their young appealing eyes. These were challenging moments of guilt, charged with endless questions I could not find adequate replies to. What if the boys were being neglected and tortured like I had been? How could I be certain that I had made the correct decision to leave them behind? Was I a coward? *Why* did I not stick it out to fulfil my marriage vows: 'Until death do us part'? But if they were suffering whilst I was in Johannesburg, they would suffer ten times more if I were dead, I told myself. Was it not better for them to live with the hope that their mother was alive somewhere and some day they would be with her? I settled for that last thought, telling myself that the one thing I lived for and cherished most on this earth was my boys. They were, are and will remain, my hope, my joy, my love, my strength and for them I would fight to the bitter end.

I struggled very hard to blot out of my mind the dreadful events I had gone through at Saulspoort. But the image of Philemon Lesejane haunted my mind. He was Ernest's brother-in-law, his wife, Christine, was Ernest's elder sister, and she and Ernest were very close. I often wonder what would have happened in the end had Philemon not come to remove me to his house. A great, good-natured gentleman by all standards. He died about ten years ago. May his soul rest in peace. Nevertheless I resolved to settle down and start life afresh, refusing to allow my recent experiences to dampen my spirit or mar my future in any way. In this frame of mind I stood up firm with my chin up, filled with fresh determination. With youth still on my side, I ventured on my second journey in life, with this thought in mind: no more castles in the air but a more realistic day-to-day approach to life.

10
Return to Johannesburg

I gradually settled down at number 1092/3/3 Merafe Street, Pimville, the house of my father, Phillip Serasengwe Merafe.

My father had been a student under his father-in-law, Jeremiah Mokoloi Makgothi, in Thaba'Nchu in the Orange Free State. After finishing his preliminary education in Thaba'Nchu, he went to Lovedale Institution, where he qualified as one of the first black printers. He worked at Mr Tlale's Printing Press *Moshochonono* at Maseru in Lesotho. Later, he worked for a short time for the *Bantu World* press in Johannesburg and finally went into business as a general dealer at Pimville. As I have described, he became a champion of civic work in Johannesburg, under the then Advisory Boards of the 1930s.

Pimville, in 1947, was by and large a slum, like all the other black areas round the cities and towns of South Africa. In those years Pimville was notorious for its 'tank' houses (Nissen huts, made of corrugated iron) and as a result the area was known as 'Ditankeng', since these houses looked like faceless, tail-less elephants, in height, width and breadth. They were also the size of a fully grown elephant: these were family dwellings, not single quarters, and served as kitchen, dining-room, sitting and bedrooms, as well as bathroom. All these houses (if my memory serves me well) were built below the railway lines, as temporary shelters for the Johannesburg black labour pool. They were finally demolished forty years after their erection — this is how temporary they became!

Merafe Street was the first street east of the railway line in Pimville. Except for a few decent houses — like the Nthongoas' and the Nkomos' next door — most looked dilapidated from overcrowding. One was called 'House Basoabile', which means 'They are disappointed' (by the owner's achievements, I suppose). Next door to each other on Merafe Street were two houses owned by my

father. His shop was on the corner, next to the houses. Pimville
Station was two minutes' walk away. These two houses were
brick-built and finished with a cement rendering. All the rooms in
both houses had properly finished ceilings and the floors were of
concrete covered with linoleum. One of the houses was rented; the
other, in which we lived, was furnished in good taste. Although the
rooms were comparatively small, the home was comfortable by the
standards of those years.

The very poor houses in Merafe Street were rented to migrant
labourers, most of whom came from Lesotho. Their 'town wives'
were seasoned 'illicit' liquor traders, and used large quantities of
water for cleaning and washing their laundry as well as the pots in
which they made liquor. This dirty water was generally emptied into
the street, which, neither gravelled nor tarred, was perpetually
muddy with pools of stagnant water. As there were no drains to
collect this dirty water, the street could stink at times.

The 'bucket system' of sewerage was used in Pimville until the
late 1970s when a water-borne sewerage system was built. Considering the fact that Pimville was established early in the century — say
round about 1918 — that community was using the bucket system
for at least 60 years, yet they survived any possible epidemics. It was
very uncomfortable, even nauseating, to inhale the smell from the
buckets lined up on every street throughout Pimville, before they
were collected to be disposed of at a nearby farm, commonly known
to the residents as 'Kwa spensel'. The sight of the buckets was very
painful to both the eye and to the inner feelings of the residents. We
used to tease my father, as a Chief 'Sisunda' on the Advisory Board
('Sisunda' is equal to Chief Councillor), about the filth and squalor
in Merafe Street where the Chief himself lived. Come to think of it,
Father took such jokes well — although, more often than not, they
were truths much more than jokes.

It was to this community that I returned brow-beaten, helpless
and lost — but certainly not having lost the fighting spirit which has
been my second nature since I have been aware of the world around
me. For as long as I remember, I have hated being a burden to
anybody, or letting myself be treated as worthless by anybody. It
was a very strange time, now that I look back. Strange, because
when I came back from Saulspoort and needed someone to help me
out, I did not feel free, in this new home, to seek the help I needed.
It was a 'new' home because the first time I had come here was
when I was on holiday and did not need anything from anyone. My

father bought me clothing as a present, not out of need, on that occasion. This time I was next to naked and deeply appreciated the shoes and clothing my father bought me, simple and inexpensive as they may have seemed then.

Without blowing my own horn, I had always been a very industrious girl. With my mother, I could not have been otherwise. I soon realised afresh that my step-mother was a very industrious and particular person too. Her house was spotless. She was also a very good cook. From what I had seen of her during my short visits, I knew she was someone I could live with. I reminded myself that my role in this household was that of a child. My mother's words reinforced my thoughts: 'Remember if you should ever be in your father's house one day, give your mother in that home the same respect and recognition you would accord me.' Among the duties I assigned myself was to get up and clean my own bedroom and the living rooms before my parents awoke. I left the kitchen to the home-help. Within two weeks this had become routine.

It was within these first two weeks too that I decided to find a job. The few friends I had in Pimville, some of them teachers, had indicated that there were no teaching vacancies locally. When I discussed the possibility of going to Orlando East to try my luck in the schools there, they agreed that this might be a good idea.

If my memory serves me well, it was on Monday, 3 March 1947, that I boarded a local train at about 7.30 a.m. But for some reason I can never explain, I passed Orlando Station and alighted at Mlamlankunzi, where I was greeted by the sight of a number of schools, all within a relatively small area. For a moment I stopped, held my breath and seriously debated on which school to go to first: a very difficult decision for a complete stranger to make. There were about two schools to my immediate right, one further on from the two, and two more facing me. Something inside me said, 'Walk straight on, Ellen.' I did just that and walked through the school gate facing me. I cannot say why I preferred this particular school. I passed the one on the left and went into the one on the right.

It was now about 9.00 a.m, and a light-complexioned gentleman was standing in the yard. He was a man of medium height and slight build. He was certainly not impressed by my appearance — perhaps he took me for a parent of one of the pupils. He introduced himself, and I did the same, adding that I wished to see the headmaster. Without inviting me inside, he said, with a puzzled look on his face, 'What do you want to see the headmaster about? Perhaps I can help.' Rather apologetically, I told him that I was a school teacher by profession, I came from Rustenburg, had come to settle in Johannesburg and that I *badly* needed a job. Still looking doubtful as if in need of an explanation for my appearance, he finally said, 'Yes, Mrs Moloto, this is a very strange and rare coincidence. On Friday afternoon one of my teachers left for home without saying a word. This morning, she sends me a letter of resignation without any warning, or even as much as serving a week's notice.' He turned and faced one of the classroom doors behind him, saying: 'You hear those children making that noise there? That is the class left by the teacher I am referring to.' As a matter of form I responded, 'It is rather disturbing for a professional person to act so unprofessionally in her job.' Deep down in my heart I would have given *anything* to get her job. He then wanted to know if I knew any teachers in the neighbouring schools who could act as referees for me. He told me that the school next door was Orlando High, that the headmaster there was Mr Godfrey Nakene and, among the staff he mentioned Mr Randall Peteni. I immediately told him that I used to know Mr Nakene and Mr Peteni, but added that I did not think they would remember me as I had last seen them several years before. His face brightened and he said, 'Wait for me here, I am coming back', then he rushed towards Orlando High School, jumped a fence and vanished into the building, leaving me there in a state of great anxiety.

After what felt like hours of waiting he came back and now invited me into his office. There he told me of the very favourable response he had received from both Mr Nakene and Mr Peteni about my performance as a teacher. 'Mrs Moloto, they both say, if I lose you, I lose a jewel in the teaching field,' he ended. There was, however, no doubt in my mind that the headmaster of Law Palmer Primary School — his name was Mr Mokale — was finding it very difficult to reconcile this 'jewel in the teaching field' with the woman who stood in front of him. I vowed to demonstrate to him that appearances are not always the best yardstick to determine someone's worth at work.

He desperately needed a teacher at that moment and I was the only person available to take over the class, who were now shouting at the top of their voices. 'Mrs Moloto,' he said, 'Let's go into the classroom.' I stood awkwardly before the children as he introduced me. It was very clear the children were not in the least impressed by me. After reprimanding the class for making so much noise, he firmly told them to behave. Then, appointing one pupil to keep order, he invited me to follow him into his office, where he gave me the class register, a timetable and a few textbooks. I then returned to the class. I had hardly been with the class for five minutes when the bell for break rang, and the pupils flew out of the classroom, as if grateful to get away from this stranger, their new class teacher.

After putting the record books in their place, I glanced through the window only to see a very smart group of teachers, both male and female. The women were very attractively dressed, as was usual. I didn't know whether to remain in the classroom or join the rest of the staff. Embarrassment was about to get the better of me when a vivacious, sprightly teacher walked in. She seemed unconcerned by my appearance and shook hands, saying, in a very friendly tone, 'Welcome to Law Palmer. Come and join us. I am Caroline Ramalebye.' In a more subdued tone I introduced myself: 'Ellen Moloto, Mrs Moloto.' I was acutely aware of my shabby appearance as I followed her to join the group of very lively teachers, chatting and laughing on the verandah. I shook hands with all of them and we exchanged names.

As we had nothing in common to talk about, I listened to their conversation, but without really assimilating the content. I would have given any excuse to get away, but I lacked the courage to do so. When the bell finally rang I could have shouted 'hurrah'.

Among the group, there was one woman who was not like the rest of the staff. In fact, she was not very different from me in appearance as far as I could see. At the end of the school day, she told me she had only been at the school a week and that she came from the Cape. We both shared our hard-luck stories. I had a lot in common with Mrs Leila Mthimkulu as regards our immediate past family life, but we were poles apart so far as our outlook towards life was concerned.

Within the first two weeks, I found myself drawn towards the sophisticated, vivacious Caroline Ramalebye as my companion. The difference in our appearance did not act as a barrier between us. Caroline, now Mrs Caswell, had, and still has, a very strong personality, and with Mrs Gladys Moletsane, born Mathabathe, another teacher at this school, had a marked influence in the school.

Except for Mr Mashala, the carpentry instructor who lived in Kliptown, all the staff members lived locally and did not have to commute between home and school. It was for this reason that, after school, we went our separate ways and I saw very little of them outside school hours. I occasionally travelled home by train with Mr Mashala.

At the end of two months, things changed drastically for me when I joined my uncle's family in Orlando. The move meant that I could live more cheaply because I could walk to work; but the change brought many other blessings as well as hardships with it. I lived more or less in the same neighbourhood as Leila and I found myself in her company more often than not, particularly on our way back home. It was in her company that I first made contact with the local shopkeepers in Orlando. Now that I lived away from home, I missed the opportunity of using my father's contacts for purchasing the goods I needed, and as a stranger in Johannesburg, this was a real need for me — a situation which the established residents of this city may find funny or not real. Through Leila, I was introduced to the local traders, and thus perhaps appeared as a more respectable citizen of their community. Through this new network of contacts I was able to put myself on a par with my colleagues in my dress, and so gained self-confidence and dignity and became independent in my own right, as a person.

By the end of 1947 I was an integrated member of the staff at Law Palmer Higher Primary School. Besides my regular classroom duties, my assignments included training the senior school team in basketball, conducting the senior girls' choir for music competitions, running the Girl Guides and supervising groups of pupils assigned to clean the school premises. Later, some of my colleagues shared with me the private impressions they had had about me when I first joined the staff. It was great fun and very revealing to get an honest assessment. I knew then I had made it in that school. I remained there for six years. It was from there that I brought home the 'Girls Choir Trophy', as conductor of the district music competition.

Not far from our school, just outside the nearest railway station, Mlamlankunzi, stood a reformatory for delinquent boys whose offences varied in degree of severity. Their ages ranged from twelve to eighteen years. Apart from Law Palmer, all the other schools in that neighbourhood refused to take any of them. For as long as I taught at this school, I shared this rare responsibility with the rest of my colleagues, and became very concerned about and attached to these boys. This concern and interest opened a new direction in my life. The boys were a challenge to all of us, including the headmaster. I was drawn closer to them when, in my second year in that school, I was assigned to teach some subjects in standards 5 and 6, where most of these boys were pupils. My direct contact with them helped me to get to know them as people with weaknesses and strengths. Some of them were very lovable and intelligent. There was no doubt that some who had landed in this institution were victims of circumstance. The fact that some were children from broken homes increased my concern for my own sons, particularly after my divorce. In the struggle to settle down after the shocking experience of my marriage, I immersed myself in some of the events taking place in my community, such as youth work training and running youth clubs in Pimville and Orlando. This occupied me in the afternoons after school when there were no extra-mural activities.

Later in the year, my interest turned to the youth section of the African National Congress. The ANC Youth League had been launched in 1943, four years before my return to Johannesburg. The leaders of this movement, Nelson Mandela, Walter Sisulu and Oliver Tambo, were young black radicals who saw the ANC as an organisation of the black élite. Their aspirations were to produce a mass grass-roots organisation. I remember the glamorous Nelson Mandela of those years. The beautiful white silk scarf he wore round his neck stands out in my mind to this day. Walter Max Sisulu, on the other hand, was a hardy, down-to-earth man with practical clothing — typically a heavy coat and stout boots. Looking back, the third member of their trio, Oliver Tambo, acted as something of a balance, with his middle-of-the-road clothes! Most of my leisure-time in the evening was spent on that. I worked very closely with Nelson Mandela, Walter Sisulu, as well as Peter Mila and Herbert Ramokgopa. I wish I could explain why there seemed to be no outstanding women in the ranks of the ANC movement at that time. If they were present, for some reason or another I missed them. I heard of Ida Mtwana but I did not meet her to work with her. I regret that to this day.

My involvement in the community as a teacher and a community worker brought me in contact with many people, and as a result, my circle of contacts and friends grew by the day. I specially valued and appreciated some of the dear friends with whom I could share the tormenting experience of being separated from my children as well as the uncertainty about the outcome of my marriage. I became active in the church, at school and in recreational programmes to keep from pining.

Towards the end of 1947, I got a rude shock when I received a summons to appear in court to show cause why my marriage to my husband, Mr Ernest Moloto, should not be terminated on grounds of desertion. Much as I had anticipated that my departure from Rustenburg might possibly end in this way, the receipt of the summons really shook me. This was my first experience of coming face to face with a lawsuit of any kind. I was at a loss what to do, and turned to my father for guidance. After receiving legal advice, as Father suggested, I adjusted my mind to appearing in court, the thought of which really troubled me. I could not bear the thought of going to court to expose our family life differences in public, much as I was very hurt and humiliated by my husband's treatment of me. Do not be fooled; it angered me more than words can tell.

I found the support of some of my closest friends invaluable during this time. Among these few friends was Dr Mary Xakana, whom I had first met when I was at Lovedale and she at Fort Hare University. She was a woman of very few words, yet in her silence she communicated care, warmth, support and silent concern. I found her a true friend, and so she has remained. The continued communication with my father and with one or two friends I trusted soothed my fears about this trying, challenging 'monster', divorce. I instructed my legal adviser — a white lawyer, for there were no African lawyers at that time — to arrange for an out-of-court settlement with my husband, for in spite of all the hurt and humiliation I had suffered at his hands I was determined never to wash my dirty linen in public. This I am glad I succeeded in avoiding.

When the day arrived, I found that I had sufficient courage to stand firm in my approach. The only setback was that my legal representative was a totally different person from the man I had spoken to previously when I visited my lawyer's office. Not that I wanted that particular lawyer, but this representative had a completely different make-up and composition — in his physical appearance and disposition, as well as his attire. The man I was relying on to carry me through this experience was tiny in stature, and timid and apologetic in manner and approach. His attire, in particular his trousers, was shabby, dirty and creased. The gown he wore redeemed him to a certain extent, but it was also just not up to the mark. I looked at him once, and immediately lost confidence in him. I there and then told myself, 'Ellen, take charge of this boat, whether you sink or swim.'

After he had asked my husband and his legal adviser to join us, I gave him no chance. I addressed myself directly to my husband's lawyer, a tall, handsome, neatly dressed gentleman with a very strong personality, and open and forthright in his approach. But I refused to allow him to intimidate me in any way.

I stepped forward and introduced myself as Mrs Ellen Moloto. My dear father, who had accompanied me to court, appeared nervous at that stage. He must have seen my disillusionment in my legal adviser, and was torn between me, his loving daughter, and the representative of the firm of lawyers he had introduced me to and had spoken so highly of. My husband, who expected us to fight it out in court, must have been perplexed and completely put out by the developments of those few minutes. On the other hand, I was determined to have it my own way and to carry out my intentions.

In a few words I told his lawyer that it was my wish not to go into court but, if possible, to settle our dispute outside court. The only demand I made was that, when my husband had got the divorce he wanted, I must have free access to see my sons at any time convenient to me, and that the court should protect me from any abuse by my husband when I went to see my sons. At that stage I read in my husband's lawyer's face a great deal of surprise and a desire for more explanation. My own lawyer stood there quite dumb. Continuing to address myself directly to my husband's lawyer, I told him that the only people who knew the whole truth about our differences were myself and my husband. Directing my eyes to my husband, but still addressing his lawyer, I emphasised that he, my husband, and I truly knew the painful experience we had gone through and that I had no intention of going into court to disclose publicly the shocking, hurting and embarrassing experiences I had suffered at my husband's hands.

On that note I continued to plead for a settlement out of court on the condition that I had free access to see my sons if and when it was convenient to me. The lawyer turned to my husband for his reaction and pointed out the constructive importance of my offer. My husband, who I suspect had expected a great deal of resistance from my side, was left with no alternative but to accept it. I later learned that the carload of relatives he had brought as witnesses were both deflated and disappointed.

As he moved away from us towards the court building, his lawyer called me aside and this is what he said to me: 'Mrs Moloto, in my practice as a lawyer, I have not come across many women who made this type of decision. You may not trust me because I represent your husband, but this one thing I wish to say; you have made an unexpected, wise decision. Although your husband may decide to hold on to the children, this must not disturb you. My experience in this practice is that the parents who force the children to remain with them and deny them the opportunity to see the other parent stand the greatest chance of being rejected and deserted by those same children when they grow older. Mark my words.' And on that note we parted.

The divorce was granted. As truly as the sun rises in the east and sets in the west, in 1957 I saw my eldest son walk into my new home at 11376 Orlando West Extension, Soweto, and six or seven years later his brother followed. They are now married and settled with their families. My elder son is in Soweto, the younger one at Umlazi in Durban. The pity of it all is that I was not able to see the gallant lawyer to say to him: Yes it happened as you predicted.

With my divorce behind me, I felt that a heavy load was removed from my shoulders. I started to plan my life all over again. I told myself, 'Ellen, you tried your very best and it was not good enough. You cannot moan over what happened; your duty is to stand up and live your life to the fullest.' Side by side with this feeling of being free from a marriage which lasted only six years, I was left as if empty — the type of feeling one has after working very hard for a stiff examination. Once that examination is over there is a sudden empty feeling, as if something is missing. For two or three months I was caught up in this uncomfortable feeling of emptiness. The longing for my sons doubled. I suddenly felt very distant from them as if I would never ever see them again. I suppose the marriage link which was snapped when we divorced had a psychological effect on me.

My ears, eyes and mind were very alert to register the challenging, interesting happenings round about me at that time. I was determined to keep myself occupied without realising that I was really trying to blot out my past experiences.

Round about that period, word got round that a certain overseas film company wanted potential actors and actresses to come forward for auditions. Without wasting time I presented myself at the studio — I cannot remember now which one — in the city. Other black men and women, some of my age, some younger, some older, arrived in large numbers. I found the audition unnerving, yet very exciting. The director, Zoltan Korda, was a very interesting person. On arrival we introduced ourselves, but were not given anything special to do. Korda had a remarkable memory for people's names, for out of the blue he called my name. I turned to him and he smiled. Our communication was without any words, yet I knew I must have made a mark. It was fascinating watching proceedings throughout the auditioning. I remember how Winnie Ramatlo and I competed for the part of a Skokian Queen. I was finally chosen to play the part and Winnie was my understudy. The film was *Cry The Beloved Country* based on the famous novel by Alan Paton. The film absorbed me completely — physically, intellectually and emotionally.

Acting in the film helped me to discover my untapped potential and, unknowingly, it became a great healer of the hurt I had recently incurred. The possibility of going abroad for the first time was raised, although not fulfilled. Winnie Ramatlo, Albertina Temba (the lady playing the leading role in the film) and I were a threesome from the Youth Club Association. We made a mark for ourselves, for the youth clubs and, above all, for black womanhood.

Looking back, I have every reason to believe that if we had known better about the benefits and implications of filming then we could have made a better financial deal. But as a section of the population which had been exploited over the years, the lump sums we received were accepted with pleasure and excitement, for they were a great financial reward compared with our salaries.

What is more, we saw ourselves as actors of standing and reputation for we shared the set with famous personalities of Sidney Poitier's calibre. I personally enjoyed working with him directly, for he played the young priest who entered my Skokian Queen's house — a house where there existed every vice and vile practice. One actress who had great potential, but who for one reason or another did not fulfil her opportunity to the fullest, was Ribbon Dlamini. If my memory serves me well, we were engaged in this film on and off from some time in 1949 to some time in 1951.

It was during the years 1948 and 1949 that in my numerous movements and engagements I met Mr Godfrey Rosenbaum Kuzwayo, a man in his early forties. There was no doubt in my mind from my first meeting with him that he was a man of character and great experience and achievements, but that he had had his share of hardship and misfortune. He was a refined, soft-spoken gentleman, with a rare sense of humour. He told me that he had been very active in the Church as the Treasurer of the African Methodist

Episcopal Church in South Africa, but he had lost interest in this work because of the disparity in the wages of the ministers of his Church who were serving the towns and those who were stationed in the country. This issue was very close to his heart. He felt that the ministers stationed in the country who were receiving very low wages were exposed to a great deal of suffering, while those in town were reasonably comfortably settled and protected.

G. R., as he was popularly known, was a compositor in the printing trade. I found out later that he had his own business in the city registered as 'Africans' Own'. Later he was compelled to sell this printing shop against his will, following the implementation of the Group Areas Act which denied black people the right to trade within the city of Johannesburg. His sense of humour and commitment to duty reduced some of the pressures and frustrations he was going through at that time, some of which were personal and linked with his private life, while others were much more of a business nature.

We shared each other's problems over a period of nine to twelve months. His problems certainly weighed very heavily on him. I got to know more about his past successes and his prospects of a very bright future. And I also learned from some of his close friends, both women and men, about some of the issues which contributed to his present situation.

When his family life completely disintegrated and he asked for my hand in marriage, I was scared, and turned down his proposal. I feared to take responsibility in that type of situation again; perhaps also I was still enjoying the few years of freedom after my first marriage. However, he persisted, and some time in 1950 I reconsidered my decision. Two main issues influenced me in accepting his proposal. My childhood longing for a home I could see and refer to as mine, even if I shared it with someone, was still unfulfilled, and remained a burning issue within me. Secondly, I had never at any stage accepted a failure and allowed it to remain unchallenged. The failure of my first marriage inside six years was a very sore point in my life. I had tried to reflect on this matter very objectively and with an open mind to see what had really gone wrong, and, more than that, where I had personally erred. G. R.'s proposal would give me the chance to test my capability in this field again, and so I accepted .

We married in 1950 and decided to start a home in Kliptown because of the shortage of houses in Soweto at that time. We found accommodation in a neighbourhood known as Paardevlei. The houses were reasonably well built and finished, constructed as three-bedroomed cottages joined together into ten to twelve units. They shared a common set of toilets built outside the cottages, which were a real hazard. The tenants were a mixture of coloureds, Indians and Africans, under an Indian landlord. The problem of relations between the race groups was non-existent. You chose whom you wished to associate with and the level to which such an association was carried. One thing was certain: we were a community with a spirit of neighbourliness which accorded respect and recognition where it was due.

Our marriage was blessed with the birth of a son, Godfrey Ndabezitha Kuzwayo. This gave me three sons in all. My husband had one daughter by his first marriage so we could boast of one daughter and three sons.

For a long time, even after my second marriage, I shut thoughts of my earlier married life out of my mind. The only time I ever came near facing it with some maturity was on one of my visits to see my sons, when I shared with my ex-husband my concern for our children, particularly in view of the fact that he was not prepared to part with them. I expressed my concern to him about the boys, and emphasised to him the importance of their being happy for the sake of their general growth and well-being. To me one very important aspect was that his new wife should be happy and comfortable, as I saw this as the only guarantee that the children would remain happy and secure. To bring it home to him, I shared with him my deep-felt wishes for the very best for both our new homes, for the benefit of our two boys, regardless of where they were at that time. Even though my own sons were not living with me, I felt totally committed to having a happy home for my second husband's children who did live with us and, I deeply hoped, for my own children when they came to visit or to live with us. The fact that I was reasonably settled in my new home meant that I was able to make my family happy.

Ernest's unexpected second divorce came to me as a real shock, and I was only too happy to have my two sons eventually come back to me as a result.

It was during our stay in Kliptown that I met Dr Mary Xakana again and we picked up the loose ends of our friendship, when she was preparing to get married to Mr Wally Xakana. I was on the committee which planned and ran their wedding programme. It was very heartening to me at that time to realise that my old circle of friends still accepted me and wanted me to share with them in their affairs, despite the stigma of my divorce.

I soon discovered that my husband and Wally Xakana were also friends of very long standing. Mary and I were now drawn together by our common interests as married women, mothers and old friends from Orlando. We lived within walking distance and so it was no problem calling on one another. Our stay in Kliptown gave me the opportunity to know Mary as a doctor, mother and wife as well as a community worker and friend. Mary attended me as a doctor during my pregnancy and attended the birth of my youngest son, Godfrey. Her eldest daughter was born about nine months before my son. For six years we were very good neighbours. (Her story is told more fully in Chapter 16.)

11
Looking to the Young

I now became increasingly aware of issues of personal and social concern in my immediate neighbourhood. Some of these gradually started fully to engage my attention and participation. It was in the course of my involvement in the community that I learned of the youth work programme run by the recreation section of the Non-European Affairs Department, popularly known as NEAD, for the benefit of Orlando children. I visited some of the clubs and made my initial contribution to this programme on a voluntary basis. Later I approached the authorities and offered my services on a part-time basis, after school hours. Initially the official reply was that as this had not been done before, it could not be done now. But my continued voluntary services finally earned me recognition with the senior officials, my application was reconsidered, and I was engaged on a part-time basis.

This appointment earned me entry into the leadership training courses run by the Southern African Association of Youth Clubs, when Miss Joan Pim was chairman.

The Association was started in 1939 and served all children in its area of operation without discrimination on grounds of race, religion, class or age. It extended its services along the Reef, including the East Rand as far as Nigel, the West Rand up to Randfontein, the Vaal complex up to Vereeniging, and the Pretoria and Johannesburg areas. I went through all the training courses offered by this body and continued working for the Non-European Affairs Department on a part-time basis. The courses were divided into the youth club helpers course, and the advanced club helpers course. None of us was prepared to leave the training in the middle. At the end of four years, as I shall describe in the next chapter, I registered with the Jan Hofmeyr School of Social Work and qualified at the end of 1955. From 1956 to 1963, I worked as the organiser of youth work with the Southern African Association of

Youth Clubs in the Vaal complex and Johannesburg areas.

The reward for this involvement was twofold. On the one hand, it augmented my meagre teacher's salary; but more than anything else, it gave me an opportunity to use my spare time creatively and fruitfully for both myself and the community. I just loved doing this type of work. It was in this programme that I made use of the wealth of knowledge I had received as a little girl on my grandfather's farm. I had lived among the peasant community there and knew the culture peculiar to them. Their music, dancing and different types of attire came back to me and I used this knowledge to produce some startling and outstanding drama performances at the Youth Festival events.

The Pimville club, where I finally became the senior leader, gained a reputation for classic performances, and it soon rivalled all the other Association clubs. The Association brought me into contact with many women, from the East and West Rand, Pretoria, Vaal Trangle and the Johannesburg areas. Nearly all the people who initiated the clubs and ran them were women and girls in the different communities. They did this on a voluntary basis. Their duties included training for physical displays of a very high standards, traditional drama presentations, folk dancing, set pieces, and handicraft skills. All these were in preparation for the big annual event, the Youth Festival, an event very close to the hearts of the members, leaders and the communities where the clubs were operating. The Festival was also very close to the hearts of the residents where the event was scheduled to be held that particular year. Indeed, the days leading up to the Festival were highly charged. It was always 'who's who?' and 'which trophy?' Members and leaders alike were excited and anxious about their performance and success.

These tremendous women and girls, who gave so much of their time to mould the future of the young people of their communities, only received what were known as out-of-pocket expenses to cover lunch and travel costs. The total amount was calculated as one half-crown (in the currency of those years) per two-hour session. Most clubs had two sessions a week, so the leaders earned eight half-crowns (one pound) a month. It was assumed that all the club leaders participated on a part-time basis, and further that they ran the clubs straight after the end of their working day, before they went home. I would love to know how much their counterparts in the white community clubs earned.

In addition to acquiring the skills needed to achieve the very high standard of performance at the Festivals, the leaders also took special training in keeping club records on which their honorarium was calculated. They kept up-to-date attendance registers for the members and for the leader herself; and financial records of the membership fees and other expenses — for example, transport costs to Festival events or on a seaside outing. The leaders were expected to maintain clear records.

I can remember the names of only a few of these women leaders whose lives refuted the uncalled-for criticism from other communities over the colour line; namely, that Africans do nothing for themselves, all they know is to go round begging for help from whites. The unsung heroines of those years who conscientiously rendered voluntary service in this noble calling, and never counted the cost, provide a true testimony to the unselfish, devoted contribution of black women towards the personal growth and development of the youth of their community.

The register and archives of the Southern African Association of Youth Clubs are somewhere in this city of Johannesburg, and contain the names of these heroines. Some of them underestimated their tremendous efforts and contribution to the point of regarding themselves as unproductive and useless in their community. I wish to call out this register and say to these women they have made a valid contribution and they should stand up to be counted. For her long service as a volunteer for thirteen years, and as a staff member from 1956 to 1981, Michael Dodo Koffie merits recognition.

As does Esther Kumalo, the first volunteer from the African community who started to work there in 1939, the year the Association was launched, and remained in that capacity for 25 years; and Winnie Ramateo, a social worker, who still holds the fort as organising secretary since her appointment to this office in 1979. She runs 70 clubs with the total membership of over 7000. They stand as examples of the scores of women who have given their resources to the Association for the development of black youth.

In addition to administrative skills, club helpers were encouraged to gain skill in the individual activities included in the programme. Traditional drama was often foreign to club helpers born and raised in the urban areas. Those of us who had known life in both the country and in urban areas had the advantage of first-hand experience of country life, including its culture — the music, dancing, dress, language, customs and values. It was only after I had gone through this training and emerged as a fully-fledged club helper that I realised the unintended harm my parents had done when they prevented my visiting the girls' 'circumcision' schools (see Chapter 4) . I lost so much, because I was only to visit these schools secretly and under stress in the fear that my family would find out. I practised some of the music and dance I heard and saw there in great fear and secrecy. Although most of the youth club instructors were white, they were well informed on the subjects they taught the helpers. However, they emphasised the technical aspects of the subjects and lacked the emotional and deep understanding of the culture, which individual leaders worked so hard to portray.

Physical rhythmic exercises were a field where none of us had an advantage over the others in terms of earlier exposure. But we soon realised that some helpers had more aptitude here than others. The way they themselves performed in class, as well as the outstanding performance of their club members at the Festival, showed clearly that some helpers had a special talent in this.

Club helpers worked very hard in each area of the youth programme in order to be able to produce a high standard of performance from the club they ran. Some emerged with distinction at the end of their training. It is both amazing and rewarding to say that they accepted their challenge and responsibility with dignity, determination and love for the work itself, as well as for the participants. You many ask, 'You mean for the love of it and no more?' Yes indeed, when you consider their very meagre financial reward, and the way in which they had to include several activities all of high standard.

Saturdays were the days scheduled for the training courses. The day started with registration and a cup of tea, as some of the helpers came very long distances to attend. The rest of the day was taken up by the specific activities. Looking back, I am intrigued by the spirit of goodwill which prevailed throughout the courses, and by the fellowship shared and enjoyed by the club helpers. Our presence there was really an outstanding achievement — but it was one which we all took so much for granted at that time, and which was underestimated by the society in which we lived.

I look back with a sense of deep appreciation for the devoted and long-standing voluntary service rendered by those women, young and old, for the individual personal growth of young black people as well as for the overall development of the whole community. These were the efforts of some of the women of the black community who (as I describe in Chapter 16) have been given the humiliating and degrading tag of 'Minors' by both their menfolk and the government of this country — and sometimes also by other communities over the colour line.

Some may challenge the description of these club helpers as volunteers. Taking into account the very poor salaries of black teachers in general, and in particular the appallingly low wages of black female teachers, it puzzles me that these club helpers never raised any serious objection to the low out-of-pocket allowances they received. My only explanation would be either that it was the result of long-term exposure to exploitation or that, from the outset, they accepted this involvement as their voluntary contribution towards the upliftment of the youth of their community — a service which has been and remains a dire need in this community.

The out-of-pocket expense allowance were collected once every three months at the quarterly meetings of the Association. The amounts received by the helpers by then had accumulated and so seemed worth more than the single half-crown earned through attendance at every club meeting. Some of the helpers, I venture to believe, saw this cash as money for buying luxury items like stockings, cosmetics and the like. Yet, let us not forget that some helpers were mothers with over-burdening responsibilities in their homes, for whom these amounts were precious as they augmented the income of the family. In such cases, the expenses allowance was used prudently as it added to the meagre wages earned from hard work, sacrifice and self-denial.

My thoughts drift back to the days when many of those good women trod the path along Holland Street to the Association office which would be pulsating with activity towards the school holidays. Helpers came and went, bringing money collected from the youth members to go to the seaside. The plans drawn up over months now took shape, and there was great excitement when the train bookings were confirmed. It was an event which everyone looked forward to. The careful planning, as well as the capable administration, were put to the test on the day of departure for the seaside camp. Park Station would look like a scene of complete confusion, despite the painstaking plans of the Association. The last-minute preparations by members created uncalled-for delays which caused everybody, club members, helpers and parents alike, panic and anxiety. What if these late arrivals were left behind? I look back and marvel at the very rare loss of luggage — or members! — and at the fact that we never had a single casualty from car or train accident. For that matter, I don't remember any members ever missing the train on any of these trips.

It was on the platform, as members arrived in groups, that the helpers showed their concern for their club members. About fifteen minutes before the train pulled out, each helper, reading from a list of their members, would call out their names to check and double-check they were all there, and to see that their luggage was together. The parents of the younger members would complicate the situation by their emotional attachment to their little ones, who were probably going away from home for the first time. I hear their voices as I write calling out to a special leader — 'Mrs X, please look after my little one; this is her pocket money, she will lose it, please keep it for her.' Such last-minute appeals, messages and requests coming from several parents at once, gave the impression that the helpers were either deaf or stupid. But there was just no time to get annoyed. The helpers were genuinely put to a test, but carried out their duties with dignity, responsibility and determination. How they managed to keep calm and composed amidst the members' chattering, the endless requests and appeals from the parents, and the last-minute instructions or questions from or to their own families, is still a question unanswered to this day. These great women exuded graciousness and responsibility.

It was a source of great pleasure and pride to watch them at the camp. Except for the rudiments of swimming received by a few at the Hofmeyr School of Social Work, none of the women could boast any knowledge of swimming, yet each one of them had a swimming costume which was worn when supervising the members on the beach; at these times the helpers were very alert. They kept a sharp eye on the young people as they rushed in and out of the sea, played on the sand or just paddled along the beach. On each seaside trip we travelled with about two male sports organisers from the Non-European Affairs Department who had received substantial training as life-savers. But the women never gave them an opportunity to display their skills to save a member in danger of drowning. No! Never! They carried out their duties very conscientiously and avoided any possibility of a member being in danger of drowning.

These women were responsible for every activity in the camp, including planning the menus, helping to prepare and serve meals, planning and administering the recreation programme, organising trips to places of interest near the camp-site, as well as their numerous administrative duties. The helpers were also responsible for the safety and behaviour of the members for the duration of the camp, up to the time the members returned to their homes. There was never a moment to contemplate the possibility of any misfortune. Each helper carried out the duties assigned to her from day to day, allowing for no mishaps.

On one of these outings, it happened by chance that our Association shared premises with a school group from the Transvaal. Our group, members and helpers alike, most of whom were seasoned campers, were astonished by the school teachers' clothes. On their arrival, it was clear that the pupils were thrilled by the sea, and, unable to wait, the pupils just rushed to the beach in their swimming costumes. They were followed by their male teachers dressed in suits, ties and shoes as if going to church or attending some important event such as the funeral of a dignitary! The sand did not seem to challenge their attire in any way. The big joke was when the waves rolled in towards the beach, as if to order us all off. Those in swimming costumes — pupils, club members and helpers — threw themselves down to be swamped by the waves, whilst the stiffly-dressed teachers tried to dash away, but not fast enough! Some ended up drenched in seawater up to their ankles or even halfway up their legs. The club members roared with laughter and shouted embarrassing yet pertinent remarks, in an effort to challenge the teachers to change their clothes for something more in keeping with their responsibilities in this situation.

They were all male teachers, note. It was hard for them, but the message went home.

At our programme review meeting that evening, the decision was taken that, during the swimming sessions, staff members of the Association and all the helpers should take responsibility for each and every young person in the sea, regardless of the group they belonged to. It was further emphasised that we should keep a very low profile in this task so as not to embarrass or antagonise the teachers. The women in our group took responsibility for this, and made a formidable task of it. Their supervision of all the swimmers created a healthy relationship with the school group for the duration of the camp. The foremost thought in their minds was the safety of all the children; the question of whether or not the teachers carried out their duties responsibly was secondary. In my experience it was a unique incident for a group of workers to arrive at a unanimous decision to take on additional duties and responsibilities to the load they already carried, in the interest of the well-being of youth. Yet this group, where women outnumbered men by four to one, undertook this task without any thought for themselves; what is more, they seemed to derive satisfaction and joy from of it. There is no doubt that while the teachers appeared to be embarrassed by this situation, they in turn appreciated the gesture very much, and learned a great deal from it.

The fact that helpers had to pay their own travel expenses did not influence their performance negatively in any way. The situation is the same to this day, but the strength of the Association has gone down tremendously from the days when the Festivals were held at the home of the mining magnate Sir George Albu in the 1940s. Members and helpers who go on these trips derive fun, joy and recreation from them; they also find them very educative. They get an opportunity to see nearby countries or parts of this country — just to see the sea can, in itself, be a mind-blowing experience for some members. Newcomers to the seaside, on their arrival, often stood back spellbound by the sight or the motion of the sea. It was very touching at times to watch their reactions.

It is a great pity that in recent years there seem to be fewer of these camps. Over a period of approximately fifteen years, the Association arranged trips to a number of places, among them Umgababa on the south coast of Natal. This was very popular and frequently used. The Strand in East London, Cape Town, Swaziland, Lourenco Marques (now Maputo), were some of the other places the Association used as sites for the popular camps.

At Christmas time in the 1950s, after the state had closed down the mission schools and lawlessness was rife, many parents were particularly willing to pay for their children to go on these trips. They often said, 'My son is safer away from home when youngsters go on a spree of fighting and slaying one another.' As well as seeing new countries and coming into direct contact with the facts of geography, the young people developed a sense of independence and responsibility. They soon became selective about their needs on these trips. At the beginning some members were still inclined to buy the wrong sort of clothes for camping, despite the talks held at the clubs about what to buy and what to bring. Towards the end of the 1950s, the change in dress, as well as the amount of luggage carried, gave testimony to the efforts of the Association through its helpers over the years.

Although the Association saw its volunteer workers as helpers, to me they had always come across as leaders. Their initiative in launching youth clubs in their areas and in running and administering these clubs; their continued interest and support for the overall programme and events of the Association; their keen participation in the training courses of the Association — all these placed these committed supporters a step above being just helpers. To this day I refer to them as club leaders.

12
Changing Roles in Mid-stream

Some of the women I met through the Southern African Association of Youth Clubs were qualified practising social workers, a
profession which I must admit was new and completely foreign to
me then. Among these, the late Mrs Anna Mokhetle took a keen
interest in my work as a helper in the clubs. Anna began to
encourage me to go back to college to train as a social worker. She
persisted because she saw my temperament, outlook and attitude
towards people as answering to the attributes expected of those who
followed this profession. At the beginning I just dismissed her
remarks from my mind, not realising that they were only pushed to
the back of my mind, rather than out of it.

I described in Chapter 10 how within two years of my
appointment at Law Palmer Higher Primary School, I was assigned
to teach some subjects in standards 5 and 6, and as a result was
brought into direct contact with some of the boys from the
reformatory, whom I got to know in depth, seeing them as students
who could do their schoolwork as well as any of their classmates.
What is more, they also accepted whatever reprimand, cautioning
or punishment that came their way, including corporal punishment,
which was not prohibited there, and was administered at Law
Palmer. These boys gave me, as their teacher, no opportunity to
view them as different from the rest of the class. It never crossed my
mind that the boys from the 'place of safety' could be rebellious.
But the relationship I established with them was not acceptable in
the eyes of the headmaster. I was very taken aback when he called
me into his office one day to confront me about my attitude towards
them.

My response was the expression of a deep-seated conviction. I
said that in my view these boys were our pupils just like all the
others in the school and as such were entitled to the same treatment
given to all other students; they should not be singled out in any way

or given a general label of 'evil-doers'. As might be expected, our discussion on this issue was charged with emotion. My final word to the headmaster was that rather than single these boys out in the manner he was suggesting, it was much better not to have them in our school at all. 'Mrs Moloto,' he responded, 'if you continue to treat these boys as you have been doing, know that you are disrupting the discipline of the school.'

Although I felt very strongly about my stand on these boys, I was shocked and taken aback by the headmaster's remark that I was 'disrupting the discipline of the school'. However, I reassured him that I never had any intention of disrupting the discipline of the school but that I would continue to treat these boys as individuals and deal with them on merit. I left his office thoroughly frustrated and disgusted. For months afterwards, one question crossed my mind: 'Why on earth did the headmaster ever accept these boys in the school when he feels so very negative towards them?' It remained unanswered. But like all unpleasant incidents, my encounter with the headmaster passed and was forgotten.

About a year or two after this, as I was busy in my class teaching, one of my colleagues, a male teacher, stopped at the door and in an agitated tone beckoned me to follow him into the headmaster's office. His words were something like: 'Hurry, the headmaster is in trouble!' The expression on his face gave me no chance to ask any questions. As we entered the office amidst screams, panic and struggle, there, right in front of me, was the boy who appeared to be the eldest of the inmates of the 'place of safety' clinging to the headmaster's tie and on the point of strangling him. There was no doubt that the situation had got out of hand. As I walked in, I shouted, 'Baloyi! Baloyi!' He turned to me and I asked him, 'What on earth are you doing?' He let go of the tie, but was still very angry when he replied: 'Every time the "Prince" (meaning Principal) talks to us, he says we are criminals and murderers. I wanted him to experience the difference between a pupil and a criminal. Aren't you surprised that you, Mistry (meaning Mistress, a term used in black schools for women teachers), inflict corporal punishment on us for various offences, but we never fight back because you treat us as *pupils*.' Naturally, I was speechless. He was dismissed from the office, and we reviewed what had led up to this situation and its implications. We arrived at the conclusion that the recognition and acceptance of the reformatory inmates as pupils in the school were basic, essential and urgent. The headmaster never discussed the incident again, but he had learnt his lesson; this I could read from the way he spoke to these boys and how he treated them afterwards.

This incident, however, forced me to think again about Anna Mokhetle's suggestion that I train as a social worker. For, much as I had been hurt and disturbed by the headmaster's remarks two years earlier, I had not taken any action on them. However, as in many instances, there is always the last straw. In this particular case, the last straw for me centred on my youngest son Godfrey Ndabezitha when he was about two years of age.

As I mentioned earlier, I had moved to Kliptown when I married in 1950 because of the shortage of houses in Orlando. Law Palmer School was in Orlando. To travel between home and Orlando I took the bus to Kliptown Station, then the train between Kliptown and Mlamlankunzi completing my journey on foot. This journey was both energy- and time-consuming. And of course I was unable to supervise the home-help. I just hoped and trusted that my helper was carrying out all her duties as she was told, in particular fulfilling the important responsibility of looking after my son. For days on end I agonised about my son's good care and good health. These hopes and expectations were shattered when my son's health showed signs of decline. All efforts to supervise the helper by some type of 'remote-control' failed, and in my son's interest and safety, I applied for a week's leave without pay to be with him. The rebuff I received from the circuit inspector about this application came as a terrible blow; I was downright disgusted. The authorities' response had a very negative effect on my attitude towards teaching as a profession. The reply, in essence, stated that I should choose between my job and my son rather than that I be given leave.

To me the message was loud and clear: 'Ellen, your services are no longer needed.' Thus, at the end of December 1952, I resigned from teaching. I have never looked back. I shared my frustrations and future plans with my husband. I remembered too Anna Mokhetle's advice. In the months of October and November 1952, I literally lived on the doorstep of the Jan Hofmeyr School of Social Work, waiting to see the authorities about registering with them to read for the Diploma in Social Work the following year. During all that period of negotiation with the authorities of Jan Hofmeyr School, my husband supported me fully, and even helped me to meet people who were influential and informed about the work of that school and who could give me an insight into what the authorities expected from the students. I regarded my registration as a student there as a remarkable achievement, which I guarded very jealously. I applied myself to my work with determination, perseverance and real enjoyment. Without being boastful, I excelled in my work there.

My course lasted three years. At the end of the first two years, I was appointed an instructor in physical education, one of my favourite subjects to the present day. I carried this assignment with great joy and diligence. During those three years, I made friends with my fellow students, some of whom I became very much attached to. My circle of friends included Winnie Nomzamo Madikizela, now Mrs Nelson Mandela, Marcia Pumla Finca, who became Mrs Denalana, and Harriet Kongisa. These three friends were far younger than me, but we had a very close and warm relationship. We gave one another moral support. At the end of the three years, we found it not easy to part.

Pumla married Cecil Denalane, also a social worker. A son and a daughter were born in this family. Pumla's first job as a social worker was with the Mental Health Society, where she worked with her office and the community-based committee where I was a member to establish the first Day Care Centre for retarded children in Soweto. Pumla Centre is named after her. She now lives in New York with her children.

Harriet Kongisa practises as a social worker in Port Elizabeth where she also serves on a voluntary basis in other community projects. We valued her rare sense of humour in that group.

Winnie Nomzamo Mandela has become a household name in all South African communities, foe or friend. She is banished to Brandfort, a rural town in the Orange Free State where she carries out an effective social work programme on a voluntary basis in the Deep South of the country.

We were an inseparable foursome. As their senior in age, I often performed the duty of chaperone when some wayward man tried to interfere in any way with one of us when we went for our cookery lessons at Wemmer in the 1950s. They all were very attractive women. Wemmer was a huge, primitive, Johannesburg city council complex, where black people from all walks of life traded. Some specialised in traditional herb dealing, others in garments or shoes, while others sold foodstuffs and traditional fermented drinks of various kinds. There was a modern kitchen where we took cookery lessons.

Marcia, Harriet and I have kept on in practice as social workers since we graduated. When I resigned from my employment with the Southern African Association of Youth Clubs, for example, I took another job which was more or less community oriented too. The state subsidised social welfare agencies have had no professional attraction for me; I have consciously stayed clear of them from fear of limited scope for imagination and initiative. Recently, however, I have been concentrating on my writing. Winnie, on the other hand, started her practice with established social welfare agencies of repute, such as the Hospital Social Work and Child Welfare Society, but was also vocal and uncompromising about the discrimination and oppression suffered by the black people at the hands of the government. Without being conscious of it, she gradually drifted away from routine social work practice and became more and more involved with soical change issues and programmes in addition, and finally earned herself the disfavour of the government. Yet in the midst of all that, if you meet her anywhere, she still radiates the strength of a determined fighter whose spirit has not been in any way dampened by any of the harassment of imprisonment, banning or banishment by the government despite the deterioration of her health; not even by being separated from her gallant husband Nelson Rolihlahla, who has been serving life imprisonment for the last twenty years on Robben Island. I talk more about Winnie Mandela in Chapter 16.

In 1963 I was employed by the Transvaal region of the World Affiliated Young Women's Christian Association. I started with them as the programme director of the YWCA Dube Centre, a job I held for about nine months. During the years I was employed by the Association of Youth Clubs, I had often crossed paths with Mrs Phyllis Noluthando Mzaidume, then staff member of the YWCA in the Transvaal. Round about 1963 I started visiting her home because she was stricken with cancer. It was during these visits that Phyllis pleaded with me to take the position of General Secretary of the Transvaal YWCA, a position she had held for several years: 'Ellen, I genuinely request you to take over the Transvaal office as General Secretary,' she told me. I repeatedly told her I did not feel competent to do so, but she insisted. After a series of requests, all of which I turned down, she sat up, looked me straight in the face and said: 'Mkhozi,' (meaning friend; it was the way we addressed each other), 'if you do not take the office of General Secretary in the Transvaal, the YWCA will *die*!'

For the first time I read something unusual in her face and voice. I promised to consider her plea and to return the next day with my answer. By the time I left her, I knew I had no alternative but to accept that challenging request. At the same time, I was scared of the women in this Association; they were over-powering and they appeared to be perfectionists. In addition to this, I was frightened of the responsibility of the work I was expected to do. I did not feel equal to the task.

The next day I called in at her house to say 'How do you do?' — and also to tell her that I had decided to take on the office. She did not ask for my reason, and perhaps I did not give her the opportunity to do so. I said, 'Phyllis, for your sake I will take this post and will expect you to assist me where you can.' She just smiled and said, 'Thank you, Mkhozi, I am happy that you have accepted my request.'

Within two days of this agreement, when I passed to check on her, she asked me to sit down and talk to her. This puzzled me, as I had never gone in to see her without taking a seat: I always spent three-quarters of an hour or so with her. I sat down without question. She turned to me and told me she thought God was inconsiderate with her. She told me of a white priest from the States who was healed of cancer. She could not understand why this did not happen in her case, particularly since her children were so young and still needed a mother's love and care. For the first time I had to face the reality of Phyllis's condition. I was stunned and dumb. Completely lost for words. As if this was not enough to unsettle anyone, she continued: 'Mkhozi, one more request, please see to it that on the day of my burial, the YWCA banner is carried in front of my coffin. You promise, Mkhozi? She looked straight into my eyes and blinking away her tears, waited for my reply. There was dead silence for a few seconds, as I composed myself and controlled my voice so as not to give in to crying.

'Mkhozi,' I said, 'I have not started to take that office; you are also aware of how strongheaded are some of the YWCA women in the leadership role. How on earth do you expect me to begin to tell them what to do about you?' 'Don't worry,' she replied, 'you will have no problem.' At that moment my concern was more about the funeral than about the YWCA women in the leadership. I had no courage to ask her why she was so sure she was about to die. She never quite shared with me how my appointment was going to be processed without advertising the post. She must have already consulted with some of the senior officals within the Association.

I had been three weeks in office when I noticed that Phyllis's health was deteriorating by the day. My mind was in turmoil. I could not think clearly. There were many questions I could not answer. Amongst these, the topmost was 'Who is this woman who has the courage and insight to appoint someone to replace her before she dies? How come she is so certain about her departure from this earth? She dares even to give instructions about what should happen at her funeral; who is she?' As the chief speaker on the day of her funeral I had to collect information about this noble daughter of Africa, and she had given me plenty to talk about.

Phyllis Noluthando Mzaidume was born on 5 February 1920 into the Maseko family in the district of Idutywa in the Cape Province. She received her primary education in the local school where her family lived. Her secondary education was at Healdtown, where she matriculated in 1937. In 1940 Phyllis received her BA degree at Fort Hare. Her first teaching post was at Orlando High School where she remained for two years, from 1941 to 1942. In 1943 she accepted a new teaching post at the Wilberforce Institution in Evaton where she taught until 1947.

It was during this time that Phyllis demonstrated her interest in a new women's organisation which had penetrated the black community. As a Tri-Y member, she instituted a section for young adults in the World Affiliated Young Women's Christian Association in the Transvaal. She was one of many young girls who participated with interest in the programme of this Association. She worked with the founder of this organisation, Mrs Madi Hall-Xuma, a black American from North Carolina and the wife of Dr A. B. Xuma, one of the early presidents of the ANC. They were joined by other older women to plan the programme and management of the organisation.

At the time Phyllis joined the ranks of the 'Y' as a volunteer, round about 1945, the Association had already been in existence for about five years. Its history goes back to 1940 when Dr A. B. Xuma returned from the States with his wife. They settled in the Sophiatown of old. Madi must have been very lonely when her doctor husband was engaged in his surgery for long hours, and she finally went out to look for the women of her new community for company. She invited them for tea to discuss issues common to all women. This contact gave birth to regular meetings in different homes where the women shared in many things. At its inception the name of the new organisation was Zenzele which means 'do it yourself'. As founder, Mrs Xuma, who had been a staunch member of the YWCA in the States, and who at that time was serving on the World Executive Committee, directed and geared the programme of this organisation to that of the YWCA.

When she left teaching at the end of 1952 Phyllis accepted a job with the YWCA as the first paid black staff member of that Association in South Africa and as General Secretary of the Transvaal region. She started to organise the clubs around the Reef. In 1954 the first YWCA club was established in Johannesburg; this gave birth to all other clubs in the Transvaal and to this day is seen as the mother club. When the Association spread beyond the magisterial area of Johannesburg, this meant more involvement and more work for the regional office and for its General Secretary.

The programme of the Association in the Transvaal and in all other regional associations was carried out through extensive, detailed planning which ensured that the activities were meaningful and effective. Leadership training courses were geared to develop leadership potential in members and to prepare them for roles within the Association and their communities. A leadership school was planned and started in 1963. It inaugurated a new three-year cycle in the work of the South African Council. It was first held at Wilgespruit Fellowship Centre from 5–15 July. Forty selected trainees from all four local associations met for in-depth lectures on YWCA history and purpose. Following the lectures, the trainees participated in classes according to their interest: they could choose between Bible study, book-keeping, how to work with young people, or programme planning in adult clubs.

All trainees were involved in practical work related to their field of study. Those who belonged to the Bible study group led morning and evening prayers; others who participated in the recreational programme gave instruction in activities such as folk dancing, drama or singing; the group trained in the appropriate skills gave instructions in handicrafts. The members on the whole found this programme relaxing, rewarding and stimulating. One of the last events Phyllis ran before she became very ill was a nutrition workshop in the West Rand. She did much and said little.

This is the woman who laid the foundation for YWCA work among the women and girls of the black community in South Africa. This is the woman who set the pace and model for YWCA work in the Transvaal as first General Secretary of the Transvaal

Young Women's Christian Association in 1953, an office she relinquished at the end of March 1964 after 11 years of service.

At that point in time my image of the women in the leadership was hazy. Without wishing to discredit some of these fine women, who had great ability and intelligence, I will highlight some of the issues. During my first two months with the Dube Centre, I was in a great deal of uncertainty about whether or not, in the absence of a job description, I was doing what my employers expected. Prior to starting the job, communication with the chairman and members of the committee was supportive and normal. Shortly after I had started work though, the lines of communication became blocked, frozen — just at the time I needed to share my thoughts and feelings. At the end of four to six months, I knew for certain that I was in the wrong job. There was very little said in words, but a great deal was transmitted through negative gestures. Towards the end of that year, my back gave in and I had to have treatment at the physiotherapy department of the General Hospital for several months.

When I discussed the Transvaal job with Phyllis, I explained that my relationship with the management committee at the Centre was not an easy one. From her sick-bed, in her gentle but firm manner, Phyllis reassured me that the problem I had identified was not new to her. To use her words, 'Mkhozi, I know, and I have lived with those problems.' But she went further and explained that this type of relationship problem was peculiar to the Johannesburg club, and that the Transvaal problems were more work-related than anything else. She warned me that relationship problems might arise within the Board, but that destructive sub-groups were not likely to be formed. But she went further, and said if there were any such sub-groups within the Executive Committee, or for that matter within the Board of Management, there were always provisions for dealing with that type of irregularity.

Now that I look back on those occasions, I marvel at the strength, deep insight and determination of thought displayed by Phyllis when she negotiated for what I now see as one of her last duties before her death. Her last words to me were, 'Ellen, do it the only way Ellen can do it. Follow the broad principles, objectives and goals; interpret and approach them in your own way. Not for one moment should you ever want to do some of the things they will say were agreed with me. Remember this is the way with human behaviour. Be Ellen all the time and never Phyllis for one moment.'

This to me was the real core of her counsel. I could not ask for more. I can only attribute this clarity of assessment and judgement to the high degree of regard, commitment and concern she had for her job. Her objectivity stayed with her to her dying hour.

It was with this legacy from a great, simple, clear-minded leader that I ventured into my new job with the hope of support and sharing from and with the committee members and Board. The legacy I internalised. It became part of me, my very second nature. It became a pointer in times of doubt and distress. It became an inspiration in the midst of discouragement and inclination to surrender and resign.

I have still to meet someone who could judge individuals and groups as accurately and objectively as Phyllis. She talked to me at length about the YWCA in the Transvaal and in Johannesburg. For obvious reasons I have refrained from discussing individuals. I can only say she shared her opinions, impressions and assessments about individuals in both the Johannesburg and the Transvaal settings in depth and she did this with the minimum of malice and bitterness. This was Phyllis Noluthando Mzaidume born Maseko. '*Lala ngo Xolo, Uli sebenzele ntombi ya se Afrika: Izwe la ko Kweno.*' ('Rest in peace. You have served your country, daughter of Africa.')

It became clear, on my first day in that office, that Phyllis had been ill for a long, long time. In the light of her continued illness, the disjointed records here and there, along with some lapsed reports in between events, gave testimony to her competence and capability as a person, and as a worker. Mrs N. Mbambo from Brakpan had kept the office going as assistant secretary, working with Miss Thoko Twala as her stand-in. I spent about a month in the office, studying the records and reports, and preparing for my plan of action in field work. This period gave me an opportunity to know and assess the members' active interests, commitment and participation in the general programme of the Association. This paid off, because those members who had the interest of the Association at heart started to look for new premises. From 1954 the Association had shared the offices of the Jan Hofmeyr School of Social Work, at No. 3 Eloff Street, Johannesburg. Some time towards the end of 1962 and during 1963 there were negotiations for new offices which was located at the Congregational Centre, De Korte Street, Braamfontein. This change of location was yet another factor which contributed to the difficulty of discontinued and disorderly records here and there. Some records were traced months after the office was established. Finally, however, the office regained its regular momentum.

The fact that there were established events, such as Board meetings, leadership training and refresher courses, workshops, regional and national conferences, as well as established adult Tri-Ys and Y-Teens groups, made it easier for any worker to put the Association back in motion.

As soon as I took over the office of the Transvaal region as General Secretary, my mind unconsciously dropped the Centre and concentrated on the programme of the branches and clubs of the Transvaal. This region extended as far south as the Vaal complex, with Evaton, Meyerton and Vereeniging having established clubs. It stretched 400 miles north beyond Louis Trichardt, embracing Elim Hospital and district, penetrating into the country with mission stations such as Valdezia and Kurulen; it extended north-east to Tzaneen, Duiwelskloof and Phalaborwa. There were other clubs and branches round Pietersburg and Potgietersrust. Similarly, along the Reef, there were branches and clubs along the East Rand, stretching from Germiston, touching Benoni Springs, Brakpan, Nigel and Heidelberg. It reached the mining communities of Geduld and Turf Mines, Dunnoter and Marievale, and the new township of Natalspruit as well. From these towns the movement spread into country towns like Witbank and Piet Retief in the Transvaal, into Vryheid in Natal, and crossed the boundaries of South Africa into Swaziland. In the West Rand it was established in Krugersdorp, Venterspost and Potchefstroom. In the Pretoria area there were clubs and branches in Lady Selborne and Atteridgeville.

It was within this geographic setting that I took office. The outline of my job description included the management and administrative work of the office of the region; maintaining established committees; establishing new ones according to the needs of the Association and its approval; promoting a healthy image of the Association through the Public Relations Office of the General Secretary; planning for and participating in all meetings of the Association embracing the areas of fund-raising, programme-planning, personnel matters and Executive Committee issues. Last, but by no means least, I was to undertake field work through branches and club visits, and report on these. At the beginning, I was also my own typist and office secretary.

The first time I saw my job description, I was shaken, and told myself inwardly, 'No person can accomplish anything in such a wide area of work description.' Then the thought suddenly struck me: someone had done it! Phyllis had done it. She had set the guidelines for those who were to take over from her, and I was that person. I often wonder to what extent this load of work cost her her life. With this thought in mind I started to put the Association back into motion by organising the appropriate committee meetings and getting to know committee members with their individual and collective thinking. It was at that level that the programme of the Association was reviewed and launched. Plans for field work were discussed, dates were set for staff visits and for the staff and Board members' visits.

The major activities in urban clubs and branches were centred on establishing the clubs in their vicinity, maintaining the clubs, and making sure that they were founded on the principles, policy and purpose of the YWCA. This organisation could be summarised as a fellowship movement of women and girls, with a commitment to a Christian-based 'triangular purpose', involving the development of body, mind and spirit for Christian leadership in our divided communities in South Africa. It was during this period in the life of the black communities in South Africa, when YWCA clubs were in operation, that a foundation of community-minded commitment was laid. Hitherto the women's groups or organisations outside the churches or political settings were focused much more on individual gain than on community development where community people work towards improving their surroundings and neighbourhood.

From the outset, the YWCA programme's emphasis was on the training of women and girls at different levels. A leadership training course was planned for the branches and clubs, to be carried out not later than the first quarter of every year. Each branch or club was allowed a limited number of delegates who either participated in all the courses, or chose special courses. The course was run over a weekend. In addition to a personal growth training course, which involved all delegates present, there were usually specialised courses in such areas as keeping the accounts of the branch, writing minutes of the club, preparing an agenda, and chairing a meeting, to improve the management and administration skills of the committee.

The workshop and refresher courses, on the other hand, were run on inter-club, inter-branch or inter-branch – Club levels. These dealt more with the programme of the Association. These events were held twice a year depending on the demand from members. They developed craft skills within the Association, and social studies related to human rights, the legal status of women, and all other related aspects. In all these events the Association provided experts to promote specific aspects of the Association's programme, from within the Association membership or, where necessary, from outside.

Each year the Transvaal region had an exhibition with a well planned syllabus, which included different home skills in knitting, sewing, baking and canning. Refresher courses were run to improve the skills of members in these areas so that they could produce high quality articles for their homes and the exhibition. Members developed self-confidence and independence by being proficient and capable in specific fields.

Workshops were organised for a major study related to a specific community problem. I recall one such event run by Phyllis in the late 1950s or early 1960s. This focused on the high infant mortality rate in the black community. A two-day workshop was run on planning for motherhood. Here members carried out supervised practical work for the duration of the programme.

The involvement of members at management level in these programmes developed in women and girls a selective and analytical approach. Members were offered an opportunity for informal organised learning. This experience gradually changed the image, outlook, performance and the achievement of many women.

After trying my hand at events within the urban communities, working with groups and individuals who had relatively good access to resources in their neighbourhood, I was encouraged to explore the rural areas. The achievements of the clubs along the Reef convinced me that I was capable of achieving some success even in the rural areas. After making all necessary enquiries about the President and Secretary of the Zoutpansberg area, I wrote to them and we agreed a date for my arrival. They also gave me detailed instructions on how to get to Valdezia. When all the train bookings were confirmed and the train ticket purchased, I packed my weekend bag and my provisions for the journey, making certain that I had enough money on me in case of any emergency. As far as I was concerned, I was fully armed for my trip. I made sure my office requirements were covered — I had my receipt book, petty cash vouchers, record book, and had prepared the Saturday programme. I felt well geared to my work. The exuberance and urgency of a worker in a new job gave me extra drive.

My first shock was the excessive heat and the dry barren, look of the countryside on my arrival at Louis Trichardt station. The people looked tired and listless. I soon spotted the man who had been sent to meet me at the station. We greeted each other and introduced ourselves. He said something which I did not grasp — and made no effort to grasp — because I was so involved with what I saw around me. Although I had not expected to find the same type of person and conditions in Louis Trichardt as those in Soweto or Johannesburg, what I saw there was far below my expectations; I was touched by the apathy and listlessness I observed in the people. I finally settled down, emotionally and physically, and accepted the facts as I saw them. But right through the journey to Valdezia I kept asking myself whether or not what I saw was real.

On my arrival, I met Mrs Bertha Maboko, the President of the area. We were scheduled to leave for Tlangelani, the venue of the event, but first we settled down and had something to drink. The event was not a leadership training course, refresher course, or workshop in particular. It was a mixture of all three, because it was intended as a forum for meeting the membership and establishing their needs.

Like a town woman, I was well dressed, though by my own standards my outfit was fairly simple. Early in the day I felt comfortable and perfectly at ease. But from 8.30 to 9.00 when the crowds started to arrive, I noticed that most of the women who attended seemed unmistakeably shaken, emotionally or physically, or both. At first I thought that there was a communication barrier because I could not speak Tsonga. But in our midst there were nurses and teachers who acted as interpreters in our discussions. I felt there was more than a language or communication problem. As I moved among the members, talking to groups, I could sense discomfort and tension. Much as I tried to ignore this feeling, it built up. I managed tactfully to communicate my concern about the general atmosphere to Mrs Maboko, and asked her if she thought I was causing the members embarrassment in any way. She reassured me that there was nothing of the sort; but she did let me know that some of the members had walked as much as four to eight miles on an empty stomach as the drought in the region had been so severe that many families had gone for days without food. In fact, she continued, some of the members had walked this long way to get something to eat, more than anything else. You can imagine my shock at that.

The problem which I had sensed, but could not identify, was explained. I stood there dumbfounded and ashamed of the very clothes I wore. I realised though that if I changed my attire I might be misunderstood and even aggravate what was already a bad situation. I consulted the President, and we both agreed that the discussion was serving no good purpose if the members were so hungry and wasted. The whole focus was shifted to preparing the meal within the shortest possible time. What meal was being prepared? There was a huge three-legged pot in which mealie-meal porridge was being cooked and another huge pot where bones, sinews and joints of meat was being cooked to go with the porridge. The President confided that the branch could not afford good meat and, in any case, there were so many members that the better type of meat would not suffice. At that point the gravity of the problem of the Zoutpansberg residents hit me between the eyes. I was speechless. I could not account for my own feelings of guilt about this situation, much as I told myself I was not to be blamed for it.

We in the leadership hurriedly prepared the meal, helped by those members who had some energy. It was just fortunate that the bones and sinews had been simmering for hours. The food was soon ready and members were supplied with plates from the Mission Youth Centre at Valdezia, operating under the auspices of the Swiss Mission Church. It was moving to watch those women line up impatiently to receive a share of the meal. When my turn came towards the end, I received my share and joined a group at the table. The meal as such was far from tasty, but that experience of sharing with the Zoutpansberg members in their plight was both rewarding and fulfilling. I think it was for that reason that I enjoyed that meal. After consultation and lengthy exploration of the situation, we identified some facts which could be to the advantage of the members. These included:

That many members had skills which, if properly channelled, could alleviate the present conditions of the individual and her family.

That although there were no funds to buy materials to make articles, there were seeds of wild fruit in the veld which could be used as beads to make ornaments. The members mentioned that fact with confidence.

That the members of the YWCA in urban areas could be helpful by selling these ornaments, or buying them themselves, to enable the Zoutpansberg members to earn some income, no matter how little. I committed Board Members without their approval.

That we should buy seeds at a reasonable price and distribute them to members in order to launch a vegetable garden project, no matter how small-scale. (The question of the drought and absence of water was real, but it was shelved.)

That we should embark on a campaign of promoting the bulk-buying of powdered full-cream milk in order to combat the frightening spread of kwashiorkor, a malnutrition disease among children. The drought and intensive heat also increased the incidence of gastro-enteritis among children.

All these ideas came out of the brain-storming session which was conducted after lunch. My observation during that session was that the members appeared more lively and confident in facing the future. I credited this liveliness and confidence to two thing. First, to the meal, which was by no means nourishing; and, second to the possibility of implementing the ideas which came out of the brain-storming session. Both these factors, I felt, and still believe to this day, contributed to the sudden change of mood among the members. Perhaps I should also not rule out the possibility that my observations were more in my mind than real. Did I observe what I wished and hoped to see? Whatever the true facts, I went back to Johannesburg with these data for the Executive Committee of the Board of Management of the Transvaal region. With them I hoped to develop a meaningful programme with the sole purpose of improving the quality of life for the residents of the Zoutpansberg community. My hope was to use the YWCA members in that community to implement these ideas. I arrived in Johannesburg inspired and hopeful for a future with possibilities and progress.

The Executive Committee and the Board of Management of the Transvaal region were predominantly made up of black women. These were my employers. This was an experience for me which held several frustrations as well as some expectations and hopes, later followed by numerous exciting accomplishments and achieve-ments. I found the members of the Transvaal region and Executive Committee at Board level very supportive, as well as determined to learn in this new situation of being an employer. That feeling permeated the whole Association. It reinforced me, encouraged me, and through it I improved in my performance by the day. I was determined, through the acceptance and support of these black women, to do my very best as their employee, despite my appallingly low salary. I held a deep and sacred feeling within me: that Phyllis had proved that a black woman can successfully serve other black women, even as their employee. The only way I could confirm this and prove Phyllis correct was by doing the same.

On my return from my first trip to the Zoutpansberg area in the North — and from all other subsequent trips to Tzaneen, Phalaborwa, Duiwelskloof, Itsoseng, Klerksdorp — I brought a full report to the Executive Committee and the Board. After careful study of the report about my Zoutpansberg visit, the Board embarked on a major event, preceded by a workshop.

After registration of delegates and identification of their interests, members were split into groups and the weekend workshop went into operation. The Board members had brought a variety of provisions, sufficient to cater for the whole weekend and more. The Association centred its attention on nutrition. Full-cream powdered milk and *Pronutro* (a high-calorie/protein food supplement) were highly recommended as the best foods on the priority-list of each family. Milk powders from different manufacturers were listed, with their prices for comparison. The distance of the source of supply was considered in terms of transport or postage costs. In addition to this, there was discussion about vegetable gardens. Spinach and tomatoes were recommended as the first vegetables to be grown. The Association was assigned to provide seeds to be distributed to members who showed initiative by coming to ask for them. The Board also offered to work on the question of fund-raising, to buy beads to supply to the members with skill in bead-work on condition that a small percentage would be deducted from the sale of the products and kept by the Zoutpansberg area management committee, to buy beads from time to time, when need arose. (The paradox of buying seeds during a drought seemed to make mockery of the vegetable gardens, though.)

This workshop was followed within nine months by a Board members' visit to Zoutpansberg. A bus-load from Johannesburg brought Board members from all over the Southern Transvaal — from Johannesburg and Klerksdorp, Lichtenburg, Vereeniging, East and West Rand, Pretoria — the occasion was an exhibition to display the handicraft skills of the members and to motivate the women to exploit that potential. Board members brought their own pocket money to buy from the local members. They brought a donation of beads from the Board as well. It was indeed very rewarding to catch the smiles on the faces of the women when they sold their products to the Board members.

That evening, the jubilation at a concert registered the achievement of the Association in that area. We shared our meals, our accommodation, our bathrooms — a long-established tradition of the YWCA which has done much to promote and maintain the spirit of genuine fellowship among the members. Even at that stage, it was altogether impossible to define the measure of success in any form, except playing it by ear and feeling.

About six months after this memorable Board visit, I went again on my rounds to the Northern Transvaal. I was able to do this as we had had a windfall from one church in Switzerland through a chance contact at a meeting in the city. This contact brought us the first car for the YWCA regional office in the Transvaal. This is how I managed to cover the long distances.

It was on this visit that I was confronted by a member of the Valdezia branch, Mrs Ann Magadzi, who declared that she was interested in going to Rorkes Drift to learn weaving. To me this idea sounded far-fetched. At first I dismissed what she said, and gave no second thought to it. It was when she confronted me on my second visit about the same topic that I realised Ann was serious about going to Rorkes Drift. In fact she had also done her homework, as far as she could. According to her, she had seen the church authorities and discussed the possibility of sponsorship, and she would start at the school inside two months if she was accepted. I tried in vain to make her aware of the possible snags I envisaged along the way. These did not deter her plans. My last question to her was what she intended to do when she completed her training. Boldly, she replied, 'I intend to come back to teach my people to do weaving.' It was at that point that I felt Ann was going in for a disaster. I pointed out to her that on her return she would be frustrated as she would have no equipment or raw materials to start the project. Her reply was, 'I will see about that when I return, at the end of six months.' We parted on that note, and I wished her well on her new venture. All efforts to stop Ann from going to Rorkes Drift had failed. She was determined. Nothing, just nothing, would stop her.

On her return she wrote to tell me she was back and she invited me to Valdezia. I gave her time to settle down and meanwhile visited the Pietersburg area and other places at Ga Mphahlele and the Botlokoa clubs. On my arrival at Valdezia I was pleasantly surprised to find that Ann had started what she termed a weaving home industry. Everything done in that small rondavel appeared very primitive and unproductive; but one thing was certain — everywhere I turned there was organised activity. The material and equipment were all very primitive, slow and unappealing in my judgement; but Ann's initiative and creativity were both unsurpassed. I watched in silence for about fifteen to thirty minutes; then chatted to Ann about other matters, not related to the programme she was engaged in, but related to the overall work of the YWCA.

Amazingly enough, my indifference did not seem to dampen her enthusiasm in any way, or so I thought. She took up a specimen of some square rugs made of raw sheep wool. She displayed these rugs and spoke to me about them with feeling and appreciation and about the achievement of the trainees. Out of concern for Ann I showed some interest, but deep down I felt that she was just wasting her time.

Ann worked with three trainees, girls between seventeen and twenty years of age. From their appearance they were typical country girls, without — or with very little — school education. They were working in a rondavel with barred windows, against burglars. The windows were more or less on a level with the height of these girls when standing. Each girl was using the bars on the window nearest to her. They had wool round their waists and the two ends of the wool were fastened to the bars. Each girl had a comb made from river reeds, with evenly spread and smooth teeth. According to Ann, she had spent much time teaching and helping the girls to produce the best combs possible. This was all the equipment Ann had.

Ann's interest and her active participation with individual trainees, her firmness with them, and her demand for standard quality in their production began to influence my attitude to her project. By the time I left for Johannesburg, after being with Ann for one-and-a-half days, I was convinced by her application to her work that she had a plan with objectives and purpose and that, although this plan was not entirely clear to me, Ann was very clear about where she was going.

About six months after her return from Rorkes Drift, we finally sat down to evaluate the project. Although the results appeared primitive, they were there and they were real; and with them was Ann's determination to achieve the task she had set herself. I asked her if she thought there was any way in which I could contribute to the project. 'Ellen,' she responded, 'this rondavel is not YWCA property, it is a Youth Centre of the locai church. From time to time when they have events in here, we have to give way and thus disrupt the continuity of our programme; perhaps you know someone in Johannesburg who would be willing to help us build a small workshop here in Valdezia, where these girls and "Y" members would work from.' I promised to do what I could to help.

Within two weeks of my return, I embarked on an investigation of possible resources to meet Ann's request, and was referred to an organisation called SAVS, South African Voluntary Service. It took some time for the President to accept the home industry programme at Valdezia as an educational programme, but once that was achieved, this organisation undertook to build a home industry cottage at Valdezia on condition that the residents of the community participated in the actual building, with the members of SAVS from the University of the Witwatersrand. This to me was a dream come true. SAVS went to Valdezia, over 400 miles away, and built the cottage, working with YWCA members. In 1976 when I left the employ of YWCA, that home industry cottage was the pulse of women's involvement in the Pietersburg area. They had acquired new equipment in the form of weaving machines. The women had started to produce beautiful woven covers for couches and cushions, using wool with beautifully blended colours, and were also knitting school jerseys and sewing uniforms for church women's prayer meetings. In the course of time, I could not resist the temptation of buying some of their well finished products. To this day I value the purchases I made from that Centre very dearly. They are as beautiful as they are serviceable, and they hold very dear memories for me which will remain with me for a long time to come. This contribution was the result of that imaginative, creative and daring woman, Ann Magadzi who, through her dedicated leadership, guidance and selflessness, equipped some simple country girls and women to be creative and self-reliant.

Unhappily, the venture survived only nine years. When I met Ann again in 1981, and asked her to tell me about the project we all so valued and loved, her face became clouded with hurt, anger, and perhaps shame too, as well as complete helplessness. 'Is there anything wrong, Ann?' I asked. She gave me an abrupt reply, 'It is a long painful experience I never want to relate, Ellen.' 'Has it terminated? What happened, Ann?' I pursued. She continued, 'I can't do anything, anything, Ellen, to bring back that project to life. My only consolation is that twenty-one women and girls who received training from the "Home Industry Cottage" are now operating as individuals, each one of them doing their own thing and making a living out of that for their families.' As she made this last statement, I read from her face a ray of hope, some redeeming factor was relayed across. 'That is very gratifying, Ann,' I replied. 'It is a tremendous achievement, by both you and the trainees as well as the Management Committee. We cannot ask for more.' On that note the discussion was closed.

Yes, during my time with the YWCA, I worked with many women of integrity and with a high sense of duty in whatever they did. Most of these women will never be heard of or seen on any record. But their achievements in the field of literacy programmes and other initiatives should be more widely known.

In another project, some members who lived in the Zoutpansberg area (known as Gazankulu today) clubbed together on a campaign against gastro-enteritis which had taken on epidemic proportions during the late 1960s in that community. Through YWCA programmes, and the concerted efforts of the doctors from Elim Hospital, local nurses (themselves YWCA members), the local agricultural demonstrators, the Swiss Mission Church and, in particular, through the efforts of Mrs Catherine Schneider, the wife of Rev. Theo Schneider of the Christian Institute of Southern Africa, the disease was fought at all levels and on all fronts.

The first front was the correct preparation of food for the infants. Mrs Schneider prepared a detailed account of how to keep the babies' bottles clean, and how to prepare the feeds. She did this step by step for each group and even for individual families when the need arose.

The agricultural demonstrators gave their know-how on how to construct a 'pit-hole' latrine of a standard size for a homestead. The doctors emphasised the need to dispose of all types of refuse. They drove home the danger of exposed faeces around homes and public places.

The social worker motivated the YWCA members to embark on the role they saw themselves playing in the whole plan, and how they would put that role into action. In this setting I was staff as well as a catalyst using my social work training. We formed a formidable team and we received in return formidably rewarding results from these biannual events.

The husbands of about three-quarters of the women in this community were migrant labourers in cities like Pretoria and Johannesburg. Some sent money home at regular intervals, but others were very irregular, while the rest had long stopped sending anything at all. Those husbands who came home when on leave wanted to rest and relax in that time as they had been under continual pressure working in the city, and so failed to contribute to any meaningful improvements in and around the home; others spent a portion of their leave at home and the rest in the city. The rest did not bother to come home for one day. They had established new homes in the cities and often had new wives and children.

After analysing their problem, these women came to one conclusion: that they had to plan their lives on the assumption that their husbands would be away from home for the better part of forty-five weeks a year. Their solution was to plan whatever project they embarked on on the basis of the work-party system, a practice I have already described, and prevalent in all rural black communities.

Organised like this, these women took the unanimous decision to launch their own campaign against the epidemic of gastro-enteritis which claimed the lives of many children in their community. They agreed to start with the disposal of refuse of any type, concentrating in particular on any filth which accelerated the breeding of flies, which were singled out by the doctors as public enemy number one. They agreed that each woman would provide the materials needed for building a pit-hole latrine — cement, bricks, a door, corrugated iron, a seat and all the small items, like screws, nails and door hinges. In addition, the women should provide themselves with the best disinfectants to keep the latrine fresh. The importance of keeping contact with the agricultural demonstrator at all levels was emphasised at that stage.

The women then formed groups in the different villages to dig holes, with the agricultural demonstrator present to give advice on the measurements and other technical details, to make certain that each latrine in every home fulfilled the health requirements.

Within six months of implementing this project, I went on one of my scheduled visits there. It was some time in March. There had been heavy rains and as a result the countryside was beautifully carpeted with green grass, with the many trees in full leaf. Thatched huts could be seen, some on the hilltops, others in the valleys, the rest clustered together on the veld — with white-washed latrines in the background giving a very pleasant finish to the setting of these communities, scattered across the countryside as far as the eye could see. These marvellous women had also moved into the community schools to dig holes and erect latrines for the school children.

In one day I covered between 120 and 150 miles, travelling all over the Zoutpansberg area to make sure that I could give first-hand confirmation of the existence of latrines in the rural areas. They were there all right, and I was able to go back to the Board Meeting of the Transvaal region within a month to give a very stimulating report about the advancement of living conditions in the rural areas. I could hardly believe what I saw. I entered several latrines to make sure that they were in use. Each one of them was well finished with a firm seat. There was a solution of Jeyes fluid in each latrine to render the air fresh. Except for only one, they all withstood the heavy rainstorms of the late 1960s and the early 1970s.

With these two programmes — correct feeding of infants and disposal of refuse — accomplished, there was a sudden decline in the high rate of gastro-enteritis among the children. With that too came the general restoration of good health. It was rewarding to see the healthy, bouncing toddlers at the YWCA events accompanying their mothers. They had beautiful, smooth shiny black skins and bright eyes. Kwashiorkor had miraculously disappeared, and the mothers' slogan was: 'A "Y" home must have a latrine.'

In recent years, too, through other social agencies, women are being trained to carry out health programmes, such as general health, care of the eyes and disposal of refuse. All these are carried out in the villages by rural women. These women form a large band of unsung heroines in the black community in South Africa. They labour day after day, not seeking publicity or recognition. Their reward is embodied in the joy and satisfaction their neighbours receive from their untiring service and contribution.

The YWCA carries out similar programmes and projects in eight other regional associations in South Africa. Each region determines the needs of its residents and forms plans to meet such needs, doing their best amidst constraints and limitations. Some of the members are humble and unassuming. Yet, as forceful and long-suffering women of this community, they have rendered a tremendous contribution towards the alleviation of suffering and dire need within their communities. We shall contine to salute them for their commendable, selfless service.

In this attempt to develop leadership potential within its ranks, the YWCA promotes overseas travels for its members and staff. By doing this, they are acquainted with the involvement of their peers in other countries near and far, and are involved in the programme of the Association at inter-association and international levels.

My own involvement for the last three years in the 'Y' has been as a National Finance Chairman/Honorary Treasurer, an office which has kept me in close contact with the Association. In this role I have had an opportunity to come into close contact with individuals and groups of the Association, many as volunteers and a few as staff, to assess their involvement and commitment and to hail them boldly as heroines of distress.

When I was elected President of the first Black Consumer Union in South Africa on 17 March 1984, I felt confident that my practical involvement and participation in many community programmes in Soweto and elsewhere had fully prepared me to accept this office, with all its responsibilities and demands.

It is in the new Black Consumer Union that I serve, with Joyce Thembi Seroke as Vice President. In addition she carries a load of work and responsibility as the National General Secretary of the World Affiliated Young Women's Christian Association in South Africa. The team of stalwarts in the Executive Committee of the 'Y' who give voluntary service include, among others, Virginia Gcabashe, Natal President of this organisation who also serves in the Executive Committee of the South African Council of Churches. They are an example of many other women with deep commitment in the service of their community in this Association and in many other women's organisations in the black community.

13
I See My Sons Grow Up

My rapid professional achievements, first in teaching then in adjusting from teaching to social work and finding employment; the extension of my circles of friends and complete acceptance by them despite the stigma of divorce I brought with me from Rustenburg; the recognition I received socially; my part in the film *Cry the Beloved Country*; and my new status as Mrs Kuzwayo and finding a new home; all these built me psychologically, emotionally and physically, but they could not wipe out my lasting, dear memories and longing for the loving sons I had left behind in Rustenburg: Matshwene (Everington) and Bakone (Justice) Moloto.

I can never thank my late husband, G. R., enough for his understanding and acceptance of me with all the problems I brought from my previous marriage. The support he gave me during those turbulent years in my life, from 1951 to about 1964, could only have been given by a mature, seasoned, loving and understanding husband. He died in 1965, and I remember him only with respect and gratitude. I recall with deep appreciation the regular festive season trips I made to Rustenburg every year to see my sons, on which he accompanied me whenever it was convenient for him to do so. If it was not possible, he happily bade me goodbye and wished me well on my journey. These visits made it possible for me to keep some contact with my children, feeble as such contact seemed. It was hard too to endure the humiliation and insults from my ex-husband which accompanied these visits.

One blessing which came my way was the birth of my youngest son, Godfrey Ndabezitha. It is true that he could not, and did not, replace the two older children; yet, on the other hand, his presence was a great comfort, joy and healer in many ways. He gave me an opportunity to express my motherhood, deep-seated emotions of love and care, and the sheer satisfaction of living with and for one's offspring.

The forced separation from my two elder sons has not left me without scars. It was a traumatic experience with a disquieting influence on my outlook as regards accepting and trusting other people. Now that I look back on this whole experience, I begin to see why I take so long to trust and believe in other people. I pray and hope this will have no ill-effects on me in later life. As a result of my earlier experience, I unconsciously protected my youngest son with excessive care.

It is going to take a long period of time to eradicate those harrowing traumatic events I went through in Rustenburg. The fact that they did not leave me with a warped mind and unending bitterness is in itself a great blessing. The writing of this book has offered me an opportunity to relive these past experiences with a certain amount of objectivity and maturity, as I struggle to understand analytically why what happened, happened. Talking about such experiences in a way I have never done before will hopefully air them and expel them from my whole system.

My early community involvement on my arrival in Johannesburg from Rustenberg was more of an escape mechanism from continued pondering and pining over my children than anything else. In addition to that, I was determined to prove to myself and to those around me my real worth. It was when I was going through the traumatic experience of a disintegrating home and the unsettling divorce proceedings, that several doubts started to cross my mind about myself: my integrity, my self-image, my worth. 'Am I really the person I think I am?' I asked myself secretly. Most of my efforts and achievements thereafter were embarked on as a real test of who I was in reality, and to what extent I did or did not contribute to the failure of my marriage.

It was during the time when I settled down in my practice as a social worker that I became continuously haunted by the thought of the sons I had left behind. It soon became very clear in my mind that I was not prompted by sheer enthusiasm to do all the things I did, but that, in fact, I was all the time trying to run away from my past. Most of the tasks I undertook, I threw myself into wholeheartedly. I believe it was really to justify both my innocence and capabilities, that is if I was at all innocent.

From March 1947 to 1956 I find that the range of my involvement demands that I pause and ask, why? In the first week, for example, I obtained a job as a school teacher. Within the first three months I had obtained a part-time job with the Non-European Affairs

Department. During the first twelve months of my arrival in Johannesburg I had found the leaders of the African National Congress, and joined the ranks as a Youth League member and become its Secretary. Amidst all these activities, round about 1950, I had received a part as an actor in *Cry The Beloved Country*. In the same year, I met a man, the first and only man I admired on my arrival in Johannesburg, who became my husband and father of my third son. He died after only fifteen years of married life — another experience that left me shocked, bewildered and terribly shaken.

The other effort which I treasure as a major breakthrough was enrolling with the Jan Hofmeyr School of Social Work and obtaining a Diploma in 1955.

Yet all these achievements did not wipe out the longing for my sons. Round about 1956, my thoughts drifted back to the boys with particular intensity. I controlled this longing only by yearly visits against terrible odds and humiliation. Strange that these hardships did not deter me from the thought of planning one visit after another to see them.

One day I was speaking about my sons, who were then in Rustenburg, to an elderly lady who was assisting in the home and looking after my youngest son. She told me not to fret about the situation, and reassured me that my sons would come to me some day. Her prediction came true in 1958, when I saw my eldest son, Matshwene Everington Moloto, who was then about 15 years of age, walk into my home. For a split-second, I could not accept this as true. It was much more like a dream. However, as seconds and minutes passed, I realised that his presence was a reality. I can never ever successfully share with readers of this book the overwhelming hold that experience had over me. I was puzzled by the bravery of this young person, his very determination in this complex city of Johannesburg. I was shaken inside me by mixed feelings of joy, hurt, anger and shock. At that time I had not realised the emotional, psychological and physical injuries my son had received during the time I had been away from him. My only consolation over the years has been that he found me alive and in sound health. I shudder to think what could have happened if the worst had befallen me. To this day I am most grateful that my life was spared, despite some very threatening experiences.

The struggle to have him 'influxed' into Johannesburg was another nightmare. I moved heaven and hell. One factor was a real blessing in disguise. As I have already mentioned, it is a custom for all first-born children of a marriage to be born at their mother's parents' home. This was the case with my first son. My father's home was in Pimville which was in the Johannesburg magistrates' area and so my son had a right to live in Johannesburg. I clung to that one loophole and my eldest son was finally influxed. But his brother, born in Rustenburg, missed that privilege which to a white child is a right, according to South African standards and legislation, even in a case where parents of such children are new arrivals from overseas.

My eldest son lived with us from the time he arrived in Johannesburg. I was naturally anxious about how my husband was going to accept the boy and relate to him as a step-father. My only comfort was that I had done my homework. From the time my husband had suggested marriage, I had told him in no uncertain terms that my topmost priority at the time was to make sure that my children were happy wherever they were. At that point I saw getting married to anyone, no matter how good his intentions, as an encroachment into my family life and its well-being.

It was when he realised that I was very firm and adamant about my stand with regard to my sons, that G. R. reiterated that these boys would be part and parcel of our home, our comfort, our love. In short, that they would be the children of that family. He lived up to ninety per cent of his promise, bless his heart.

Within a very short period of his arrival, it became very clear that my son had suffered many bruises, both physical and emotional. The scars were obvious. This set my mind in motion about his brother. I became very concerned about him and this intensified my longing and anxiety for him. His names, Justice Bakone, rang in my mind all the time. I felt that he was left alone, torn by the sudden separation from his brother and the violent departure of his mother. These feelings gnawed deeply into my whole being. My youngest son, from my second marriage, Godfrey Ndabezitha Kuzwayo, born at the beginning of 1951, was aware that he had brothers in Rustenburg and, as I had taken him along several times at Christmas-time when I visited them, he often asked about them. Although this was done in a very child-like manner, somehow it brought some relief when he enquired after their well-being: '*Bo aubuti ba tla leng mo gae? Nna kea ba rata*' ('When will my elder brothers come home? I love them'). It is amazing how those simple remarks from a boy four or five years old built me up and gave me hope and courage for things to come.

When I received my first offer to go overseas in 1961, Bakone was at Tigerkloof Institution in Form III; I visited him there to bid him goodbye. He matriculated there and registered at Fort Hare University in 1965, before being expelled for political activity in 1966. He took a teaching post at Matseke High School in Soweto and later in Mafeking. He returned to Fort Hare in 1968 and was again expelled and refused entry to any other university. After the black leaders' consultation with the authorities, he registered with UNISA, the University of South Africa, which offers correspondence courses without residential facilities. By this time he had been living with us in Soweto since December 1964, and it had become very clear to me then that he was dedicated to the cause of liberation of the black man in South Africa.

The dismissal of students from the black universities has become habitual with the various departments controlling African education over the years; in fact it has become a way of life. I often wonder to what extent this has become a very good excuse and cover for the authorities systematically and 'legitimately' to deter the educational progress of the black child. It is too frequent to be accepted as impartial — or reasonable. Parents' representations to some of these universities have not brought any noteworthy results. These unfortunate unrests at universities, sometimes even at high school level, have strong political undertones. In a recent incident in 1983 here at Ibhongo High School in Dlamini, Soweto, pupils requested the removal of a white headmaster. On other, earlier occasions these pupils strongly objected to white teachers carrying firearms into the classroom. There is hardly a family with children of school-age which has not been subjected to some victimisation at some time or another. My son suffered with many others at university. Sufferings and intimidations in these institutions, resulting in mass expulsions of students, are the order of the day even now in the 1980s. Six high schools in Saulsville and Atteridgeville in the Pretoria districts were closed in 1984, because students opposed the system whereby an age-limit is imposed on entry into certain classes — a system particularly unjust to black students who may not be able to *start* school until they are in their teens, for instance, because they have been working to put another sister or brother through school first. One student has died, many have been injured during the schools' unrest.

All efforts to register Bakone (Justice) as a 'legitimate' resident in Soweto failed. After doing intensive soul-searching, I happily told myself that Bakone was my son; he had been forcibly separated from me at the age of two, and now at the age of twenty he was denied the right to live with me in Johannesburg because of the artificial and unjust laws of influx control, laws which made the blacks of South Africa foreigners in their country of birth. The instinct of motherhood had the better side of me and, without looking for any reason or excuse, I happily settled down, permission or no permission, with him and the rest of my family in the normal way families do all over the world, including the white community of South Africa, even the foreigners from Europe.

My husband was supportive all the way. He accepted both my sons from my first marriage. His daughter, who was the oldest of the children, was the only girl in the family. There were no marked relationship problems amongst them, except for the common daily children's tiffs experienced in every home. By and large, we were a happy family with a minimum of differences and petty quarrels. In the course of time the boys looked up to my husband as a father, and his daughter looked up to me as a mother. I could not ask for a smoother transition in setting up a family.

Who knows to what extent this refusal of permission to live with his mother pushed Justice towards his involvement in the black political movements? It was at this time that black consciousness fever was mounting, with Steve Biko, Barney Pityana and others concentrating on the South African Students Organisation (SASO) whilst Justice was assigned to head the University Christian Movement (UCM), a multi-racial student organisation. He himself was also a member of SASO. This goes to confirm the truth that has been reiterated again: that black consciousness did not necessarily promote racial hatred. Steve Biko, one of the champions of that cause, reiterated time and again the importance of *healthy* race relations in South Africa. He rejected and detested racism.

Among some of Justice's commitments with UCM was the task of working with university students of all communities and language groups to promote literacy among the black people, a project highlighted as first priority in South Africa by blacks. That need is still a reality to this day. His duty was to mobilise university students to give a small portion of their holiday time to implement that programme. He was deeply involved in this from 1969 to 1971, travelling the length and breadth of South Africa, east, west, north, south. He gave his mind, body, soul and emotions to this programme. He slept and dreamt literacy twenty-four hours a day. I was always concerned about his safety, until he knocked at the door, home from these travels.

As a mother, my sixth sense told me that he was treading a sensitive and rather dangerous road with the government, much as he was involved in a very noble and very fulfilling programme for both instructor and participant. One day, as we sat chatting about our respective work, I shared my fears and feelings with him, and suggested that he relinquish this job. He calmly analysed his job in comparison to mine, and requested me earnestly to show the difference between the two. In all sincerity, the UCM and YWCA programmes were so similar in objectives and content that I accepted his comparison. He finally said, 'If anyone should decide to arrest me for the literacy programme, you should know you are the next in line for your YWCA work.' On that note we closed our discussion.

He continued with his organisational work in as many universities as he could cover in South Africa within the given time and other constraints. We all accepted as routine his work situation. His employers arranged for him to register at Albert Street, where all blacks go for employment registration when they start in a new job — I would go further, and add that this is a calculated process by which influx control regulations are implemented and administered. He went there one day in September 1971. My anxiety and secret prayers were all centred on his registration — that he should be successful. I cherished hope against hope. However, with the load of work on my desk, my concern about my son's registration drifted out of my mind. In a strange way I forgot all about it.

With my attention focused on my office work, I was disturbed by a knock on the door. As I said, 'Come in,' in walked Bakone's personal friend and colleague, Basil Moore. I could see at first glance that something unusual had happened. His lips were parched, he wore a crest-fallen face. I fired two or three questions at him: 'Basil, are you ill? Is there anything amiss?' The painful reply was made with a dry hoarse voice. He spoke in an unnatural way: 'They have taken him. They have taken him.' This reply did not mean much to me. I looked at him with genuine puzzlement on my face. 'Basil, what do you mean? Who has taken who?' 'The police have taken Justice,' he replied. His reply still did not register on my mind at first. I heard the words, but they did not mean anything. When he repeated his message, the words he had first said made sense. 'Where have they taken him?' I asked. 'I don't know.'

For some seconds — perhaps minutes — we stood perplexed, gazing into space, speechless. Breaking the spell, I said, 'I understand, Basil. If you hear anything, ring me. If I should hear something, I will come back to you.' We parted.

The office suddenly became small and empty. I felt crowded and short of breath. My mind was in turmoil. I sat at my desk, gazing at nothing, thinking nothing; my world as it were had come to a standstill. I tried to search for an answer for many questions to solve one problem. 'Where have they taken him? Will he contact me? Will they allow him to contact me?' Suddenly a thought crossed my mind and stuck; Bakone is mature and intelligent and, all things being equal, he will come back to me, no matter where he is. He will either phone or write. I clung to that.

I could not apply my mind to my work though. I became more and more restless and agitated. I moved between my chair and the window overlooking the street. There were moments when I peeped through the window with the hope of seeing someone I knew to talk to or, by some miracle, to see Bakone himself. More often than not, I ended up staring into space with my mind blank, not registering anything.

It was during one such moment, when my mind was blank, that I heard a knock on the door. I don't remember saying, come in; all I know is that I turned, stopped and stared. As if in a dream, my son, my dear son Bakone, walked in accompanied by a young white man whom I soon got to know was a plain-clothes policeman. Within the space of a few hours, he appeared taller and thinner, his lips dry, as if he had not eaten for days on end. I was lost for a moment about what to do or say; then suddenly we were in each other's arms. I led him to the office couch where we both sat down. I took him and placed him on my lap, tall as he was, with his legs dangling on the floor. The instinct of motherhood took complete control of me. I kissed him.

As I started to speak to him I noticed the white 'gentleman' becoming furtively restless. We painfully ignored him and this seemed to disturb him as he started to pace up and down the office. Bakone informed me that when the police told him he was going to be banned to Mafikeng — a small town near the Botswana border, some 200 miles from Johannesburg — he emphatically told them he would not be taken without seeing me. He insisted and that was how he got to my office. My assessment of him was often correct.

The impatience, anxiety and anger on the policeman's face was pressure enough to push me into putting as much as possible into the limited time I had at my disposal to talk to my son — the time, I felt, Bakone had forced out of the policeman because he is who he is. The resentment on the policeman's face was unconcealed and it mounted as more time passed.

I embraced and kissed him, to reassure him of my love, but without allowing this to trouble further his disturbed emotions. Gripped with tension, hurt, anger and downright disgust at the cold-hearted treatment of the black people by the government of South Africa, and handling a situation which affected me directly as it involved my son, I looked into his distraught face and gave him his farewell verbal provision, unplanned and unrehearsed:

'Life has never been a bed of roses for black people in South Africa. If you had done anything subversive, the law would have been even with you. You have been involved in a very noble engagement, where you have gone out of your way to plan a very worthy programme in the form of literacy classes for the under-privileged section of this country. You are now taken to task by the powers that be and you can easily be locked up for an effort which could have earned you recognition, honour and special respect in a normal, sane-minded country. Here for this noble gesture, you are facing prosecution. This says to me, in this country if you are black, and you embark on a most respectable worthwhile project for your community, you become a threat to the rulers of this country. Remember nobody ever kicks a dead dog. This action by the state should never ever dampen your spirit. On the contrary, let it inspire you, reinforce you with new zeal to do better, when you get your next chance. Wherever they take you, be calm, never forget the values, standards and all that our family has stood for in the past and will stand for in the future.'

I then kissed my son again and, holding his hand, escorted him out of the building as far as I could. I then bade him farewell and rushed back to stand at the window to watch the direction the car he was travelling in was taking.

Long after the car had vanished from sight, I remained as if stuck to the window, my eyes fixed on something I could not see or point out to anyone. Then I realised that I was staring at nothing, that the numerous cars which congested the streets had not registered on my mind for the greater part of the time I stood there. As I started to become aware of my surroundings, I was seized by feelings of bitter anger, hate and disgust with the rulers of South Africa. And at that moment a thought crossed my mind, as if in a whisper from a friendly neighbour, 'Ellen, remember South Africa is your country of birth still. You have no business to give in to any form of intimidation or brain-washing by any human being.' With this thought, I felt a curtain which had obscured my thinking torn into two. I placed all the happenings of that late afternoon to the back of my mind, put my office in order for the next day, locked up, and went home.

As I reflected on the unexpected drama of that afternoon, I emerged with a spirit of triumph. I went home with a fresh determination to be committed to the struggle of the black man for as long as I live. This spirit of victory and achievement came from the courage my son portrayed during our last sharing before he was taken away by the police. We had communicated mutual support, mutual understanding and acceptance, mutual suffering and commitment for the cause of the black man in South Africa. Much as we accepted all our shortcomings and limitations as individuals, we still believed that a contribution by every member of the black community, no matter how humble or small, can add to the efforts and contributions of many others. The results would be measured at the end. To give up and fold our hands is to accept death before it takes over; defeat before the enemy proves his worth.

On my arrival home, I started to plan my practical support for my son. From the short, emotionally charged moments we had in my office that afternoon, I knew that my son was banned to Mafikeng for three years. He had also given me a telephone contact there. We had also mentioned the possibility of phoning his father, who was then the education planner of Bophuthatswana and coincidentally was living in Mafikeng.

At that time in my life, conditions and the trend of developments dictated the direction I was to follow. My son was banned to Mafikeng. I had never been there, even for a flying visit. I hardly knew any person I could request to keep an eye on him to give him moral support. The one and only person I could fall back on to do that was his father. I was compelled to clear my mind of all the 'cobwebs' which had developed when our marriage broke up, and to put aside some of the resolutions I had privately made at the time of the break-up. I swallowed all my pride and acted in the interests of my son to make sure that someone who cared would stand by him in my absence. After several efforts, I got his father on the phone and informed him about Bakone's plight, and requested him to do what he could to help. I asked him to tell Bakone I would be coming soon to see him. I deeply appreciated his cooperation and willingness to help at that time.

There I was then in September 1971, a working mother with a son banned to Mafikeng. I had no car. Thank goodness for the friends I had. Jane Phakathi offered the use of a car for the day. 'Ellen,' she said, 'here is the car. I will drive you to Mafikeng. Yours is to put in petrol.' I stood there, speechless at this generous, selfless offer. 'Jane,' I said, 'I will never be able to thank you enough.'

Word had already reached me that my son had been dumped in an empty house somewhere in Mafikeng, so I next turned my mind in search of what essentials he would need in this situation. I looked thoroughly, and selected what household utensils I felt would be useful. I packed the old gas stove which had not been used from the time our house was electrified. The few saucepans which were not used regularly were added, along with other bit and pieces useful in a home.

My first trip to Mafikeng with Jane and her husband was too long, although Jane travelled at the fastest the speed limit permitted. At times she exceeded the speed limit to accommodate me.

We did not have trouble in finding Dr Moloto's house. It was clear on our arrival that we were both expected and welcome. Within a short time we were served with tea, and there was preparation for lunch. I only stopped for my tea, then excused myself to go over immediately to my son's place. I made certain not to hurt our host. I explained my anxiety about my son and gladly requested that my friends stay for lunch while I went ahead. There was no doubt that the cook had gone to great pains to prepare a tasty meal for us. The tantalising smell from the kitchen and the pangs of hunger in my tummy tempted me to stay. But the longing for and anxiety about my son pushed me to walk out and join him. Going alone was logical as we were all aware that Bakone's banning order allowed him the company of only one person at a time.

To this day I can still see that tall lanky figure of my son waiting impatiently for me to appear round the corner. The moment I set my eyes on him, I was filled with pain and urgency. I half-walked, half-ran towards him. His long arms stretched out to hold me, as he dashed forward calling out, 'Mma, Mma'. We embraced, kissed, laughed, cried in the street, and finally we took each other's hands and walked towards his house. 'I saw the car arrive and recognised it as belonging to thePhakathis. You took a long time to come over,' he said. I explained that we were offered tea. Further, that I did not stay for lunch because I was pushed to come and see and be with him. He soon understood my predicament, and we just sat and talked about everything and sometimes about nothing. I could not believe I was reunited with him.

For the first time he described in detail the restrictions of his banning order and some of its limitations. He highlighted the following points:

That he was allowed only one visitor at a time. If he spoke to more than one person at a time, it was an offence for which he could be charged, convicted and imprisoned.

That he might not enter any school, church or publishing office.

That he must remain within Montshioa township, except on his way to work, when he must not stop anywhere.

That he was forbidden to go more than ten miles out of Mafikeng from any point, for any reason.

All these restrictions had far-reaching implications. Mafikeng being such a small town, it was out of the question for him to find rewarding work in terms of remuneration and job-satisfaction. He was compelled to take the first offer he received in order to keep the 'wolf from the door'. He was never quite certain of whether or not he could use a (shared) taxi. Even if he did not know the other commuters, he never knew how the law could interpret his presence in the taxi. (These taxis operate on fixed routes, and so can be hailed by more than one passenger at a time.) In later years, he found himself facing the problem of not knowing who his true friends were. It can create a real problem when two 'friends' knock at your door as a banned man within five minutes of each other — and then a policeman walks in shortly after. You begin to wonder whether it is a genuine coincidence or a well-planned trap. He had several of these experiences which brought him twice before the courts.

He has reflected on that period with great pain and deep resentment, especially when he recalls how the police shifted the responsibility and task of policing him from their hands and, in effect, forced him to police himself, by observing all the regulations they imposed on him. To him most of these were no offences, but a way of tormenting banned people. Every time we reviewed his breaking the banning order, he always explained the fact that it was unfair that he was made his own policeman whilst the police were paid to to that job. So when he was summoned to appear in court for any of these offences, Bakone always displayed outstanding courage, whilst I was always in great fear and pain for his *safety* and *freedom*, much as these had been limited.

On every visit to Mafikeng, my last words to him were invariably, 'Take care'. We both accepted it to mean extra care about mixing with people, regarding their number and their trustworthiness. Despite all my efforts to sound a word of warning, Bakone fell foul of the law, once when he attended a party and, on another occasion, when he was with more than one person. I went down on both occasions to give him moral support during the court proceedings. I was in great fear about the outcome of these trials. On the first occasion, there were nerve-wracking moments while the prosecutor stated his case. I sat in the courtroom strained, isolated, cold. The judge finally cautioned and discharged him, with a very strong warning not to be seen in the company of more than one person again. That night I spoke to my son very strongly, pleading with him not to do anything which was likely to bring him before the courts again. After expressing his frustration and feelings about the way some of the police hounded him and the influence some of these practices had on him, he promised me faithfully to stay clear of any possible offence.

About nine to twelve months later, I received a report that he had been arrested again for breaking his banning order. That report just finished me. I concluded that this time he was going to get a jail sentence. My journey to Mafikeng was made in depression, fear, anger, hurt and despondency. I felt I had no choice but to go, for I feared that he would be all by himself. By the time I entered court, I was just a bundle of nerves. This time a special office was used as a courtroom, because all other courts were occupied.

After the furniture had been arranged and we had taken our seats, I enquired after the defending counsel, why he had still not arrived. Embarrassed and rather shaken, my son explained that because of the distance and the expense involved, he was unable to come. Further, Bakone said that he was going to conduct his own defence. That really was the last straw. I sat there going through hot and cold flushes, completely unnerved. I felt like screaming and walking out of the courtroom; but something glued me to the chair.

Before the proceedings started, the judge checked with Bakone when the defence lawyer was coming. Bakone explained that he was going to conduct his own defence. The judge wanted to know if he could furnish him with a certain book to help him. He explained that he had his own and he showed the book to the judge. After that the case proceeded. Right through the proceedings, I sat tense in my chair, keeping to the rules of the court, doing what was demanded of me, but also concerned with my innermost feelings about what the ultimate outcome of the case could be. The possibility of a jail sentence chilled me utterly, but I saw no alternative.

He was given a sentence suspended for three years. I gave a sigh of relief.

That time when we parted, my last words to him, after communicating all my feelings and pleas through my eyes, were simply, coolly and meaningfully said. 'Majase. (A nickname he picked up from the university.) You know what my prayer, ardent desire and plea are.' I said no more. From that day he served his banning order without any further disturbing incidents. However, he shared with me his loneliness which had brought about his court appearance and expressed his dearest wish for me to help arrange his marriage.

'You can only understand my plight, Mma, if you once experienced what the serving of a banning order and its implications are. It is very hard to live alone under these circumstances. My continued plea with you, to arrange for me to get married, is prompted by this loneliness. In addition, I love Vuyelwa and I always cherished the day we would live as husband and wife. I will appreciate anything you do to expedite our marriage, particularly since my movements are so drastically restricted and monitored.'

Let it be known that the trauma I went through in the three years my son was banned to Mafikeng is nothing unique. It is the torture and suffering of hundreds of black parents. Mothers in particular have endured such torments from the time the black population of this country raised its voice against the callous, discriminatory and oppressive laws of South Africa. Even prior to the year 1912, which marks the birth of the voice of the black people through the African National Congress, there is a record of intimidation of black by whites, of inhuman beatings, unlawful arrests and gruesome tortures. Black people have been killed, sometimes under the mere pretext that they are thieves or trespassers. How do people live with the knowledge that they killed another human being for such a trivial offence as trespass or thieving? Or even, as was reported in 1984, for removing nine cents for milk from a window sill?

The present-day detentions without trial, bannings and banishments, life imprisonment, all mean heavy burdens for the parents, children, close and distant relatives, friends and neighbours who are forced to endure the endless torture of those they love, in the name of 'maintaining the security of the country' or 'justice'. My son Justice's sufferings when he was forcibly removed from his home and banned to Mafikeng for three years put me on a par with many other mothers of the black community who suffered the same or even greater hurt and pain.

It was under this pressure from Bakone that I considered my son's request to facilitate his marriage to a Miss Vuyelwa Mashalaba who was at that time in her fifth year at the Medical School at the University of Natal. He had told me much about her but I had not met this woman who really sent my son crazy at the thought of her. My son's banning order placed responsibilities on me which, under normal circumstances, fell outside the sphere of the would-be groom's mother. First, I had to counsel my son not to get married simply because he needed company and because he was lonely and under pressure from the police. He must be sure he loved the woman he chose to marry. In addition, I had to visit Vuyelwa, and get her response to the marriage proposal. Remember, I did not know her temperament, or what her attitude and general outlook on life were like. Would she take me to be a forward, nosey mother? All I had learnt from my son about this young woman was that her home was at Katkop in the district of Maclear in the Transkei, a place not accessible in the rainy season — needless to say, we had heavy rains all over the country at this time. Further, that she was the youngest of seven girls, alone with their mother, as her father had died when she was five years old.

I thought my son was very optimistic to hope that a mother in that situation would allow a prisoner, even a political one, to marry her daughter. However, I set forth first to introduce myself to Vuyelwa in Durban, and then to visit her mother in the Transkei. Indeed, my fears were confirmed when the proposal was rejected on the grounds that Mrs Mashalaba could not deliberate with me on this issue without a representative from the Mashalaba family. I was forced to return home disappointed.

But the firmness which I had recognised in Vuyelwa when I met her surfaced very strongly after her mother turned down my son's request. I shall never know what transpired between mother and daughter, but the long and short of it was that Mrs Mashalaba wrote two weeks later to accept my son's proposal, which she was prepared to treat as a matter of urgency to meet my son's desperate position.

To me this was a breakthrough, in that it put aside the traditional, lengthy negotiations by both parties on behalf of the prospective bride and groom. Negotiations which, because of drawn-out deliberations, often leave underlying tensions which in some cases have serious effects on the relationships between the two families! This situation has sometimes damaged the foundations of the young family at a very tender age.

The letter I received from Mrs Mashalaba in a sense made up for the unhappiness I had gone through at Katkop. It reassured me that the Mashalaba family had no objection to their daughter getting married to my son; that because my son was serving a banning order and was living under such very depressing circumstances, Mrs Mashalaba gave her consent that I go ahead to arrange the marriage of our children, and that I notify her about the date so that she could be with us on that day. I read that letter several times to make sure I was not making a mistake. I could not believe what I read. I was overwhelmed. I phoned my son and gave him that very exciting message, and promised him to be in Mafikeng that weekend. That visit in February 1972 to Mafikeng gave me great joy. On arrival he reported the progress he had made. They had set the date of the wedding for 26 April 1972. From that day we made the necessary arrangements to get them married.

On the other side of the scale were the instructions from the Department of Justice. These arrived, cold and dry, to inform us that the only people allowed at the wedding celebrations were the bride and bridegroom, the priest to marry them, and the parents of the couple. As might be expected, those instructions sapped all the joy and excitement out of the good tidings from Mrs Mashalaba. I was frantic with disgust, anger and complete disrespect for the authorities. I found them petty, small-spirited and very cheap in giving such instructions on an occasion like this. I deeply regretted having given them recognition and respect by asking their permission.

On the day, Mrs Mashalaba was with us and she brought one of her daughters along. At the start, the going was not at all easy in our relationship as we were meeting for the first time since our first unhappy contact. But it was good for us to accomplish our common mission. By the end of the day, the hardship and hazards which confronted us in a sense brought us together and cemented our relationship. I soon realised I had a friend and a sister in Flora. In later years, our friendship grew from strength to strength with the arrival of our grandchildren, and I began to admire and really respect Flora Nomaliso Mashalaba, born Moyo, for her achievements with and through her children. As a teacher's widow in the rural areas of South Africa, she had managed to provide her seven daughters with support and guidance of the highest calibre. To this day, I don't stop marvelling at this.

Time and again we look back on Bakone's and Vuyelwa's wedding and ask ourselves why they had to send a policeman to guard over the events of the day the way he did. Did they think we were going to bomb the buildings instead of celebrating? Throughout the whole day the policeman just harassed us. The neighbourhood residents were kind enough to offer us their homes to house our guests, but we were still expected not to serve them with food. I was really impressed to see women take a stand, and insist on housing and serving the guests despite the harassment and intimidation. One poor black policeman spent three-quarters of the day standing in sweltering heat. The officiating priest, on his own initiative, dished out food for the policeman and served him at his post. Without any shame or hesitation he accepted the meal and ate it heartily. The priest calmly remarked afterwards, 'This might have a message for him.' It was really amazing to see the residents of that small community rally round for an event which was planned and announced overnight. The mothers gave all they could to make the wedding a success for families they were seeing for the first time. Some of those young families have remained dear friends to Vuyelwa and Bakone.

Again, I could see the communal element which underlies the basic social structure of the black community in this country, cutting across the educational, practical, religious, social, economic, and sometimes even the tribal, barriers at a time of crisis. Our children's wedding day is a clear example of this phenomenon. It was very significant that the womenfolk more than anybody else stood by that communal tradition when they opened their doors to those of our guests who came from outside Mafikeng. Except for my son's immediate neighbour, I was seeing most of these women for the first time that day. The only person they had known and lived with was my banned son; they did not even know his fiancée at that stage. Yet when the police entered their homes to order them not to house or feed our guests, they reacted with unanimous defiance.

Here were women who had offered assistance to a neighbour being threatened with arrest for doing so; they took a very firm and resolute stand, unmindful of the cost they could pay for what they did. I have never been able to express adequately my heartfelt gratitude and appreciation, to those gallant women.

14
How the State Sees Me

As I write this chapter in 1983, I am sitting in full view of the Atlantic Ocean, at a point where I can raise my eyes and catch a glimpse of Robben Island where many of the political prisoners from the black community are still serving jail sentences, ranging from twelve years to life imprisonment. The irony of it all!

This mixture of beauty and pain takes me back to 19 October 1977, when, at about half past four in the morning, a harsh rap on my front door startled me from sleep. Heavy steps moved towards the back, then paused halfway. Suddenly torchlight at my bedroom window announced the presence of intruders. The words, 'Maak oop', ('Open up!') were sufficient for me to know that the new arrivals at my home were the security police.

That early morning visit started a long-drawn, five months' painful ordeal in detention at Johannesburg Fort. To this day, I ask myself, detention for what? I end up swallowing my own rhetorical question; there never has been a reply.

My first move was to rush into my youngest son Godfrey's bedroom to alert him to the arrival of the police and to give him courage to face up to the reality of that moment. He was the only person with me in the house. All this happened very quickly. All I said to my son was: 'The police are here, stand by as they search the house whilst I am washing.' I then let them in.

They handed me a document from the Minister of Justice and Prisons granting them the authority to search my house and to arrest or detain me. I was still very shaken by what was happening but I found an opportunity to consult with my inner self and come to terms with what was obvious. I hurriedly read through the document, with my son present somewhere nearby. Then, without alerting the honourable officers, I quickly moved into the bathroom to refresh myself. I had almost finished dressing and putting on my shoes when one of the three officers peeped into my bedroom and with an angry look and in a harsh voice ordered: 'Kom jong, kom jong, toe maar, toe maar.' [Come, man, hurry up, hurry up']. Trying to play for time, I responded, 'I am still dressing.' 'Kom, kom, kom'; he was becoming impatient and pushed me out — yet without ever touching me. I kissed my son goodbye and joined the policemen (four of them, two whites, two blacks) in their car. My mind was blank from that time until I realised that we were driving towards Protea Police Station. I resigned myself to the inevitable and waited for what was to follow.

I really don't remember getting out of the car, nor walking in any direction, but I was finally ushered into a long, badly lit hall or passage, with many black men and one or two white security police, one of them rather harsh like an army lieutenant. All black men, young and old, in that passage-like hall were moved with compassion and angry hurt to see me enter. But they were helpless. I supported them and cheered them up by being cheerful myself and strong. Dr Nthato Motlana, who was sitting uncomfortably on something that looked like a small suitcase, stood up to join Mr Vella Kraai, the shopkeeper, George Wauchope and others; they all congregated round me to give me moral support. I soon realised that all the members of the 'Committee of Ten' were there.

The Committee had been formed in 1976 during the unrest in Soweto, when the youth of that community expressed their anger and frustration in many ways as I described in Chapter 3. They burnt government buildings, and attacked institutions related to any government structures and any persons linked to such. In particular, the youth had openly spoken very strongly against the Urban Bantu Council (UBC), an institution which represented the Soweto local authority, and finally forced its closure.

It was after this that the community residents with civic awareness felt that the situation could not be allowed to continue. This concern was expressed by Mr Percy Qoboza, the editor of Soweto's local paper, who wrote an article in that paper inviting all concerned residents to a meeting to review what was happening, particularly with regard to the UBC.

That meeting, attended by about 200–250 Sowetans, after some deliberations about what was happening, agreed that there was a great need for the community to make an in-depth study of the local authority — its functions and duties, its funding, and so on. To implement this, the meeting chose ten people, nine men and one woman, to follow this schedule: that they do their best to complete the assignment inside three to six months; that as soon as that is done, they report back to the group that elected them. Because they were ten committee members, it was called the Committee of Ten. I was the woman member.

Our Committee came up with a blueprint inside six months, and we presented our findings to the group which had elected us. The group approved the blueprint, and instructed the Committee to call a meeting of Soweto residents to present it to them. The authorities banned the first and the second meetings called. A third meeting was never called. That did not dampen the spirit of the Committee which went on with the other duties related to its organisation, and on 19 October, like me, all Committee members were detained.

It was a reunion under very depressing yet challenging circumstances. I had been there for about 30 minutes when Thenjiwe Mthintso, another woman, was brought in. This relieved my concern about being the only woman in that 'crew'.

Now started a long empty, tedious, uncalled-for five months of sterile life at Johannesburg Fort, from 19 October 1977 to 13 March 1978. Many things happened. Most of them were sad and meaningless and others were very revealing and challenging; strange to say, the rest of them were often ridiculously amusing and stupid, and were dismissed as such.

In addition to the monotony of those five months, I was at times stunned to discover the type of people employed as warders, male and female alike. Time and again I puzzled: what measuring yardstick was used to appoint them? There was a good number of black female warders among them. They were, by and large, all human, and carried out their duties to the best of their ability with dignity and responsibility. To this day I shall not understand why they were called 'Vakashi' by their white counterparts who were themselves addressed as 'Nona'. ('Vakashi' is a Zulu word meaning 'Visitor'; 'Nona' is the respectful way black farm labourers address the Afrikaner farmer's young daughter.) I felt terribly insulted on behalf of the black female warders by this unequal form of address, for they were equal in all respects to their white colleagues, judging by the way they carried out their duties.

At the time of our detention there was a marked change in the circumstances described by the women who had been in detention the previous year. They had often talked about sleeping on the floor, without a bedstead. Shortage or sometimes even absence of warm water was another source of complaint.

Among some of the most moving experiences they shared with us was the poor way in which the black female prisoners were clad, regardless of age. They narrated with deep hurt, anger and humiliation the compromised situation endured by women prisoners. They were allowed no panties and were not even supplied with cotton wool when they were having their menstrual flow. The detainees of 1976 stuck their necks out and challenged the prison authorities about this humiliating and degrading situation, and with great excitement they reported the positive change which came out of the stand they took. Each woman prisoner was subsequently issued with panties and cotton wool when necessary. Whether this change is still observed is another matter. I strongly feel to this day that the stand the detainees took on that one issue has left the prison officials with a stinging message — that is, if they have a conscience. Only black women could achieve that victory for their fellow prisoners. Joyce Thembi Seroke told me this story.

Most of the discomforts of sleeping on the floor, having no warm water and having no regular change of clean bed linen were not in force when I was detained in 1977. All the same, we still had our own dissatisfactions. One thing which hit us was lack of privacy in the bathroom. We insisted on getting a latch put on the inside so that people coming in would find themselves compelled to knock on the door. We were bargaining for this change with the male lieutenant when he put his case of why the bathroom door should not be latched from inside: 'This will encourage bigamy', he claimed, vehemently. Whilst some giggled, others just burst out laughing. We assumed he meant lesbianism, but didn't know the word. We ultimately won the day and got the latch for the bathroom as well as a light. By the time we were released, the broken windowpanes and doors were all repaired. We were thus spared the harsh, stinging, late winter, with cold winds and rainwater leaving us suffering from endless coughs and headaches.

Those of us with regular ailments found it a treat to get away from the cells to see the doctor. On my way to the doctor, I had the opportunity to rub shoulders with, or just pass, groups of prisoners serving their sentences. Just to say 'Hello', 'Good morning' or 'Good afternoon', meant a great deal. My route passed through the quarters where white women prisoners were housed. As usual, I compared and contrasted the surroundings. It was amazing to notice the relaxed mood of these white prisoners, many of whom

were uninhibited, shouting 'Morning', and one or two calling out
'Hello Skweeza' — Soweto slang. On my way back to the cell, I felt
fresh and light from being away from the monotonous atmosphere
of the cells and enclosure, day after day, hour after hour. A health
hazard becomes a blessing in disguise in prison.

The best days were when we had a visit from the International
Red Cross. Prior to my detention, I always had imagined that any
form of imprisonment, be it criminal or political, would inhibit the
offender to the point of being timid and subservient. Amazingly,
the reverse is true. We looked forward to the Red Cross visit, as our
forerunners in the field had already prepared us how best to receive
the representatives and to understand the conditions under which
they were going to interview and speak to us. On that day I went out
of my way to titivate myself to the best of my ability under the given
circumstances.

Red Cross representatives walked with us from the cells, past the
prison officials. These warders looked very annoyed, and perhaps
humiliated, by the sight of black women prisoners — detainees —
being escorted by such distinguished gentlemen. I laughed at
nothing when we passed the prison staff just so that they would hear
me make a noise, to regain my personality in some way. I regret
that I shall never know for sure how they felt about this.

Life is strange in that for every twenty joys you have, you can rest
assured that at the end of the road somewhere one single mishap
can mar that joy and beauty, leaving misery in its place. During my
detention, I experienced moments of happiness, but was surrounded by the perpetual pain of the young girls, aged from only 12
to about 18 years, who were detained under Section 6 of the
Terrorism Act and who were separated from me by just the wall
which divided our rooms (or, to be accurate, our cells). I myself was
detained under Section 10. Section 10 means being put away in
prison, cut off from your family, friends, neighbourhood, community, work and worship; it means denial of all your freedom of
movement and, to some extent, your freedom of speech. On the
other hand under Section 6 you are open to severe interrogation at
the hands of the security police, some of whom are callous and
ruthless. Of the many detainees who died in detention, the majority
were in under Section 6.

Here I was then, in detention at the age of 63, permitted to read
books and newspapers, granted change of clothes and fresh food
from my family and friends, allowed visits by my family at specified

intervals, able to see the doctor when necessary. And all the time I lived side by side with youngsters under Section 6 who were separated from me by nothing more than a wall and who were denied all the privileges I enjoyed. These young girls could not be visited by their parents or any one else; they were refused fresh food and garments; they could not possess or read a book or a newspaper, except the Bible on request; they were not entitled to see a doctor when necessary unless permission was granted by a senior prison officer. These girls, above all, were open to interrogation, a practice which is more often than not accompanied by severe assaults, restricted diet and painful isolation. Here too, the Children's Act legislation had no effect.

It was an invidious position, at my age, to listen to these young girls talking amongst themselves about their very terrifying plight. At other times I could hear them singing Sunday school hymns, their favourite being 'Amazing Love'. It was a heart-rending situation. Some days, hour after hour, I sobbed in vain, when the conversation of these children penetrated my cell. If I had had my way, I would have fled from hearing those innocent voices. Just imagine how they yearned for justice, peace and love in their country of birth. In the process of seeking all these, they had been brought to this place. There I was, with my own problem of being detained, as well as having to live beside these young girls — with all their thinking and suffering — when I had absolutely nothing to offer them.

Frequently there were moments which took my mind back to incidents related by some of the women who were detained in 1976 — Joyce Seroke, Debra Matshoba, Vesta Smith, Jane Phakathi, and many others. Did they feel the way I felt then? Would I have been better off then, in detention with my friends? The reality was I was there, now, and no wishful thinking would change the situation.

Certain days of the week were better than others, as we looked forward to a visit from relatives or a meal from friends. On the days when nothing exciting was expected, we looked forward to the arrival of the post. Now that I reflect on those days, there was never an empty day at the Fort, even if some more than others were tainted with sadness or misery.

Christmas Day for me was the worst of all regarding my feelings and mood. I woke up that morning very angry and distressed, and with the naagging questions on my mind, 'Why am I in prison?' 'What am I detained for?'

At about seven-thirty in the morning, when the lieutenant's assistant did her rounds, I was still in bed, fuming with anger. In an artificial manner she wished me a 'Happy Christmas'. That alone sent me hopping mad because I knew it was false. I just lay numb and dumb like a statue. The officer was infuriated by my silence and ordered me to get up and make my bed. That remark triggered something in me I had never anticipated or contemplated. I lashed out about my children left at home, motherless and lonely on Christmas Day — a day when families came together: 'For what?', I asked her, adding that she should keep her good wishes to herself and leave me in peace. I ended, 'This bed is mine and so is the cell too, and I will attend to these, if and when I am ready to do so.' Having said that, I pulled the sheet up and covered my head. By the time I lifted my head to look around, she had left. It closed that episode.

Amidst all these times of despair and anger, there were many saving graces. It was during this period that I received support from quarters I never expected. Individuals and groups rallied round to help in any way they could. Through different organisations and individuals, both the white and black communities assigned themselves tasks which they carried out regularly for the five months I was in detention.

One of these organisations was the Urban Foundation, which came into being in November 1976, in response to the unrest in Soweto. At the height of the disturbances there, a conference of business men in Johannesburg was held at the Carlton Centre to see what contribution businessmen could make. The response was impressive. Many black people were invited, most of them teachers, nurses, social workers, traders and others. At the close of the conference, a decision was taken to launch the Urban Foundation with the broad purpose of improving the quality of life for the deprived communities in the country.

The main areas which the Foundation has tackled are housing, education, and business enterprise in Soweto. Since 1977, many new homes of quality have been built in Soweto. To some people in Soweto and outside, including whites, there is continuing criticism that the housing scheme is creating a middle class to divide blacks into class structures within the country. The 99-year leases which were seen as a breakthrough when introduced are now seen as an insecure piece of legislation when assessed against a background of the thousands of people who once owned private and communal property on full title deed and have been dispossessed by this very government.

There are many black people who severely criticise the Foundation as an arm of the government which tries to make some blacks comfortable to protect the white community. In some quarters it is seen as sheltered employment for whites. There is a cry from the black community that together with the housing and educational projects, the Foundation needs to be seen to be doing something about employing blacks in managerial positions in preparation for senior posts within the Foundation.

In a country riddled with so much racial discrimination and poverty and deprivation directed at one racial group with no political rights, an organisation like the Urban Foundation needs to be involved at all levels. I have served on the Transvaal Board of the Urban Foundation, and have been severely criticised for it. Although I remain on the Board, there are some aspects of its operations of which I am highly critical, and I intend to see them changed.

The representatives of that organisation were the first to visit me within a week of my detention to express their solidarity with and concern for me and my family, as well as to offer their legal expertise. They will never know what this meant to me, a mother and widow, who left her youngest, unemployed son alone in the house. I was unnerved, not so much by the actual detention, but by its ramifications for my job and employers. Would I have a job to go back to? The rent for the house I called home was another great worry to me. If the West Rand Administration Board did not receive rent for two months, would they lock the house up? And if so, what would become of my son, and me on my release? How could I help my son find a job while I sat in prison? Numerous questions riddled my mind. They went unanswered, and left me painfully helpless.

The Urban Foundation in short offered the assistance of their organisation wherever it was needed. It was after I had given this office Power of Attorney that I could think properly. In addition to running my home and all related matters, different representatives from that organisation paid me visits whenever it was possible. Their legal representative services were invaluable, to say the least, and cost me nothing. What more could I ask for? This was the only organisation, I suppose because of its unique foundation and composition, that found it possible to arrange to pay me regular visits when I was in detention.

But other organisations too provided detainees with welcome comforts. Members of the well-known women's organisations, Black Sash and the World Affiliated YWCA, joined with women from other organisations, such as the Dependants Conference, to provide us with fresh, wholesome meals, interesting and entertaining literature, and handwork material. They prepared a weekly roster for delivery of meals to our group in detention. To those who have not had a taste of detention, this may appear as a trivial gesture, unworthy of mention. To those of us in detention at that time, we looked forward to those days, to that hour, with great expectation and appreciation.

Another event which meant a great deal to me was receiving mail. All friends who found time to compose a line or two to me when I was at the Fort will never know what those letters meant to me. It was at the end of another sterile, empty day, when each one of us was locked in our individual cells, that I managed to communicate with some of my relatives, friends and sympathisers either by reading, re-reading and digesting their correspondence, most of which was loaded with powerful supporting messages, or by sitting in my bed to reply to some of those letters.

I am well aware that some of my dear friends were distressed because they were refused permission to visit me during that time; some of them were too scared even to ask, but they too were very much perturbed. I have no doubt their prayers and ardent wishes were equally rewarded.

Let me take this opportunity to thank each individual who for one reason or another was given permission to visit, particularly those who were not members of my family, as well as those whose efforts to visit were turned down.

I would like to thank in particular: Justice J.N. Steyn, Executive Director of the Urban Foundation, Mr C.S. Menell, Transvaal Chairman of the same organisation, Mrs Helen Suzman, who came as a friend, Mr Geoff Budlender, who listened to many of our problems during that time. How we beamed with joy to meet him! Mrs Joyce Seroke and Mrs Sheena Duncan's correspondence kept me alert and going, as did letters from friends who wrote only once. My children's visits and those of my relatives were deeply appreciated, but they always left me sad and nostalgic. I dragged through that mood for hours and sometimes for days on end. It is very difficult to describe the pain I suffered.

It is amazing that some of the casual friendships I made as far back as the late 1940s and early 1950s became some of my strongest pillars during detention. I became ill in jail, and the diagnosis indicated a need for surgery. I was shocked to learn from the surgeon that I was booked for an operation. My response to him was very frank and firm, namely that no one would operate on me without my knowing exactly why I needed an operation. When he insisted — I must say in a supportive way — I told him in no uncertain terms that nobody was going to cut me open until it was made very clear to me why the operation was necessary. Remember, I did not know the surgeon; I had only met him in detention. Who was he? Why was he working with prisoners? And this sudden, new medical condition — was it caused by prison conditions? I needed someone I trusted to share my fears and concerns with before I could accept the surgery.

At that stage I asked the prison lieutenant to phone a woman doctor friend of mine, Mrs Elaine Morris, who worked under her maiden name, Dr Hammer, and ask her to come to the Fort for my letter, in which I informed her of my plight, requesting her to consult with the surgeon about my condition, and find out if surgery was the only treatment he recommended. She confirmed by letter that this was so, and she strongly advised me to consent to it for my own good. She came in at a time when my mind was plagued by doubt, suspicion and uncertainties. Strange that Elaine has always been a friend and never a doctor of mine at any time. Yet it is equally true to say that in times of ill-health she has been my confidante over many years. She has always provided support when I was confronted with any alarming health problem. Yes, I have called on her in the middle of the night. I have always received a warm response. She has fulfilled that role with complete dedication, support and respect for me. To this day that relationship continues. In addition to that, she ran many errands for me while I was in detention such as doing my shopping and other household duties which the Urban Foundation could not fulfil.

I want to make it perfectly clear that many women in my community would not only have been willing to do this for me, but would have loved and enjoyed doing it. My requests were made with no consideration for race or colour, but were put forward on a long-standing relationship of tested friendship. She visited me at the hospital and kept her profession in very low profile without denying me the warm guidance and confidence we shared over the years.

During my term of hospitalisation — in fact, from the time the security police escorted me for registration with the hospital clerical staff — I was treated by the police as one who had committed a serious offence. I read the mood of anger and disgust, clouded with complete helplessness, from those clerks; but they did not fail to transmit support, concern and profound care and solidarity to me in their silence, with their faces looking down in hurt and disgust. I regarded the male security policeman escorting me as very insensitive, and when he turned to me and said, 'How can they be given the responsibility of collecting money?' I considered him out of his mind. The one dirty look I gave him was loaded. He did not say another thing.

On my admission to the ward, several nursing sisters and some matrons — some friends of mine, other just acquaintances — streamed into the ward, both out of curiousity, I suppose, to say, without expressing it, 'We are with you'. Some of them broke down and wept. I found myself in the unusual situation of having to comfort them and reassure them that I was fine and that I would manage. The limit in this case was when two female black officers or security police took turns twice every day to sit and guard over me; I suppose the authorities wanted to give the impression that I was the most hideous black woman 'criminal' or 'terrorist'. The irony of it all became obvious when I consistently introduced my guards to the scores of visitors, friends and relatives who did not stop coming to the hospital to say, 'How do you do?' This had an unexpected effect on my guards, because they suddenly burst out, saying they did not see why they had to guard over such a respectable adult person. I took no notice of their remarks. The long and short of it was that within three to four days of being in hospital, the guards sat at a distance from me, like some strange and well dressed, healthy 'patients' or 'visitors'.

At the end of ten days, with the operation fresh and the pains still intolerable, two white security police, one man, one woman, arrived to take me back to detention. I was shaken by the sobs of the nursing staff. Their hurt was aggravated by the police remarks: 'Maak gou jong' ('Be quick, boy'). I took it all in my stride. As we reached the door of the prison, the female police officer turned and mockingly asked: 'Are you coming to fight for your people's freedom?' I dismissed her and her question with the contempt they deserved in one look, and not a word. The message registered as she went pink in the face in her silence.

The door of the prison opened and the female white warder who received me from my high-handed escorts beamed with an unmistakeably warm smile which puzzled me. She turned to me and said 'Welcome. Do you feel better, Ellen?' My mind failed me at this unexpected warmth and I struggled to find the appropriate words to respond. When I turned to study the reactions of my two previous companions, they had not only disappeared, but the door behind me had been shut before I could say my 'Adieu' to my short-lived, precious freedom. Within minutes of my arrival at the lieutenant's office, I was ushered back to my cell, with the clink from the heavy bunch of keys endorsing my most unwelcome arrival, as if saying, 'You have no choice, Ellen; adjust to the inevitable'. My fellow detainees, Thenjiwe Mthintso, Mathabo Pharase and Rebecca Musi, all young girls of my children's age group, received me with love back into the fold. Needless to say, the first two weeks after the operation were torture: I suffered acutely from abdominal pains. The prison authorities expected the cell to be spick and span, notwithstanding my operation.

Of these three fellow inmates Mathabo Pharase had appeared very offhand, even to the point where she could easily be misunderstood as unkind and very uncaring. A day after my return from hospital, she informed me that from that day on I should never clean my cell as she was taking it upon herself to do so. In her firm, yet not so serious, manner she left no doubt in my mind that she meant every word she said. Every time I tried my best, in the most becoming words, to thank this easy-going, tall, thin girl, with a sometimes very haughty nature, she would dismiss me as if I had said absolutely nothing or as if I was speaking rubbish. So I stopped thanking her for this generous offer, and told myself that one day I would get my chance; and this is it: Moradia (daughter) of Pharase, you possess some hidden, rare, treasured talents of love and deep-seated sympathy and concern for human needs. I have no doubt that what you did for me in detention, on my return from that painful operation, is what you have often done for other people in different yet very related situations. I shall never accept that you were showing this unusual generosity and hidden compassion to me alone. I can only say that yours is a gift to be nurtured and maintained. Thank you once more, Mathabo. I am grateful to have had this opportunity to know you better.

I spent the better part of five months with these young women in detention. We had our mid-day meal together daily. From ten o'clock in the morning until about three o'clock in the afternoon we played different indoor games in the open enclosure and enjoyed the God-given sunshine and fresh air. We chatted, teased and laughed at each other, sometimes enjoying idle talk, at other times sharing meaningful current events related to the lives of the black people as individuals. We also discussed local and national issues affecting our community. The young girls aged 12 to 18 years in detention under Section 6 of the Terrorism Act were often our greatest concern and our topic of discussion, because they were our immediate neighbours and there was just no comparison between their plight and ours. There was no way of running away from the misery of those children. My three young fellow detainees really supported me through this very challenging experience with their calm and profound dedication and committed involvement.

Another pastime we enjoyed immensely, although I must admit we took a long time to cultivate it, was handicraft. Occasionally, we engaged in this as a group, but on the whole we found it a very relaxing exercise when we were on our own in our cells after lock-up, where our only means of communication was through shouting to one another. Our favourite craft was tapestry, we each came up with different finished articles. We derived great pleasure from that.

Most of the material we used for handicrafts was supplied by Black Sash and some by individuals like Helen Suzman. As a student, handwork was one of my most detested subjects. However, when I found myself in the situation I was in, I had no choice but to try my best in that field. It was after a month or two that I discovered that I was not as helpless as I thought myself to be. Among the articles I completed were an embroidered table-cloth which covers an eight-seater table donated by Jossie Thandie Emery now in Bristol, England, and three tapestry articles which are not artistically done but considering the circumstances under which I was compelled to make them, I take great pride in these.

Thenjiwe, who had really suffered a raw deal from several different detentions, including being restricted under Sections 6, 10 and 22 at different times, made fun of some of the most painful experiences of her life. She shared with us an episode when she was detained in the Transkei in a prison at Lobode, a name which finally appeared on one of her tapestry articles. The joy and peace of mind we derived from some of her previous experiences which she shared with us were amazing. To know that she had survived some of those hideous incidents and could share them with no mark of malice nor expression of bitterness gave us the opportunity to see our own plight with the minimum of resentment, thus saving our energy to complete the detention we were subjected to. She is a woman of small stature but strong moral fibre.

Another evening pastime activity was reading. It kept us company when we were locked up in our individual cells with no one to share or communicate with. It was a commonly accepted practice for each of us to limit the time we spent on a book so giving each other the opportunity to read it too. Newspaper-reading was also a regular engagement, with each of us assigned to compile current events on specific topics so that we could all be more less up-to-date with the daily happenings, as well as keeping in touch with our community on the specific events of that week or month. The exercise for the mind from this assignment was invaluable. Again, Thenjiwe, with her long record of experience in several detentions, motivated us in that direction.

Looking back, I have reason to believe we were privileged to have Thenjiwe Mthintso as a fellow detainee. The fact that she had been exposed to different levels of detention, either in South Africa or in the 'baby boy' of South Africa, the Transkei, meant she had become seasoned and to a great extent immune to the emotional trauma which accompanies prison life. This to me was a great help; and within the very first week of my detention I quickly adjusted to the high-handed attitudes of the wardresses, particularly the white ones. Thenjiwe was cool, calm, composed and very unruffled by the appearance or even the presence of the most officious wardress. Not once did she verbally indoctrinate me, but her actions spoke much louder than words, and their message was loud and clear. However, these endless detentions had not left her emotionally and physically unscarred. But despite some very unfortunate afflictions, Thenjiwe still has much to offer, particularly in this soul-rending and nerve-wracking situation.

I never had an opportunity to share these deep-seated sentiments with her before we parted at the Fort. It is my ardent wish that she will get access to this book somewhere, some time and accept these humble words of appreciation. If that is not possible, then I hope that her son, Lumumba, whom she spoke of with deep longing when in detention, will come to know of his mother's contribution from this book. Keep it up, Thenjiwe, wherever you are.

Three weeks before my release I had a unique experience. It was

about three o'clock in the afternoon and we were parading before
our cell doors for the final day's inspection before being locked in.
Three white men walked into our enclosure unannounced. Without
disclosing their identity, they asked for Ellen Kuzwayo and Rebecca
Musi. I stealthily eyed them with suspicion concealing my subdued
anxiety; I did not recognise a single one of them. I responded, 'I am
Ellen'. 'Come with us,' one said. I started to ponder what the next
surprise would be: Was I going for interrogation under Section 6?
You can imagine the fright which shook me and sent my pulse
beating ten times faster for about two to three minutes as I prepared
myself. But I was determined to conceal my fright.

Their gentlemanly attire reduced my fears. All the same, my
mind swiftly moved from one thing to another in an effort to find an
answer to the questions, 'Who are these men?' and 'What can they
be looking for?'

After the clanging of the keys and the opening of the first gate,
we were ushered out — in the usual ladies first style — without
anyone uttering a single word. The same routine continued for the
second and third gates. It was clear that the shortish bulky
gentleman who kept opening the gates and ushering us out was the
leader of the group. Outside the lieutenant's office the same man
turned to me saying 'Come into the office, Mrs Kuzwayo'. How
strange that I should be addressed this way whilst in detention: this
was one of the thoughts which crossed my mind. My fellow detainee
was ordered to wait away from the office out of sight and, I
suppose, out of earshot too.

I was given a seat across the table facing the man I had presumed
was the leader of the group. The second sat in line with the leader,
but in a corner, with his arms folded across his chest, looking
straight ahead and mute. The third man sat behind me; I can only
guess that he was there to record the interview, but that is no more
than a wild guess. And I still didn't know who these men were. The
hope I had cherished of having the 'support' of the lieutenant (the
only officer who seemed to have any human feelings at the Fort)
was dismissed by her absence from the office, which was so much a
part of herself. Later on, I could have kicked myself for even
allowing such a thought to cross my mind.

Without introducing himself, the 'leader' of this trio started
telling me about their mission, namely, that his department was
thinking of releasing me, but before this could happen they had
come to talk to me. I looked up and asked him who he was. He

replied, 'I am the Minister of Justice'. Startled by this disclosure, I responded, 'Are you Mr Jimmy Kruger?' He nodded, and, I continued, 'I feel honoured and privileged to speak to you, sir'. His reply was that he too was honoured and privileged to speak to a leading member of the Soweto community. I felt mocked and insulted, and gave a firm response: 'No Minister of Justice would be honoured and privileged to speak to a prisoner.' Silence. I continued: 'This is besides the point. What is it you have come to see me about, sir?'

The conversation then became involved. I was told that they were considering reconstructing the schools programme, and so I should go to Cape Town. My very first reaction to this was that I was to be banned there, but he reassured me that this was not the case. I then expressed my concern that it was suggested that I was in some way disrupting the schools programme in Soweto. He denied this but I strongly felt this was the case and replied, 'By implication, this is what you mean'.

I now made it abundantly clear that I was particularly disturbed about my job and my priority on my release therefore would be to find out if I had a job to go back to. Then and only then would I be in a position to arrange a holiday at the seaside; and in that case, my choice would be to go to Durban to be with my son and his family. I had hardly completed that statement when the Minister raised both his fisted hands and banged the table, saying, 'That son of yours who gave the government so much trouble'. In a flash I responded, 'On the contrary, the government gave my son unnecessary trouble.'

I paused and continued as I felt it unnecessary to make an issue out of this matter, 'This is besides the point. Can we go on?'.

At that point fear of a longer detention was far from my mind. Uppermost at that time was the recognition of the fact that I had been offered the chance of a life-time, that of a black woman in South Africa having an interview with the Minister of Justice and Prisons. It was without precedent, and one which I intended using to the full. Our interview centred on the need for better communication between the black people of South Africa and the Nationalist government, and I let him know of the black community's long-standing dissatisfaction; that whilst the state saw it fitting to plan the future and destiny of our community, the black people themselves saw this as a futile, sterile exercise; that government-chosen leaders could never enter into any meaningful negotiations with the government on behalf of the blacks because as state employees they would say only the things the authorities wished to hear. I concluded: 'The day the government of this country agrees to sit round the table with the black people's own chosen leaders about the political aspirations of that community, then and only then shall we all begin to see the dawn of a new day of anticipated peace and calm within the country.'

Needless to say the Minister did not take this at all well and our interview ended. Nevertheless, I felt I had made my mark — even if it cost me another five months' detention.

Much as the Minister had indicated that preparations for my release within three weeks were underway, when we parted I doubted whether this would come to pass. To my amazement then, two weeks later, I was called to the front office where I met a security policeman in the presence of the lieutenant. I was issued with a letter of release, which also ordered me to hand in my passport or any travel document in my possession. As the passport was not on my person, and it was clear that it would have to be handed in before my release, I called on the Urban Foundation to send my legal advisers to the Fort. They contacted my son for the passport, and after receiving it from him, handed it over to me with the strict instruction to hand it to the security personnel myself. These instructions I kept to the letter.

From the time I received my letter of release, I was overwhelmed with conflicting emotions. Out of nowhere I developed a feeling of hurt for my fellow detainees whom I was leaving behind. This tore me apart, for I was longing to go home, yet the thought of leaving the others behind now hit me hard. It was much easier to share the news of my release with Mathabo and Thenjiwe than with the Section 6 detainees. Their response, *'U hambe kahle u nga silibale'* ('Go well, and keep us in your thoughts'), remained in my ears long after my discharge. I have never met Thenjiwe again, but I have seen Mathabo twice. Of the girls detained under Section 6 I have only met Baby Tjawa and Masabata Loate. Perhaps I have met others, but without knowing it. I never saw them, we only talked through the cell wall.

It would have made a great deal of difference if we had all been released at the same time. I often wonder whether these are calculated moves by those in authority to sow the seeds of mistrust amongst the detainees. The obvious outcome for those left behind is to start asking questions within or among themselves: 'Why has so and so been released? Why not me? Why not us?'. All the same. I have reason to believe that there is great awareness within the ranks of those black people of the kind of psychological tactics used by the police.

Other moves which can create suspicion within the black 'leadership' (I use this word with reservation to mean those people the masses often look up to, even if they are not vocal or in the forefront of community events) include suddenly granting a passport to someone who has been branded a troublemaker, whilst those who were similarly branded are denied a passport. The community raise their eyebrows and ask, 'Why him?' 'Why not us?'. Certain circles in the black community are well aware of this attempt to divide us. Let us all be warned.

When my luggage was packed and I was ready to go home, I was summoned to the last ritual of prison life. This has left a sour taste which will remain with me as long as I live. After having to state what I had left in the lieutenant's office on my arrival (for example, whether I had had any money), I was instructed to take possession of my personal belongings. These were my wristwatch, some jewellery and a little money. I was then ushered into an office where they intended taking my fingerprints. At this I saw red. Something just stuck in my throat. I felt so angry and annoyed at being subjected to this final humiliation. I was lined up with a number of new prisoners, presumably there for criminal offences, in a passage which served as a reception area. I asked myself, 'For what?' Then I lashed out verbally at a bulky wardress who was in charge, and told her in no uncertain terms that I did not see any reason why they should take my fingerprints as I had committed no offence, nor had I stood trial in any court of law. Much as they exhorted me to stop talking, I ignored them and continued saying my piece as I saw this as the only channel open to me to express my grievance and hit back — even if it served only to humiliate the prison personnel for a moment in front of the new arrivals.

The warders were both very angry and embarrassed, whilst the new prisoners were stunned and terribly frightened by my performance. But it really eased me inside. I am very grateful to this day that I had the courage and strength to do it. It made me feel much better at the end of everything.

After they had taken my fingerprints, my hands were soiled with the tar-like liquid they use, and there were no facilities provided to wash my hands. I lost my temper again and demanded soap, water and a towel, all of which were provided. I see the lack of these facilities as another tactic by those in authority to degrade and insult black people in prison. To this day I see their quick response on that occasion not as a simple answer to my request or demand, but much more as a means to save themselves more embarrassment in front of the new arrivals.

The final insult came when I was collecting the cardboard boxes I had packed my belongings in. One security policeman offered me a lift back home. I gave him a dirty look and muttered 'Over my dead body'. That day seemed so much longer than all the others I spent in the Fort. I knew even at that moment that someone from the Urban Foundation was waiting outside to pick me up. That alone was a great relief and support. I could not wait to shake that person's hand.

As the prison doors closed behind me, my eyes were dazzled by the bright sunshine. My sense of direction and time were both confused. Several cars were parked nearby, and some men were standing round as if to watch me emerge from that notorious entrance. My mind was so preoccupied with the seemingly enormous baggage of several cardboard boxes that I was forced to halt to find my bearings. Some of the men were unmistakeably reporters, others had the appearance of plain clothes police. Suddenly, my eyes caught someone I recognised, a friend, in the person of Mr Michael Rantho from the Urban Foundation. I must have shouted something in my excitement. I really do not remember for certain what my first reaction was. All the same we ended falling into each other's arms and embracing whilst tears just rolled down my cheeks.

The emotional upheaval over, we packed my luggage into his car. As I tried to make sure my belongings were together, another security policeman interrupted, saying, 'Can I help take you home?' In anger I retorted, 'Get thee behind me, Satan!' I never saw him again. You may ask: Ellen, how did you know he was security police? He was a strange *white* man who did not disclose his identity; he stood apart from the reporters. In my mind, he was a security policeman, because in the South African situation no white man without an axe to grind would choose to help an unknown black woman particularly on her release from detention.

One of my boxes disappeared in the commotion and I have never recovered it. It was lost with some of my most treasured correspondence from dear friends both in and outside the country who comforted and supported me during those turbulent months. If you ask me to guess where I think it vanished, all I can say is, 'Your guess is as good as mine'. After I had packed what I thought was everything and had taken the front seat of Mick's car, he drove off. I had no idea which way because my sense of direction at that point was completely disoriented. He spoke to me, asking questions or giving me news, but nothing registered. I was thinking of home, of my children, my neighbourhood and its people. I longed to get there, but somehow I was frightened — very much frightened — though I could not say what I was really afraid of.

We arrived at sunset. Teenagers were playing along the street for lack of a sports ground. I sat motionless for a couple of minutes, taking advantage of the few moments while Mick walked round the car to open the door for me. Trying hard to collect myself, I finally managed to step out of the car and stood for a few seconds next to him, half-happy to be home, half-paralysed with unaccountable fear. Two little girls with loose wraps over their heads, aged about seven years, approached me and, as if in fright and joy, started shouting at the top of their voices 'U mama, u mama' (Mother, Mother), the custom of my nation where every mother is every child's mother. In no time the whole street was crowded with boys and girls, some of them just toddlers, rushing towards the car and surrounding me shouting, 'U mama, u mama, u mama' and fondly throwing themselves into my arms. For a second I was tongue-tied but soon responded to this warm, loving reception. I kissed them all, clean and grubby alike. Their different condition did not affect our mutual response.

As their excitement dwindled as spontaneously as it had swelled and run over, they began to disappear, and their place was soon taken by the adults. These were certainly not as numerous as the children and they were also far more composed, even subdued. They were formal, yet very warm and welcoming. After the usual interactions and exchange of formalities, my opposite neighbour, Mrs Makhoba, turned to the others surrounding me saying, 'People, let Mrs Kuzwayo go into the house and rest, we shall go there and see her'.

It was in my house that my children came forward and kissed and embraced me. I sat on the couch and received a string of visitors who walked in and out of the house to welcome me back and to expressly thank God for sparing me. I was touched by a group of not less than ten women and girls, some of them very simply dressed, some of them bare-footed and most of them holding bibles, all unknown to me. The opening words of their spokeswoman were: 'Mrs Kuzwayo, you do not know most of us and some of us you have not even seen once. Most of us know you from hearsay when people talk about your community involvement and overall commitment to the service of your people. We have thought of you when you were in detention, we identified with you and are therefore coming to express our solidarity with you as one with us and of ours as a black woman as well as a Christian woman.' At the end of this speech, they sang a hymn, read from Psalm 23 and prayed.

That group finally ended the fears I had had about the reaction and attitudes of my people. I had received outstanding support and acceptance on my return from detention and I survived and thrived on that. As I sat on that couch, I did not stop marvelling at this warm concerted reception from all levels of that community. It made my day.

The strangest thing was that I could not as much as stand up from that couch to go to bed that night. Suddenly the resistance I had put up in detention, both emotional and physical, deserted my system without warning. I collapsed without passing out, and spent the night on the couch. When I came to, the next day, I was not the same Ellen I had been twelve hours earlier. My response to this condition was to see the doctor, who gave the first diagnosis as threatening heart failure. The friends who gave me support during my detention did not stop enquiring after my well-being. Again the Urban Foundation, on learning of my poor state of health, hurriedly arranged for me to be seen by a specialist, in addition to many other personal services. I shall never have adequate words to thank them and the many other friends who stood by me then.

PART THREE

Patterns Behind the Struggle

15
Finding Our Strength

As I observe people's perceptions of me in the communities where I move, and then place my findings against the cold attitudes and harsh responses I get from government departments, I am completely thrown off balance. While I really believe that my community and country accept me as an asset, my government sees me not only as a liability but as a threat.

During the last ten to fifteen years, I had been able to serve my community in many different ways. The courage, generosity and support of my people have over the years helped me to carry a load that under ordinary conditions I would not have found easy to bear. I am amazed when I observe the power, strength and self-confidence that are born of involvement in work on behalf of one's own hard-pressed people.

There are some very awkward aspects to such intense involvement. Even when I began writing this book, for example, trying to concentrate my thoughts and express them clearly, people were knocking at my door at the rate of three or four a day, each one with a problem which he or she expected me to help solve. Their needs included finding accommodation — applying for a site, or buying a house, helping an old, sickly pensioner who needed someone to share the rent, electricity and water bills with, or just finding an outside room or a garage for hire. Always, I have tried to help, and often have done so successfully. But those successes in turn have added to the long list of people with different needs who return with other problems or who need extra help, all urgent, and demanding an immediate response.

I share this plight with a few other community members in Soweto who are seen by their neighbourhood as appropriate people to be approached in times of crisis. I can never be too grateful to the University of Witwatersrand for providing me with an office in which to complete the writing of my book!

I also find myself approached to play a more formal role in a number of organisations. The following are a few of those in which I have served: World Affiliated Young Women's Christian Association, as National Finance Chairman (sic); the Committee of Ten, as one of the Committee members for six years from 1976 to 1982; Zamani Soweto Sisters Council, Consultant since 1978; Maggie Magaba Trust, Chairwoman since its inception in 1979; A re Godiseng Chelete Basadi (Black Women's Endeavour to Understand Investment); one of the founders and first Treasurer from 1980 to 1983; the Urban Foundation as one of the founder Board members in the Transvaal as well as Board member at national level since 1982; the Black Consumer Union, launched on 17 March 1984, as its first President.

I have been proud of the faith placed in me by all these organisations. But once in my life I was called upon to do a task which shook my whole being as it involved me mentally, emotionally, physically and, I have no doubt, spiritually too.

It was on my release from detention, when there was very alarming talk that eleven students — ten boys and one girl — who had been arrested under the Terrorism Act were facing very serious charges which could lead to long prison sentences, or worse. I had only been out of detention myself about two months when I received a letter from Advocate Ernest Wentzel, a leading Johannesburg lawyer, well-known for dealing with political cases. He wanted me to see him in his office. When I delayed responding, he sent me a second letter expressing the urgency of the matter he wished to talk to me about. This weighed rather heavily on my mind, with the scar of detention still very fresh in my memory. But his letter, which should have clarified the issue and thus eased my mind, was vague as well as pressing and when I arrived in his office, I had numerous unanswered questions on my mind.

Advocate Wentzel started by outlining in detail the case of the eleven students, emphasising the gravity of the charges they faced, and expressing his fears of what the outcome could be. Genuinely puzzled by this story, as I had absolutely no contact with this case, I bluntly put a question to him, 'What has all this to do with me, Mr Wentzel?' It was only at this point that he disclosed to me in his gentle way the need to find a social worker of repute and an unimpeachable record of service in the black community, to plead in mitigation for those students. It was hoped in this way to reduce the possibility of heavy sentences — then estimated at nothing less than life imprisonment for some, without ruling out capital punishment for one of them.

But, I simply could not come to terms with why this lawyer was sharing this very delicate and challenging subject with me. Looking straight into his face, and very much agitated, I replied, 'Why do you tell me all this? It has nothing to do with me.' He continued to share with me his fears for the outcome of the case and revealed that after consideration he had concluded that he could not find anyone better qualified than myself to make the plea in mitigation for the students.

I frankly told him that the fact that I had just been released from detention alone disqualified me from carrying out that assignment, as it might have an adverse influence on the court; further that this would place me in jeopardy with the authorities, who already saw me as a troublemaker and might thus find good reason to put me back in prison. I completely turned down the request. No amount of persuasion would change my mind. I was too disoriented by my recent experiences to accept the challenge.

Yet Advocate Wentzel did not give up. He painted a picture of the judge expected to be on the Bench that day. He said he needed someone who would be able to get through to the humanity of the man. He needed in particular a social worker who would be able to describe in court some of the very oppressive conditions experienced by the majority of the young population in Soweto. Everyone had advised him to approach me. But my reaction to this was precise, simple and clear; that there were many of us with my training and experience in our practice in Soweto.

His last words to me were: 'I approached you because I have great fears about the outcome of the sentence. I appealed to you in the firm belief that you are the only person who would bring home to the judge the truth about the conditions and circumstances which contribute to some of the seemingly negative behaviour of youth in Soweto. I am not saying your mitigation would have a favourable effect on the sentences of the day; on the other hand, I have a hope it might. If some of them end up with life imprisonment or capital punishment after your mitigation, then we shall say we tried, and our best was not good enough. Now that you say you cannot, when the worst comes to the worst,we shall have nothing to test what could have been our best performance against the sentence they will get.'

It was at that point that something sparked a completely new feeling in me. Fear, doubt, hesitation, all three deserted me. I turned to Advocate Wentzel saying, 'If I am the last and only person you placed your hopes on for this case, in the name of the black child, I have no choice but to plead in mitigation for their safety and for my conscience. If they get life imprisonment or capital punishment after I refused to assist, I will carry a guilt feeling to my dying day.'

I had hardly left his office when I found my mind immersed in the decision I had made. Had I done the right thing? Would this involvement not have repercussions which would see me back in prison? Was there still a chance of backing out of this arrangement? But if I did that, what would happen to the students?

There was still about a month to go before the trial, and I passed a very tedious four weeks, endlessly reviewing the decision I had made. This was often accompanied by sleepless nights spent in an effort to reconcile myself to this very frightening commitment which left me frantic and quite isolated. I did not share my decision with my family and close friends, to avoid severe criticism and possible ridicule from them for making a martyr of myself.

The fateful day and hour finally arrived and found me still full of doubts, regrets, fears and completely withdrawn from any possible source of support, encouragement and understanding. On my arrival at court that morning I felt completely numb and cold. The unfamiliar location of the court and its surroundings in Kempton Park added to my bewilderment. I moved from one end of the corridor to the other in the hope of bumping into the defending counsel or someone I knew. Instead, the interior seemed to be full of black and white uniformed police who all appeared very unfriendly, or so I saw them. Here and there were intimate groups of ordinary people who I assumed were either relatives of the accused or their close friends. I finally collected myself and sat down in one place hoping to see the advocate or his colleague walk in. As I raised my eyes I saw Mathabo Pharase, one of the women I had been detained with. We were both so preoccupied with our own thoughts that we greeted each other very casually, just a 'How do you do?', both cool and vacant.

At about eight fifty-five, I could not contain my panic, and at that point approached one of the court officials to find out the whereabouts of the lawyers' offices. I walked in after a distant 'Come in', to find the gentlemen on their feet ready to go into court. They didn't dismiss me ungraciously, rather, as they walked out they left me with the impression of how much depended on me. But I still had not received the support I had so much hoped for.

Five minutes dragged by. I was experiencing hot and cold flushes. I was aware of the heavy thump of my heart, and my short intake of breath in between. As people moved into court, I mingled apologetically with them and found myself a protected seat amongst the spectators.

I fixed my eyes on the steps leading from somewhere under the building from where I expected the accused to emerge. I was very keen to see them as I knew nothing about them, yet, when they finally walked up the steps, I felt a cold chill run down my spine. They were so composed and very strong, a condition which strangely unsettled me. I suddenly felt altogether unequal to the task.

I listened with great interest to Mr Montsisi, the father of Dan Montsisi, the first accused. He pleaded the case of his son with courage, composure and absolute conviction. He encouraged and inspired me. The priest who followed, on the other hand, sounded frightened when he was called to testify about Dan Montsisi as a member of his congregation.

When my name was called to enter the witness box, my mind was in complete turmoil. At that point, I turned to the long-standing, living practice of mine, which has seen me through some of the most awesome experiences in my life. I handed over the challenge which faced me to the 'powers' which were fed to me by my mother in my early childhood, as the 'foundations of living': 'Nothing is too big or difficult for the Creator', and 'Always turn to Him when you are in need'. Those words came alive at that moment of reckoning.

I remember very clearly standing in the witness box with my hand up, saying, 'So help me God' as I faced the judge, still in the grips of fear. When he started questioning me I was completely at a loss as I did not know how to address him. This was my very first experience in the witness box. The quick-thinking, supportive interpreter handed me a piece of paper on which he had scribbled: 'Address the judge "Your Lordship".' You can be sure I still made mistakes, but I managed.

I did fairly well with the advocate. He asked for my name, established my profession and occupation, and asked me to say why, as a social worker, I saw the black children in the country as very deprived. My response to this was to highlight the complete absence of recreational facilities in the form of playgrounds and leisure equipment; to point to the overcrowding in homes where ten to fifteen people living in a three-roomed house was a common condition; to describe how the youth gathered on street corners at night; to explain that parents — mothers in particular — had to leave their young children sometimes as early as four o'clock in the morning and come back long after six or seven o'clock in the evening, in a desperate effort to augment their husbands' appallingly low wages.

It was against this background that I appealed to the judge to see and understand the life of the Soweto child. When I thought that I read doubt on his face, I supported all that I had said by outlining a very nasty and recent experience that the Orlando Home for Children had had. Thugs had walked into the children's Home at night, ignoring the staff on duty there, and had removed the TV set donated to the Home by some well-wishers. The children, all aged less than twelve years, were left shaken with fright, puzzled and robbed of the best, last and only instrument of joy and entertainment they cherished in their lives. This offence the police, perhaps for reasons beyond their control, failed to investigate to the fullest, and it was left to the staff to discover the stolen TV set, which they brought back, reporting their find to the police.

In his amazement the judge wanted to know whether what I had just related was true. I reminded him that I was giving my evidence under oath. That was sufficient. There was no doubt he was puzzled beyond all understanding, but believed my story, which was true in all respects.

Unfamiliar with court procedure, and accepting my first evidence as final, I was taken aback when the prosecutor took over from the defence advocate, displaying an attitude of impatience and superiority. After reminding me that he had heard that I was a social worker of standing in Soweto with long dealings with youth, he wanted to know if I had any knowledge of Black Consciousness, and what my opinion of it was; further, if I believed in it. A very loaded question by any standard. I was rather disturbed by his arrogant manner, but I felt the need to give him an unflinching and convincing reply. 'Yes, I know something about "Black Consciousness",' I said. I went on to tell the court, interrupted by the prosecutor's retorts and unsettling interjections, that I saw it as a very significant period in the history and life of the black people in South Africa; a stage when they had been compelled to pause, stunned by the overwhelming impact of political events, and assess who they were, where they came from and where they were going. The prosecutor's irritating interjections were undoubtedly affecting my speech and disposition at this stage.

Unexpectedly, the judge, seeing my predicament, I suppose, addressed me by name. I raised my head from the gradual droop it was taking and looked up startled. 'I am the only person in this court you should address yourself to and be conscious of. Be free to express your convictions and beliefs without any inhibition.' I took in the message, resumed my courage and followed his guidance to the letter with confidence. I ended up saying that, to me, Black Consciousness was an institution, a process whereby blacks in South Africa were beginning to take a serious look at themselves against the perilous political plight of a history of close on 350 years, and to find a way of redeeming themselves from that crippling situation. 'This is our dilemma,' I finished. 'I believe in Black Consciousness.'

By now I was very tired, having spent two hours in the witness box, and dry from my non-stop presentation, I appealed to the judge saying, 'My Lord, am I allowed to drink water in your court?' His subtle support and protection from the haughty prosecutor had fully restored my confidence. With a wry smile, he then ordered that I be given a glass of water and let me drink it at my leisure. I recognised a clear and unspoken expression of justice and felt good.

I had hardly taken my seat with the rest of those who had come to court when suddenly someone took me in his arms and crushed me, almost squeezing the very last breath out of me. As I turned to see who this very brave person was, I saw a man who looked beside himself, as if under some strange influence. All he said to me was, 'You are not an ordinary woman, you pleaded like a man, only a man could speak the way you did.' Before I could respond or ask a question, he was kissing me and thanking me. He was one of the parents of the eleven appearing in court that morning. I was just overwhelmed both by the mill I had been through in the witness box and the unexpected response of this parent. I sat huddled in my seat as if nailed to it.

When sentence was passed, four were found guilty including Dan Montsisi, who was sentenced to four years; the other three received shorter sentences. The remaining seven were given a warning and discharged.

Another major challenge to me came in 1978 when some of the community voiced deep fears concerning the effects of a spate of new legislation, and in particular, the Fundraising Act (no. 107 of

1978). This Act prohibited any but recognised church and religious organisations from raising funds without first obtaining a certificate from a 'Director of Fundraising'. Rumour — subsequently confirmed— had it that this law gave the government power to investigate all accounts of such organisations in banks and building societies, and to examine the objectives and intentions of the organisations. The government could take action against any organisation without a fund-raising certificate and freeze their funds, which would then be forfeited. The fear was that this legislation would be used to force the closure of many black self-help organisations.

In the absence of any meaningful social welfare system, such organisations are of vital importance to the survival of the black community, carrying out as they do a variety of programmes and projects geared to maintaining the home and developing the community, as well as providing a basis for a sound community support structure. Any threat to them would be an extremely serious matter.

Working along with staff from the newly formed Legal Resource Centre, we were able to organise a seminar on the nature and likely effects of the new legislation. A large number of community-based organisations sent representatives, and clarification of the issues involved helped them to organise their future activities so as to minimise any possible harm from the new law.

But perhaps my greatest challenge has come with the development of women's self-help groups in Soweto. In 1975, when I was still General Secretary of the YWCA in the Transvaal, some of the very talented women of this organisation started to express their burning desire to go beyond the circles of the YWCA to work as volunteers within the community at all levels. This urge grew more and more, championed by women of the calibre of Bertha Makau who was very proficient with her hands in many fields, and who had perfected some of her skills as an occupational therapist at Coronation Hospital where she had worked for about 20 years.

I remember only too vividly how Bertha came to talk to me in the 1960s and early 1970s on many occasions about her deep-seated desire for volunteer community service. She repeatedly shared her thoughts with me 'Ellen, *Nnake* ('younger sister', a common Setswana intimate expression), please help me to launch a community club for unemployed Soweto women to teach them to use their hands.' And Bertha would stretch out her gentle, seemingly frail hands, saying, 'There is great wealth in these hands, if only people would learn to use them. I have augmented my family income and achieved many things just using these hands. I am dying to share my talents and skills with others who can also become just as skilful and proficient.' This was Bertha's daily wish.

When she was pensioned from the hospital, Bertha did not wait for the women and girls to come to her. No doubt finding too much leisure-time on her hands, she started to share her skills with the young women in her neighbourhood. It was from her efforts that one of the first contemporary self-help women's clubs was born, and run in the home of one of the instructors in Soweto. It was later known as Soweth (Soweto Women's Thrift Club). Maria Hlomuka and Emily Ngwenya worked with Bertha. As their numbers grew, the leaders found premises in the neighbourhood where they all lived, the Chiawelo Centre in Moroka township.

The dream of many years was fulfilled. It gave the members an opportunity to develop skills of their choice, hopefully to end up self-reliant and self-sufficient. This achievement became the talk of the neighbourhood and YWCA circles as a real breakthrough.

When I took up a new job with the School of Social Work at the University of Witwatersrand in May 1976, I lost touch with the club as time did not permit me to visit them as frequently as I wished. Yet at the back of my mind this achievement was a real source of inspiration, indicative of the potential creative power black women possess. I felt that great possibilities could come out of it with proper management and planning.

On my release from detention in March 1978, the talk which engaged the minds of many people in the field of social welfare activities — academics and consumers alike — was the new legislation on fundraising, already mentioned. And it was during the seminar which dealt with this legislation that I made contact with members of other self-help women's groups in Soweto, unknown to me up to that time.

There was Imizamo Yethu (Our Efforts) whose delegates on that occasion included Elizabeth Mpenyane, Florence Kkhasibe and Angeline Hlahane. Then there was Entokozweni Welfare Centre Women's Club at Moletsane, the only group run with the help of social workers working at that Centre. Itekeng Club was represented by Mrs Rose Masombuka, wife of the Methodist Church minister at Jabavu, with other members of that church who were also in charge of the Ikageng Club in Diepkloof. The YWCA and

Chiawelo Centre self-help groups were represented by Bertha Makau and Maria Hlomuka.

It was at that seminar that delegates of all these self-help women's clubs, some established as early as 1973, first met and made meaningful contact. They decided to meet again to formulate a way of working together so as to receive maximum benefit from their common resources of funding, expertise, personpower, accommodation if necessary, and relevant equipment.

That impromptu meeting became the cornerstone of an umbrella-body which brought together some of the self-help groups operating in Soweto. They included the YWCA, the Women's Club which met at the YWCA's Dube Centre, Entokozweni Women's Club with premises at Entokozweni Welfare Centre at Moletsane, Soweto Women's Club in Chiawelo Centre in Moroka, Itekeng and Ikageng, operating under the auspices of the Jabavu Methodist Church and Diepkloof Lutheran Church respectively, and Imizamo Yethu which met in a garage workshop at 1341 Dube Village. These clubs were scattered all over Soweto.

Early in 1979 two delegates from the umbrella-group approached me formally to request me to give my services on a voluntary basis as a consultant. They brushed aside all my 'feeble excuses' and I finally accepted their request. I have remained as such to this day. My acceptance was not a simple matter. Here was a new organisation with very new coordinating responsibilities, for up to six self-help clubs whose purpose and intentions were to improve the lot of the black woman and the black girl who had missed the opportunity of formal or informal education. This condition had left her semi-literate or totally illiterate.

The clubs had all committed themselves to programmes of developing different handicraft skills with emphasis on laying-out, cutting and sewing, knitting, crocheting, hanger-covering, embroidering tray-cloth covers and so on. The sewing and knitting were geared to making school uniforms, particularly gym-slips and jerseys for all school age groups. The materials used were purchased with funds collected from the affiliation fee (10 rand) and by individual clubs, and an extra five rand a year from the clubs' membership fee. The umbrella-body expected to generate funds from the sale of the articles.

It was at my insistence that it was agreed to appoint a book-keeper as treasurer to supervise the accounting of the umbrella-body, and advise the member clubs. We finally agreed on

Mr Ephraim Tshabalala, a social worker and treasurer of SABSWA (the South African Black Social Workers' Association). Much as we had all agreed on principle to having women in every position of importance, it was not possible to find a woman book-keeper at that period. For the period he remained with us, Mr Tshabalala served us without any qualms. He did his work fully and to the best of his ability.

Although the Executive members and general membership had no experience of actual book-keeping, the repeated mention of accounting, and the discipline of bringing a receipt for purchases even if they amounted only to a single cent, left a very healthy and indelible mark on the minds of all participants, and prepared the ground for the future running of their associations. It was during that period that several courses of money management were planned and run for the women's groups. In addition, a group of members came together to carry out on-going studies in money management. That sparked off another interest in the area of investment. Another small group was born out of that study, A re Godiseng Chelete Basadi ('Let us invest money, women'). It has great possibilities for the future. Women have started to visit financial houses like Old Mutual and the Stock Exchange to do on-the-spot investigations. This was unthought of before this programme.

It was against the background of this Council that an unknown white woman walked into my office unannounced with a companion early in 1979. She was on a mission which was undoubtedly foremost in her mind, judging by her whole countenance. As she walked in, I certainly withdrew and, I am sure, sulked too — a defence mechanism I often resort to against the intrusion of white people. They have a tendency to come into an office run by a black person without an appointment or any warning; something they would never accept from us — perhaps from anyone for that matter. My hostile or resentful reaction, however, did not seem to touch her in any way. Her companion, white too, did react to my attitude, but she supported her friend without saying a word. She looked familiar.

I wanted to know who they were, their mission, and why they had come without an appointment. I also pointed out to them my tight schedule, and my desire to know in advance whoever was coming to see me.

To my surprise, my new contact was totally unruffled by my

questions. She moved forward easily, and graciously introduced herself in her deep voice as Elizabeth Wolpert and, turning to her friend, introduced her as Jennifer Kinghorn. Her name rang a bell. I suddenly remembered I had met her for five minutes when she had collected a friend at my home a few days earlier.

Mrs Wolpert explained that she had arrived the day before from London to establish if there was a group of women in Soweto involved in self-help projects for themselves and other women in their community. She went on to say that she had done her homework in the city and in Soweto and everybody had directed her to find Mrs Ellen Kuzwayo, and that was why she was in my office without an appointment. She added that if she was fortunate enough to find what she had come for, she would catch the evening 'plane the next day to return to London.

There I stood, deflated, telling myself, 'Ellen, you could have been gentler with the ladies'. The only amends at my disposal was to adjust with a minimum of apologies and explanation. I did not stop to marvel at the thought of a white woman coming all the way from London to find a group of black women who were struggling to help themselves.

Turning to Mrs Wolpert, I told her that she had come to the right place at the right time, as the women met every Tuesday (this was a Monday) to discuss their plans and administer their programme. I went on to tell her they met in deep Soweto at Entokozweni Welfare Centre, and that it would certainly be difficult for her to find the venue alone. I offered to meet her so we could drive there in convoy; this was my way of making up for my curt manner earlier. But thanking me for the offer, she only pleaded with me to give her the address and the time of the meeting. I warned her that the women were not very well disposed to visitors who came unannounced, but said I would do my best to pave the way for her. At this the two women left.

Afterwards, I examined the way I had received my visitors and was forced to recognise the harm my detention had done to me. I saw the dents it had left on me, the unseen, emotional scars I had suffered, as well as the need to help myself out of that rut: 'So this is what is left of me, Ellen?'

As arranged, Mrs Wolpert arrived about half past nine, after I had cleared the air with the members of the Executive. She walked in gently, cautiously I am sure, still having very fresh memories of the day before. She received a very warm welcome, which made up for the hurt of the previous day, I hope.

After the normal introductions and settling down, I watched our visitor out of the corner of my eye very stealthily, making sure she did not notice my eyes were on her all the time. Throughout the deliberations, she sat quietly, listening to what was said, whilst the members of the group carried on with their transactions undisturbed — not disregarding their unknown guest, but also not being in any way inhibited by her presence. I was the only one caught up in my own personal debate — about my guilt feelings, perhaps, and also about the group interaction and our new contact.

Elizabeth Wolpert did all in her power to conceal her emotions but her flushed cheeks and nose, and her eyes glittering with suppressed tears all betrayed her. This woman with her strong personality kept a brave appearance to the best of her ability, which in itself touched me, as I found it very strange for a white woman to be so moved as to come all the way from England in search of a group of black women.

Before the close of the session, she could not contain herself. In one sentence with a subdued voice she remarked, 'I will return home very happy because I have seen with my eyes what I came to look for'. She expressed her appreciation for the efforts of the women, and without any hesitation she told them how touched she was by their determination, commitment and vision, and in turn made her commitment to contribute 3000 rand to their project from her own pocket. She ended by saying, 'This contribution will be my personal assistance and it has nothing to do with what I have really come about'. That puzzled me all the more. Right through these deliberations I could not miss the unexpressed emotions cutting across the table between our visitor and members of the Council: the excitement, mixed with the unmistakable doubts of the Council members. In my role as stealthy spectator, I ended up feeling very awkward and clumsy as I read the fluctuating mood of surprise, of hope, of disbelief and of excitement. The saving grace in that meeting was the honest and committed manner in which Elizabeth Wolpert handled her presentation, so leaving the women reassured and secure.

As we walked to her car, and when there was no one within earshot, she said gently and softly in her very deep voice, 'Mrs Kuzwayo, my real reason for coming to South Africa is to come and launch a Trust in memory of someone very dear to me, a black woman who nursed me as a child, called Maggie Magaba'. I heard every word she said, but without grasping the entire meaning of that statement. She continued by saying that the Trust she contemplated would be launched in recognition of the black women of South Africa, and it was for that reason that she wanted it to be established and administered by the women of that community.

I pointed out to her that there was just no way that could happen, as this was a very foreign concept to black women who had neither the knowledge nor the skill to run a Trust. She reacted very vehemently by insisting that, like everybody else, the women would have to learn these new skills and take responsibility for the affairs which affected them. 'You realise this is a tremendous responsibility?' I asked her. Perhaps she was unaware of the mammoth task she was contemplating and the inadequate position the black women were in to carry out the task, which would demand expert knowledge in accountancy, administration and a clear understanding of the basic principles and functions of Trusts.

As our discussion developed, it became clear from Elizabeth's speech that the name 'Maggie Magaba' had a very deep personal and emotional meaning for her, and that she was determined to express these feelings in some tangible way; further, that to do so she needed the cooperation of black women. Finally, our discussion reached deadlock, as Betty (as I later got to know her) was adamant that under no circumstances would this Trust be left in the hands of men, be they black or white — or, for that matter, even any women other than black women. She ended her talk by saying, 'The failure of people in the administration of public funds is not peculiar to particular race groups, but is a universal human weakness. Whilst I admit that there are black women who for one reason or another will misuse public funds, I also believe that there are many others who are honest and honourable. It is this group of women I am looking for, women who will be willing to work with me and to learn and who will run this Trust. In fact, Mrs Kuzwayo, I have every reason to believe that you and Mrs Sally Motlana can come together to find other women in your community to launch and run this Trust.'

As I struggled to highlight what in my mind would hinder our progress in this regard, fully convinced that it would be both premature and unwise for us to accept this great responsibility at that stage, Betty turned to me, saying, 'Mrs Kuzwayo, I appeal to you to accept the chairmanship of this Trust, and formally request you to approach Mrs Motlana on my behalf to work with you to find another two competent women in Soweto to sit on this Trust'. Suddenly our discussion had moved from the level of the capability of black women to run a Trust to finding competent women to run that same Trust in Soweto! I ended up promising to approach Sally Motlana, letting her know our reply, and taking it from that point.

Eventually, Sally and I agreed on choosing the two extra trustees from established women's organisations in Soweto. We felt the two women must have shown committed participation in the programme and overall work of their associations. As consultant to the Council of Soweto Women's Self-Help Organisation, Betty had already requested me to represent that group on the Trust, whilst Sally represented the Black Housewives League as its President. We agreed that the National Council of African Women and the YWCA qualified as organisations from which the trustees could be chosen, and agreed on the names of Magdeline Mokgata and Joyce Seroke of those two organisations as appropriate members to serve on the Trust. We informed Betty of the progress we had made.

Before too long, the Maggie Magaba Trust was formally established and its bank account opened with a cheque for R10,000. Briefly, the terms of reference of the Trust were as follows:

To maintain and promote the women's self-help movement in Soweto; to ensure its growth and development.
To give financial assistance to women faced with very challenging situations within their immediate families; situations which make it totally impossible for such women to take regular gainful employment.

This started the very long drawn-out, steadfast implementation of a detailed involvement between Elizabeth Wolpert and all her helpers and colleagues in London on the one side, and the Maggie Magaba Trustees as well as the Executive and general members of the Soweto Women's Self-Help Coordinating Council on the other. Towards the end of 1980, the Council took a new name which gave it a completely new image and character: the Zamani Soweto Sisters Council. (The word 'Zamani' means 'Make an effort'.)

The first significant assignment of the Trust in that year was to send two delegates from the Council to London to observe the involvement of women in community self-help programmes, with the purpose of bringing new ideas into the work of the women in Soweto. Maria Hlomuka and Florence Mkhasibe were chosen as delegates from the Council; Maggie Mokgata accompanied them as a trustee. On their return, the delegates could not wait to share their impressions and experiences with us, some very revealing and others understandably confusing. One of their impressions which hit me, and also brought back the memories of my first trip to London in 1961, was when one of the women shared with us her surprise when she saw white men sweeping the streets of London. My mind at that point drifted back to when I too had walked through London and suddenly saw a row of white men digging a section of the street. I stopped spellbound and listened to the men talking to each other in a kind of English I could hardly understand.

The other delegate told us of the contacts with English women who had become their friends in a way very different from South African friendships over the colour line. She told of one outstanding experience while they were visiting women's workshops to observe how they were run and their training sessions conducted. By chance, they had walked into the Quilters' Guild workshop and had received a very warm welcome and ended up enrolling in the name of Zamani Soweto Sisters Council, as well as paying their enrolment fee as members of the Quilters' Guild, an organisation their hostess, Betty Wolpert, had never heard of.

So they came back home talking about the sisterhood they had established on their first visit overseas. This was the discovery which Florence Mkhasibe, Maria Hlomuka and Magdeline Mokgata brought back home from London to share with those of us who looked forward to the day when our opportunity to be in the overseas delegation would come, and also to those of us who, because we were not granted passports, had to be content with the impressions and experiences of our friends. (For me at that point, obtaining a passport to travel out of the country was a fantasy, a dream, only wishful thinking.)

Florence and Maria, as truly conscientious ambassadors of their association, returned fully equipped to share with their fellow members, as instructors, the skills they had acquired in London. Of the three skills they had observed, silk-screening, Chilean collages and quilting, they concentrated on two, collages and quilting, and excelled in their production. It was very inspiring and very joyful to walk into the workshop to find Zamani Sisters absorbed in their work, each one of them determined to produce the best quilt or the best collage.

The slower ones, or those who joined later, were assigned to do patchwork and to produce cushions, which also demanded skilful techniques, but which were less taxing because they were smaller, easier to handle and quicker to complete: the cushions were used as a preliminary stage to help the trainees command the skills and gain the confidence to produce quilts.

In later weeks it became very clear that Maria's interest and skill in the collages, a technique she learnt from the Chilean Women's Workshop, exceeded that of her fellow delegates. Maria emphasised the importance of their historic aspect as a medium as well as a process of self-expression and healing. Through this technique Maria brought home to all of us the fact that whilst we suffer under the political laws of our country, many people in other parts of the world also suffer, but find in creative work a way whereby they can escape some of the destructive pain.

Side by side with the intensive work coming out of that first 1980 visit to London, was the production of a film, *Awake From Mourning*, by Elizabeth Wolpert. This film was the effort of Betty, Maggie Magaba trustees (Magdeline Mokgata, Joyce Seroke, Sally Motlana, Ellen Kuzwayo the author of this book), and the Zamani Soweto Sisters Council members. At the beginning, the idea of a film seemed far-fetched and very remote from all of us in the Trust and in the Council. We planned and discussed it with Betty and finally accepted it as a very worthwhile project to work on. At that stage, it was nothing more than an idea in the air for some of us. However, there was no doubt that as black women in Soweto, becoming more and more visible as a group and with growing community responsibilities, we soon realised the importance of finding ways of generating funds for the Trust in particular, and for the Council. The film held great hopes for us at that level. The fact that the Maggie Magaba Trust had not been granted a fundraising certificate to appeal for and receive public funds made the need for the film more urgent.

Suffice to say, the release of this film, particularly after going through the Board of Censors, left all of us connected with its production with a deep sense of achievement. Its financial success has often brought home to us the pain of not being able to receive funds as a Trust because of the limitations of not holding a fundraising certificate, but we have not stopped appreciating the publicity it has generated about the work of the Trust and of the Council. Until we met Betty, the thought of making a film never crossed our minds. It has liberated us all the more as black women.

The second overseas visit of the Zamani Soweto Sisters Council came after the Rev. Donald Reeves of St James' Church, Piccadilly, London, had seen the film. He extended an invitation to Zamani and offered his church as a venue for the exhibition of their work in 1982. His invitation generated much excitement and jubilation for all of us.

As well as helping in Zamani's work, the Maggie Magaba Trust supports other activities in Soweto. It pays rent monthly and buys food parcels every three months for nine families in Soweto, where the mothers, for example, are unable to go to work either because the father of the family is bedridden and has no other person to look after him, or where there is no other breadwiner in the family and the woman is an invalid. Of course, these families are a drop in the ocean in a deprived community like Soweto with a population of two million.

It is to be regretted that the Maggie Magaba Trust finds it totally impossible to continue with the project of bursaries to high school and university students because without the required fundraising certificate the Trust is not able to accept public funds.

In October 1982 a further overseas visit, arranged by the Chelsea Craft to which Elizabeth Mpenyana and Florence were delegates, was received with the same enthusiasm. Here we began to observe the relaxed manner in which delegates who had travelled before took their next trip. Except for the normal tensions which go with producing quality work, and other related problems of packing and sending away their work in good time, there was less tension on this trip.

In 1983 Jane and John Moores of Liverpool invited literacy teachers to observe literacy programmes overseas. This was another opportunity which opened new avenues of learning for those teachers and for the organisation as a whole. The Moores had visited Soweto earlier, on Betty's invitation. They made a tremendous impact on Zamani and the Magaba Trust through their warm friendship, and have since committed themselves to helping to raise funds for building a Soweto Women's Centre.

The next exhibition, run by the Balmoral Trust in Scotland, was attended by two new members from Zamani Sisters Council, Renee and Leah, and was a financial success as all products were sold.

The programmes of the Zamani Soweto Sisters Council and the Maggie Magaba Trust have offered some women of Soweto an opportunity to learn new trends of service and community development. Sometimes they have received organised formal training; at other times they have used trial-and-error methods. More often than not they have achieved fruitful and encouraging results.

The film, *Awake From Mourning*, has been a true instrument of communication at many levels within and outside South Africa. Through it we have made contact with groups of other women we had never thought of. One classic example is Die Kaapse Vrouwe Klub, a white Afrikaans women's group operating in Cape Town. They requested to see our film and invited some of us to come and speak with them. It was a very painful experience for some members of that group, who felt challenged at different levels. However, at the end of the day, after sharing on some very delicate issues, we agreed that the film was useful and truthful; further, that we should keep our link as women from two different racial groups who need to work together so as to know one another with less prejudice and suspicion and, hopefully, to explore the possibilities of a better South Africa.

There is no end to the development and growth of black women of this country. The pressing need is for these women to come forward to be involved in this process.

In the name of Zamani Soweto Sisters Council and the Maggie Magaba Trust, I express our deep appreciation for the chain of sisterhood which is gradually growing and expanding in several countries. Your moral and physical support means much to us.

I have no doubt that the new venture Elizabeth Wolpert has embarked on, namely that of creating the Black Women's Charitable Trust in London to enable these women to travel and participate in creative programmes round the world, will have far-reaching effects in the growth and development of black women in South Africa.

The Maggie Magaba Trust pledges itself to do its best within the country to work with Elizabeth Wolpert and her colleagues overseas to make this venture a success. I look forward to the day when the chain of sisterhood shall develop the potential of black women of my country and of other black countries and countries abroad to its maximum, and thus enhance their dignity, integrity, self-reliance and independence both as individuals and as productive members of their community.

16
'Minors' are Heroines

Who are 'Minors'? In the South African context, black women are classified as 'Minors'. They are even 'Minors' compared to their own sons, regardless of the disparity in age. My first experience of this very annoying and humiliating situation was some time in 1969 when I was chosen to represent South Africa at the International Training Institute run by the World Affiliated Young Women's Christian Association in New York.

I applied for a passport for that trip, and among the very first questions put to me at the immigration office was, who my male next of kin was. Without attaching any serious thought to that question, I disclosed that I was a widow, and I had my father and three sons. After establishing that I lived with my sons, the officer, quite unashamed, told me to take the forms he had given me to my oldest son so that he could sign them so giving his approval and permission for me to go overseas. He brushed aside my explanation that my son still lived with me at home, where I was in full control and responsible for everything, insisting that no progress could be made without my son's permission and signature.

In the frustration of having to be given permission by someone who usually needed permission from me, I was annoyed and very angry — but also very helpless, as I needed a passport badly. Having expressed my anger and disgust, I collected the forms and left rather ungraciously.

I shared all that had transpired at the immigration office with Everington, my eldest son. He turned and looked at me, saying, 'I will complete and sign the portion relevant on this form, Mama, not because I am willing to do so, but for you to get your passport. To know that we are here as your responsibility, and that I should turn round and give you permission to go overseas, I find it a shame and an insult.'

Although this particular degrading practice has been abandoned in recent years, many others still flourish.

There is no doubt that black women have faced oppressive social, cultural, economic, political and educational barriers. But they have never surrendered without challenging them. They have not always succeeded, but they have always put up a commendable struggle. Let me support my statement with a few examples.

Black women were scheduled to carry passes like men when this legislation was first introduced in 1913. The women in the Winburg, Kroonstad and Bloemfontein districts put up a very strong resistance under very trying conditions. Many were arrested and sentenced to long terms of imprisonment. They had to spend cold winters in jail and, in some instances, came out as permanent invalids. Their reward was a delay of about 40 years before women were forced to carry such passes. And when this did finally happen in 1955–56, it was done in a very hush-hush manner.

Even then, the women did not give in without a struggle. A huge crowd of black women gathered in front of the Union Buildings in Pretoria to register their protest in the full knowledge of the possibility of imprisonment or detention. Tens of thousands of women had travelled from all over the country. Their resistance was passive; they did not stone anyone or destroy anything. They simply sat down in front of the Union Buildings in their thousands and chanted their slogan: 'Strijdom (the prime minister at that time) you have met the women, you have struck a rock.'

Like mature adults, they sought consultation to explore avenues for negotiation — but in vain.

Some of us, however, were not beaten. I think of Annie Silinga, one of the great political fighters resident in the Cape, who steadfastly refused to carry a pass throughout her life and died in 1983 in her eighties. She was imprisoned many times for her stand, and was denied rights to any pension or welfare benefits. Even when she became crippled and lived in a wheel chair, she still refused the pass. Long Live Annie Silinga.

Earlier in the book I discussed the immense pressures brought to bear on black women as a result of the dispossession of their land and the loss, sometimes temporary, sometimes permanent, of their menfolk to the mines. At that time every duty and office in the family and community became their responsibility. It was a responsibility they carried with great steadfastness and courage. These women, their daughters, and their daughters' daughters have defied the cultural myth that black women are inferior to men and to women of other racial groups.

Take education, for example. From the earliest mission schools, black women were not allowed a free hand to explore the field of education. For too long black parents preferred to educate their boys and openly denied their girls that same opportunity: they kept the daughters at home. If they were allowed schooling, girls were encouraged to do domestic science, a subject which they ended up despising, ridiculing it as preparation for domestic service in white homes. As recently as the late 1930s and mid-1940s, girls were encouraged by teachers and parents alike to substitute science subjects — mathematics, physics and so on, with subjects like geography, physiology and hygiene. Thank God, some of the girls saw through that myth, took the plunge into the sciences and brought the truth and reality of their ability to the surface.

Before the 1940s many black women had graduated as teachers and nurses. But there, it appeared, they had reached their limit. A few of them however, some as teachers, others as nurses, started to become ambassadors into neighbouring provinces within South Africa itself; for example, women from Natal started to teach in the Cape, and vice versa. Others went further afield to explore countries like Northern and Southern Rhodesia (now known as Zambia and Zimbabwe), or moved deeper into Africa, where some of them have made a mark. Yet others, more daring still, got as far as Britain or the United States, the two countries which over the years have had a very strong attraction for the South African black woman. A number of them continued their educational careers there and either remained there or came back home, some with masters, others with doctorate degrees.

But most black women in search of higher education have knocked at the doors of the educational institutions within this country; some earmarked for black only, others established as white institutions. Against great odds they have gained entry and struggled with their studies amidst many problems, including limited funding at university, poor financial support back home and lack of basic adequate attire. All these problems have been exacerbated by relationship problems within and without the family, problems and undertones which may differ in their magnitude and severity from person to person, but which have often had far-reaching effects on the overall well-being of the people concerned. You have to be black, and live in this age, to understand the extent and weight of such problems.

In the beginning most black students graduated as Bachelors of Arts and the majority of them became teachers. In the mid-1940s the first group of black women doctors emerged. This was received with great excitement by the black community and in particular by other women who saw this achievement as proof of the fact that black women are equal and the same as any human being regardless of race or sex. The large numbers that followed and are still following have confirmed that.

Black women's educational progress has gathered momentum since then. Many have explored the fields of medicine, law, economics, commerce, administration, human and social sciences and others.

These are the achievements of black women today, who over several generations have been condemned as unproductive, unintelligent, incapable to the point of being seen as male property, whether they be single or married, and finally being categorised as 'Minors'. Through their own efforts and achievements they have pulled themselves up by their own bootlaces and have proved beyond all shadow of doubt that, after all is said and done, '*Minors' are heroines.*

At the end of this book I list some of these women and their achievements.

How can I begin to convey the suffering endured by so many black women — and the courage with which this suffering has been borne?

Let me share with you a little of the lives of four women, two of them world renowned, one famous within South Africa, and one famous only in her community, and to family and friends. I shall take the last first.

Mrs Nthaelone Manthata was born at Soekmekaar in the Northern Transvaal about 80 years ago. She is today known as Mma bo Matsepa, a name she received after the birth of her first son. She came from, and lives still in, a rural black community.

Her second son, Madikoe Thomas, born in 1938 or 1939, qualified as a teacher before enrolling at a college of higher education. Having lived in Saulspoort with my sons, and being related to them on their father's side, Tom came to live with us in Johannesburg when he decided to try his luck in the city. He soon joined the Soweto youth groups and, later, the University Christian Movement. After working for a time as a teacher, Tom was elected Vice-President of the South African Students Organisation, an important black political grouping which I have described in Chapter 3.

In 1974 he took a job with the South African Council of Churches; here issues of great social concern were brought directly before him. That same year, in November, he was detained under Section 6 of the Terrorism Act and placed in solitary confinement for seven months. As his guardian, I did all I could to persuade the prison authorities at John Vorster Square to allow me to see him or, at least, to tell me his state of health — but all in vain. Only his mother would be permitted to visit him.

The months passed and we began to hear very disturbing reports about his condition. My friend Jane Oshadi Phakathi, now a self-exiled South African living in Holland, and then a field work organiser of the Christian Institute, and I joined forces and went to the Northern Transvaal to fetch Thomas's mother so that she could visit him and give him her moral support.

It was under these circumstances that Mrs Manthata, a mother who had lived all her days in the country, a simple rural woman, yet very strong and dignified, found herself compelled to travel to Johannesburg, about 400 miles away, to face one of the most challenging situations possible. She had to see her son, if only to establish his safety and well-being. All we women in Johannesburg, who had the welfare of Thomas at heart, were completely helpless and impotent. We looked to Mrs Manthata to do one of the most difficult duties that could be expected of any parent, especially a mother.

I was very impressed by her readiness and willingness to carry out such a sensitive role with such courage. She was weeding her fields when we arrived, but within an hour she was ready to leave. She only allowed herself enough time to refresh herself and pack a few belongings, a lonely smile playing on her sad, questioning face as she geared herself for a journey of uncertainty and fear. Our reason for coming did not harass her. All she said when she realised why we had come was, 'You have come to fetch me to go and see Madikoe? I am willing and ready.' There was no self-pity or shedding of tears.

On our arrival at my home in Soweto I offered Mrs Manthata tea, but she made it quite clear that all she wanted was a glass of plain water. She agreed to take a dish of *bosoa* (a simple, traditional food) with a little meat, but no vegetables other than spinach — and certainly no rice.

For the duration of her stay we shared my bedroom. This arrangement was deliberate as it allowed me to keep an eye on her because, composed and calm as she appeared to be, any observant and sensitive person could see that this was only a front. Naturally, she was very disturbed about the unknown. This surfaced through her gestures, or through her involuntary sighs of 'Oh Madikoe!' Her visits to Thomas must have been distressing for he had been badly beaten — indeed, his eyesight has never fully recovered.

The first three or four nights were especially hard to take. They were charged with great sorrow, despair and uncertainty about the future and in particular about the behaviour of the police in charge of Thomas. This worry was something we were both aware of but were too upset to face openly and discuss. However, during her fortnight's stay, we shared our daily prayers, and it was at this time that we came near to expressing our concern in the pleas and supplications of our prayers which were our refuge, and a great source of strength and support.

Mrs Manthata came to stay with me on another occasion, again to visit Thomas, and her visits helped me understand the hurt, fear, doubt and sadness of a mother in this predicament. I was often awakened during the night by her soft sobs and murmurings which came unbidden, and were from my observation uncontrollable. I tried very hard not to respond to her sorrow in the same way, but it was very difficult not to share her tears.

The second life I shall describe is a more famous one — that of Albertina Sisulu, whose husband, Walter Max Sisulu, as General Secretary of the African National Congress, was sentenced in 1964 to life imprisonment under the Suppression of Communism Act. Those of us who knew Albertina Sisulu in the 1940s never thought that some day we would see and experience the Albertina of the 1960s, 1970s and 1980s. I knew her then as the smiling and pleasant wife of Walter Sisulu, a kind hostess who served the committee members of the Congress with tea after long and intense meetings. Who would have thought then that in 1983 we would be talking about her as someone who had endured the longest banning order, amounting to 17 years? When interviewed after the banning order was lifted, she remarked, 'If it has been lifted, I am happy because I will be able to continue my work.' And by 'work' she meant her political work.

Her active political life started in 1958 when she was arrested after having led a crowd of black women who destroyed their passes outside the Market Square Offices in Johannesburg. This was followed by her detention in 1963 when, on release from prison, she made a powerful speech in Sophiatown.

The sentence of life imprisonment on her husband in 1964 left Albertina, now the sole breadwinner for the family, even more concerned to work towards changing the political situation of black people in South Africa. In one interview, when asked if she was bitter about her husband's sentence, she gave a forthright reply: 'How could I not be bitter, after being left alone with five children and no food?' With a full-time job as a nurse with the City Health Department (where she has worked for the last 36 years), Albertina has set herself specific tasks in the national struggle. She campaigns for better education for black people; she champions the cause of the abolition of passes for black women; she encourages people in her community to fight the existence of the state-run beer halls.

Her family has a history of its own through each member's involvement in the struggle for liberation. I have no space to describe this history here; sufficient to quote Albertina herself when she remarked to one journalist, 'Jail is what we are used to here at home.'

The amazing thing about this mother who carries so many burdens is that her face is always very peaceful, relaxed. You need to see her to believe it. How she manages this is indeed a great mystery to me.

I have already described, in Chapter 12, how I first met Winifred Nomzamo as a fellow student at the Jan Hofmeyr School of Social Work in Johannesburg. When she qualified, she became the first black medical social worker in South Africa, based at Baragwanath Hospital. In 1957 she met Nelson Mandela, one of the accused in the long Treason Trial that had begun in 1956. To what extent the subsequent marriage influenced her move from social work practice to social change involvement, I do not know.

Nelson Mandela's eventual discharge when the trial ended in 1961 gave the family an opportunity to enjoy a normal life, although this state of affairs was short-lived. In 1962, when he was campaign organiser of the (then underground) African National Congress, Nelson was captured and sentenced to five years' hard labour. In 1964 he was sentenced after the Rivonia Trial to life imprisonment. He was sent to Robben Island where he remained until 1982. He is now in Pollsmoor Prison in the Cape. In the years between 1962 and 1975 Nomzamo served a banning order.

Since 1962 then, Winnie Mandela has been a grass-widow, unable to hold any job for more than two months because of the restrictions of her banning order; who nevertheless has had to find some means of livelihood in order to care for her two 'fatherless' daughters as well as meet the commitments of daily living. From May 1969 to September 1971 she was detained in solitary confinement under Section 6 of the Terrorism Act. No wonder she has ended up with heart ailments.

She was imprisoned again in 1976, and was once again banned on her release in January 1977, this time to Brandfort, a small semi-rural town in the Orange Free State — a predominantly Afrikaner province in the 'Deep South' of South Africa. For five years now, Nomzamo has been in Brandfort. When I saw her by chance in 1982, I was gladly surprised and impressed by her very pleasant disposition, her calmness and complete composure. Her charm, her singing laughter, her unchanging face and her ever-present dignity are those of the Winnie Nomzamo of the 1950s when I first met her.

Those who see her often confirm that she still practises her profession in this community. Her small home, I learn, radiates hope for the deprived of Brandfort. It is used as a relief half-way house for the hungry and destitute; a soothing, healing place for the sick; and a place of light and learning for the ignorant. Her vegetable gardens are said to be a model for the whole township of Brandfort, in her effort to arrest the high rate of malnutrition. A woman who teaches by action and example.

Long live Winnie Nomzamo Mandela, Ntombi Ka Madikizela. May God give you the strength and courage to go through this ordeal of banishment.

In Chapter 10 I described a little of my friendship with Dr Mary Susan Malahlela Xakana, the first black woman doctor in South Africa.

Mary was born in 1916 in Roodepoort, the daughter of a schoolteacher. She received her preliminary university education at Fort Hare and graduated at the University of the Witwatersrand as a medical doctor in 1947. Mary Xakana challenged and destroyed the fallacy that science subjects were out of reach for black women.

As a GP, she practised in Kliptown, Johannesburg, where she first lived following her marriage in 1948. Her two daughters, Vuyelwa and Linda, were born there. Later, because of the Group Areas Act, they were forced to move to Dobsonville, a township adjacent to Soweto but within the jurisdiction of Roodepoort. Her practice flourished and she served both Dobsonville and Soweto, where she became affectionately known as Dr Mary by both young and old in these communities.

During the last few years of her life, she concentrated on TB patients because, in her own words, there is 'much suffering from poverty and ignorance particularly in the lower income section of the community'. This resulted in her taking an active part in the Santa Care Group at local and national level. Santa — the South African National Tuberculosis Association — Care Group organises units to serve on a voluntary basis in their immediate neighbourhood to identify TB cases and ensure their regular clinic visits for treatment. They also provided these patients with the extra nutritious foods they needed to supplement their inadequate diets to aid their recovery.

After the 1976 troubles, some of the whites in this organisation who had been active participants stopped working in the black township. Dr Mary commented, 'I then made it my duty to revive these contacts by going into the city to collect donations in cash and kind to be distributed to the needy cases in the TB section of the Dobsonville clinic. This programme gives me great satisfaction.'

In addition to her responsibilities as a doctor, mother, volunteer and housewife, she decided to give some of her leisure-time to one of the active women's organisations in South Africa, the YWCA of the Transvaal. She and other women in her district started the YWCA Dobsonville club and she was chosen President of that branch. It was during this time that the local authority or possibly the police in Dobsonville sent a uniformed policeman to all the YWCA meetings. Nowhere else in the Transvaal, or for that matter in South Africa, did we in the YWCA have such disturbing, unnecessary and degrading treatment. To this day, I still wish to know whether their motive was to persecute Dr Xakana as an individual, whether they were out to disrupt that particular club, or whether they wanted to destroy the morale and spirit of the Association as a whole. Dr Mary was unshaken by these persistent police visits. The meetings went on at her house. Finally she was summoned to court about her YWCA work. She went and she was not found guilty. We never grasped the meaning of her charge.

This was Mary; an unassuming, relatively quiet person with a pleasant face, but very determined and unflinching when the occasion demanded. She was a committed member of her community in an extraordinary way, in that she held office both as a medical practitioner and as a volunteer in community work; indeed a rare combination of duties.

You have served your nation and country. Go to rest in peace, Daughter of Africa. You have left us an example of womanhood with vision and determination.

Mary Susan Xakana inspired many black women who followed in her footsteps in the medical field from 1947–1982 at the only two university medical schools in South Africa which then accepted black students. During those 36 years, and working against insupportable odds, black women have qualified as doctors and have gone out to serve the most deprived communities riddled with serious social diseases, some of them highly infectious.

Mamazana Desiree Mkhele, born Finca, set a similar standard when she became the first black woman to qualify as a lawyer in South Africa in 1967. She opened a way for other black women who today practise as lawyers in different parts of South Africa to help the alarming numbers of black people who are arrested for both petty and serious crimes, and risk being convicted undefended. Like Dr Mary, Mamazana Mkhele disproves the myth that medicine and the law are the exclusive domain of men and white women.

Other black women are gaining recognition for their people at international level. The impact Brigalia Hlope Bam made in her job at the Women's Desk of the World Council of Churches in Switzerland, for instance, is an inspiration for all of us, and we are also awaiting with keen interest the outcome of Oshadi Jane Mangena's work for her Master's degree at the University of Utrecht in Holland, on the economic and political struggle in South Africa.

In Liverpool in October 1984 I met Ntombenhle Protasia Torkington, born Mayeza, yet another reminder of the commitment of black women outside South Africa. She is registered with the University of Liverpool to read for a Ph.D. in Sociology, and is actively involved with a local campaign for social and economic change – the Merseyside Area Profile Group.

Marcia Pumla Denalane, born Finca, a social worker specialising in mental health, left South Africa in the '60s and settled in New York. She continued her studies in mental health, obtained a Master's degree, and is at present reading for a doctorate.

These women represent only the tip of an iceberg. I am horrified to think of the brain drain, of the black women alone, my country has suffered. These are the women who have been branded as 'Minors' by their country! They have modelled a life style for future generations.

Long live the spirit of those unsung heroines!

17
The Church and the Black Woman

The Christian Churches have played an immensely important part in the life of the black community in South Africa — in particular, in the lives of the women of that community. There are, of course, two sides to this coin. Let me look at the bright side first.

The Churches have been a vehicle for progress, growth and development for all black women educated before the mid–1950s: this is the age group who could not have escaped church or mission schools, the first and only institutions which brought education to the doorstep of the black urban and rural communities in South Africa from the late nineteenth to the mid-twentieth centuries.

This was the time in the history of the black people of this country when the different schools catered for a particular denomination within a community, with a few exceptions here and there. This was most pronounced in the boarding schools. Examples include Healdtown Institution which was Methodist, Lovedale Institution, its neighbour in the Cape, which was run under the auspices of the Church of Scotland Missionary Society, and St Francis' College at Mariannhill, Natal, which was a Roman Catholic school. These three churches had several other boarding schools throughout South Africa providing education for the black population during the era of the Native Education system which came to an abrupt end in 1953 when the Nationalist government took over black education. This government replaced the Native Education run by the various provincial departments with the inferior and detested Bantu Education, designed to reduce black people to the status of perpetual servants to the white people in this country.

I remember with disgust some of the popular insults from the Afrikaner community which were hurled at blacks who had a reasonable command of the English language. They were ridiculed as pretending to be 'swart englemane', ('black englishmen'). Those insults may sound remote today, but they were very real in those years. Some of the inhumanities suffered by South African blacks, yesterday and today, need to be experienced to be understood in their entirety.

Several black women in this country went abroad for the first time sponsored by their church or by a group, organisation or individual linked with the church within or without the country. Similarly, teachers, nurses, pastors, interpreters and businessmen received their preliminary education from one mission school or another.

As I described in the previous chapter, many black parents refused to see the education of their daughters as a worthwhile proposition. Those who did so took advantage of the education offered by the mission schools. Girls did not only benefit from the A,B,C and 1,2,3 lessons but also received a strict ethical training based on Christian principles and values — some too high for human achievement or expectations. These were the required standard in those years, and they were drummed into us by those in authority. Despite our shortcomings — and they were many — we believed these standards as the gospel truth, all the same.

It it that early group of black girls, trained mainly as teachers and nurses, who laid a foundation for the remarkable achievements of black women witnessed today. There is no doubt that mission schools played a very important role in preparing black women to develop the confidence to stand side by side with men in the classroom and finally enter higher education to explore new educational avenues.

In addition many African myths and superstitions were challenged — and sometimes dismissed as unreal — through formal education. The Christian doctrine taught in church produced women of character and high moral values. These characteristics can still be traced in the community to this day in those women who went to mission schools and were exposed to that type of teaching and influence. Medical practice, through the mission hospitals serving the black people, reduced some of the fears related to diseases and conditions which previously were explained as the wrath of the gods and ancestors. Some women were freed from the suffering of child-bearing. All in all, education through these mission schools came as a physical, psychological and emotional liberation to black women as they began to discover their potential and identity, even if to a very small degree.

The slogan of the Afrikaner over the years has been, and still is,

'*Sit die kaffir in sy plek*' ('Put the kaffir (black) in his place'). The Nationalist government institutionalised this by destroying the educational foundation laid by the missionaries. They seized Lovedale, Healdtown, Adams College, Khaiso and reduced them to nothing. When I passed Lovedale some ten years ago, I stopped, gazed at that former fountain of knowledge, progress and Christian values, and wept.

But then, as I said, there is the other side of the coin. One lamentable aspect of the Christian Churches is the reluctance of all denominations to allow women a free hand in training as ordained pastors, priests or ministers. And then, too, black people have always been critical of a segregated system of education designed for them by their colonists. This was true even during the Native Education era, for this system was different from — and thus deemed inferior to — the system of National Education for the ruling white race. However, the subsequent Bantu Education system was so shockingly inferior that compared to Native Education it is like porridge to cow-dung. Indeed, it brought home to me the meaning of the old proverb 'You never miss the water till the well runs dry'. Nothing could be closer to the truth.

Then again, it is truly to be regretted that the white missionaries disregarded or belittled many of the customs and traditional practices of the black community when they brought the Gospel to South Africa. For reasons best known to themselves they judged the attire, music, folklore and homes of black people as heathen and primitive. They made no effort to learn, or even try to understand, some of their rituals, their idioms, their culture in general, even if to approve of some and disapprove of others. To dismiss the whole culture of a people as primitive, and contrary to decent religions and cultural beliefs is traumatic and very detrimental for those people. I want to believe that in the long run it is also detrimental to those who militate against it.

The way of life of the black people embodied their religion. All black communities in South Africa to this day have a name for the figurehead which towers over all creation, life and mankind. This they always had, long before the arrival of the missionaries in the country. But in the black community the Creator had no particular, defined institution like the Church in the West. He was part of every institution of the community: in the home and outside the home, in work, in birth and marriage and death.

Their language was enriched by idioms, and each ethnic group laid down guidelines for daily interpersonal dealings and behaviour. Initiation schools set the standards and values of the community and had a strong influence on the appearance and behaviour of people of all ages.

When the missionaries made the initiation schools targets for ridicule and derision, they were attacking an important aspect of the cultural and religious life of the people. In the course of time, the attitudes of the missionaries succeeded in dividing the so-called Christian black people and their non-Christian sisters and brothers who were always regarded as heathens and therefore evil. The loss of status for the initiation schools also meant that moral standards were seriously disrupted, for it was through these schools that guidelines on sexual behaviour were imparted to young people.

In that community the Creator did not punish, but rather He demanded certain standards of behaviour and way of life. Going to hell or burning in purgatory are concepts which came with the modern Christian teachings. These concepts ran counter to traditional religious understandings. The religion of the black community challenged your actions, unlike the modern way of Christian teachings which, in a very subtle way, encourages an attitude of erring as much as possible whilst taking care that your errors are not exposed.

Another cultural tradition which was debased was *lobola* or *bogadi*. This is an agreement between a couple entering into marriage. It is a practice very similar and related to the dowry in Western societies. The difference is that in the former it is the groom and his family who make a presentation to the bride's family. In the past it was made in the form of cattle, but changed to cash payment when the black people lost ownership of individual or communal land.

For reasons beyond all understanding, the dowry has always enjoyed acceptance and even some esteem; whilst in general, *lobola* receives ridicule and spite from other race groups, as well as from the black community itself. In its purest form at the beginning of this century, *lobola* or *bogadi* was still regarded as a token of goodwill between the two parties, a way of raising the esteem of the bride in her new home. In some black tribal communities, it was customary, where *lobola* was given in the form of cattle, to give back a cow, which was to be milked for the offspring of the marriage when they came to visit their mother's home. The wife in that setting, even if her husband was a polygamist, and particularly when she was the principal wife, enjoyed recognition and prestige as such. She was respected and given her place in the family. I never in my life as a child in the country, heard anyone refer to a wife as 'bought property'.

Over the years however *lobola* has degenerated into a commercial transaction. Husbands tell their wives that they are a purchased commodity to be used (abused) as such. This unsavoury outlook, I believe, is the result of the disintegration of the family structure of the black people. Formerly, marriage in this community was the concern and involvement of the whole family; no young man carried the responsibility of paying his *lobola* as an individual. A young husband could remark: *'Pulane Ke mosadi oa Khomo tsa Ntate, Ke Mma bana ba Ka'* ('Pulane [the wife's name] is the wife of my father's herd of cattle, and a mother of my children'). This was a positive statement. It implied respect and recognition for the young wife.

As in every society, regardless of race, religion or class, some men had affairs outside their homes, but these were kept away from the family, especially from his wife. African men in rural communities had great respect and regard for their wives, a situation which has deteriorated in urban areas where sophistication and materialism have become the pivot around which family life rotates. The values, mores and standards of old, built on the extended family unit, have been discarded as antiquated by young and sometimes old couples.

In the rural community in which I was brought up, I witnessed the principles and values upheld by rural women who emerged from the so-called 'heathen' and 'backward' traditional setting. These women had accepted the Christian Gospel and were grappling with the transitional problems of the two over-lapping cultures. Such problems were aggravated by the missionaries' rejection of the way of life of the black people, a rejection which caused and promoted undesirable conflict for those new converts at the beginning of this century.

The tensions and undertones of those conflicts struck at the very roots of the moral fibre of the traditional black community, crippling the social and cultural institutions of initiation schools, folk-lore, music, dance, attire, ancestral beliefs, customary union marriages, funeral rites. All these were dealt a final blow by the colonial legislation of the notorious Native Land Act of 1913.

The new regime distorted the image of the Christian missionaries and as a result has had a very detrimental effect on the overall development of the Church in South Africa. Black people have seen the Church as being only passively involved in a community plagued by poverty, deprivation, denial of education and work opportunities, freedom of movement and political and economic rights. The Church's seeming indifference to these problems over a long period has been interpreted as connivance with the government — or, at least, as fear of taking a stand against it. This has meant that young people in particular are reluctant not only to take part in the affairs of the Church but even to accept Church membership.

It is difficult not to feel that in their approach to converting the black people of South Africa, the missionaries threw out the baby with the bathwater. I think of a revelation I had in 1955 when I was posted to the Transkei as a final-year student in social work. I worked at Ncora Social Welfare Centre, situated in a rural area.

In those years typical traditional rural communities existed round the Ncora Centre. You could often hear the singing of boys and girls in the middle of the night. For the three months I was there, I listened to that singing with interest and enjoyment, and later became interested in the young people who participated in it.

The girls were between the ages of 15 and 19 or 20, and the boys were of the same age group or slightly older. My critical inspection of those girls from a distance said a great deal to me. I could not stop marvelling at their very fit and healthy appearance. It was there for all to see and could not be missed in any way. I remarked on this to my colleagues who confirmed my observation and added that the community had a very organised form of sex education for young people which was strictly adhered to and practised by the youth of that community. Not one of the girls in that village had an illegitimate child.

In my capacity as a senior student I approached several mothers to find out from them the full content of this sex education for their children. All mothers in that community were illiterate, or so they appeared. They were typical traditional rural mothers in dress, manner and speech. They first ignored my questions — I suppose to save me embarrassment and disappointment. In my own way, I insisted on knowing about their 'secret weapon' in this very sensitive area. In desperation — I wish to believe — one of the mothers looked me straight in the eyes and said in Xhosa, 'You chose to follow Christianity. Leave us alone with our traditional custom.' I never attempted to find out from anyone else in that community about their sex education. All the same, I got the message straight and simple.

We shall never know the difference it would have made if the missionaries had worked with the black people in a way which combined teaching with learning. And we cannot go back to make good the evils endured by the disregard of the culture of a people. But we can say that we have learned something for the future. Who knows, black people may be called upon in some unforeeseable future to play a very meaningful role in the re-shaping of events in the history of world. What does this say to us now?

18
Nkosi Sikelel' i Afrika
God Bless Africa

Today, 22 October 1984, I am once more in London, completing this final chapter and watching on television 7,000 police and military in a dawn raid surround and seal off the township of Sebokeng. Sebokeng has a population of 180,000 and has been the scene of massive student protest in the past few months, during which many young lives have been taken. The police and military are marching through the streets in full battledress, in platoons, with rifles at the ready. Hundreds of military lorries filled with more soldiers surround the township. 18,000 homes are being searched for 'terrorists and agitators'. It is as though a state of war has been declared against the entire black population. A massive demonstration of the mighty armed strength of the regime, against a defenceless, unarmed people. A show to create terror! The *Guardian* described this action as 'the indiscriminate lashing out of an enraged, blinded cyclops'. And the London *Times* commented 'It would have been suicide for any of the people to resist at this time'.

But does this mean an end to struggle? Looking back over the history of my people's resistance through this century, I know it cannot be. Here are but a few of the campaigns black women have been through:

The 1913 Orange Free State Women's Anti-Pass Campaign, against the proposed extension of the pass system to women. They staved off the carrying of passes by women for more than 40 years. All the women who ran that campaign have died nameless and faceless.
The 1956 Anti-Pass Campaign culminating in a silent demonstration by 50,000 women from all over the country at the Union Building, Pretoria. They were contemptuously ignored by the government.

The Defiance of Unjust Laws Campaign of 1952, in which women participated and served prison sentences, side by side with their men.

The 1960 Sharpeville Massacre, where once more women were killed and wounded with the menfolk.

The 1976 uprising, in which young girls participated equally with young boys; and through which thousands of mothers suffered the disappearance, detention and death of their children, some of them as young as twelve years old.

The physical activities of a people can be temporarily contained, but the spirit behind that movement lives on forever. That alone, if nothing else, should be an inspiration for the black women. If we needed to be convinced again, two days after the massive display of military force by the authorities in October 1984, the children of Sebokeng again went into the streets in protest.

British television revealed the faces of the women of Sebokeng while their homes were being searched by the police, and the dignified, composed way they moved from room to room at the order of the armed officials on that fateful 23 October 1984. They shed no tears, showed no panic. They survived the ordeal.

When I look back over the history of women in South Africa as I have told it in this book and over the changes that have taken place in my own lifetime, I find myself amazed all over again, first by the extraordinary disabilities under which the women of my country have had to struggle, and then by the spirit with which so many of the challenges have been overcome.

These are the same women who over the past century have been compelled to remain home in the rural areas, penniless, faced with severe droughts, to mind the young and elderly, to till the land and raise flocks, as well as administer the neighbourhood and larger communities.

Gradually some of these very women decided to defy tradition and dare the cities, going first in search of their husbands, fathers, brothers, sons, then becoming trapped in the urban economy. They were forced to accept domestic work and menial earnings.

Today women from rural areas come to the cities as migrant labourers like the men, on permits granted by their relevant 'homeland governments'. These women have to have their 'homeland' passports or reference (identity) books endorsed monthly by government officials. You can see them in long queues at the beginning of every month at the segregated women's influx control office. These women are forced by poverty to leave the rural areas, and today they take jobs as road diggers or newspaper vendors as well as domestic servants.

New generations of black women have also brought about unprecedented transformation in the old loathed stereotype of the domestic servant. During the 1960s a kind of 'trade union' called the Domestic Workers Employer Programme (DWEP) was established. Leah Tutu (her husband, Bishop Tutu, won the Nobel Peace Prize in 1984. Leah deserves a good share of it) is Director of this movement. In this programme, run mostly from church halls in Johannesburg, Durban, Capetown and elsewhere, domestic workers are being trained in new skills such as fine sewing, cookery, literacy, money handling, car driving, first aid and other skills. The women of this movement are also fighting for living wages, paid annual leave, pension schemes, all of which have been denied to them in the past by their white employers.

Indeed, the determination and fortitude of black women pushes them to try their hand at everything. Now that the era of the computer is with us black women have joined such of the training programmes as are open to them and became competent in handling keyboards and punch card machines.

So began a slow but steadfast growth in the number of black women cashiers in the large department stores in the city centres of South Africa. Today most of these stores employ predominantly black women. Whilst these women have arrived there on their own steam and thanks to their unquestioned efficiency, it is equally true that they save these white establishments thousands of rands, as their wages are far below those of their white counterparts.

Many black women are also tellers in different banks in the country, particularly those established in Soweto and other black townships in industrialised South Africa, and in the so-called 'homelands'. Building societies also employ a few black women, as tellers and in other skilled jobs.

A good number of black women are prominent in large industrial and commercial firms in cities and towns, at secretarial level, as personal secretaries, typists and receptionists. These numbers are not growing fast, as there are no properly run schools for such training.

Today as I look around me, I see that black women have broken into a whole range of new occupations; that they expect a great deal in their lives, such that young women of fifty years ago never dreamed of; and welcome their ambition as a very exciting, and overdue development.

But this dynamic process among black women, revolutionary as it is, brings with it its own complications. New achievements in employment for women brings women a new kind of equality with their menfolk, at work, at home and in the community. This situation has become a threat to some men.

The changing role of the urban black woman as she makes an increasing contribution towards the family income, even brings in more money than the husband, has added to the problems of family relationships. This factor hits at the root of the traditional acceptance of the man as the head of the family, and is made more complex by the cultural dimension in the black community where the man has always been accorded a special authority as father and master, with his word the last in family decisions. Women are now taking a very firm stand against such behaviour in their husbands, who often still expect their wives to accept in silence some of their most unacceptable practices. The men may completely refuse to listen to and reason with the women, even in matters very crucial to the existence of family life.

When such feelings of threat surface they can have serious effects between spouses. These may be so serious that the marriage survives only within a very unhealthy climate, for the spouses and their children alike, while in others it may even end in the divorce courts. The divorce rates in Soweto and other similar black urban townships have risen in recent years (though there are many reasons for this, besides male resistance to the liberation of women!).

So in addition to the growing number of single women with children who for one reason or another have never been married, we also have growing numbers of divorced women in our community. They have at last won the right to own their homes in recent years: a major victory for black women.

Taking into consideration that the rate of illiteracy of the whole population is very high and that for generations black girls have had extra problems in entering schools the rate of illiteracy among women must therefore be higher than that among men. This fact makes the educational achievements of those women who have managed to excel all the more admirable. But it also underlines the need for more education, even at primary school level, for girls.

This is a responsibility black women have made their own. For more than forty years our women have worked collectively, through small and large organisations, to improve educational and social facilities, for deprived urban communities in particular. Many of these organisations have already been mentioned in this book. But there are many others.

Orlando Mothers' Welfare Association, established in the early thirties, was the brain-child of Mabel Ngakane, who was concerned about the growth of truancy and juvenile delinquency in the young Orlando of those years, the first township of Soweto. Among the issues she raised with the Non-European Affairs Department was the lack of recreational facilities – playgrounds and community centres) and the dearth of toilets in the centre city for black women. It is striking that fifty years later there is very little improvement!

I remember too, how at the close of the 1940s and beginning of the 1950s black women in Soweto formed groups known as 'Service Committees' to raise funds and equipment to build neighbourhood creches to serve as day care centres for the children of working mothers. There are now about forty to fifty of these. These are far too few to meet the demands of the population of two million people, but the government of South Africa has never valued black children, and never offered any assistance for building more of these.

These organisations and several others mentioned earlier in this book sent representatives to an historic meeting held in Johannesburg on 17 March 1984. It was attended by about 250 women representing at least 50,000 members of various organisations, and unanimously resolved to established a 'Black Consumer Union'. The delegates referred to the great economic buying power of the millions of black people in South Africa who make up 75 percent of the population.

The black women in South Africa have shown outstanding tenacity against great odds. We shall never give in to defeat. Today we remain determined, like the women of our community of previous generations, who have left us a living example of strength and integrity.

Even now, at the age of 70 years, I tremble for what the future has in store for my grandchildren and those of their age group if things continue in the state in which they are at present. I am all the more determined to join the struggle, and fight with all the means I have at my disposal for change in my country so that the coming generations can enjoy a better life in their ancestor's country.

The commitment of the women of my community is my commitment – to stand side by side with our menfolk and our children in this long struggle to liberate ourselves and to bring about *peace* and *justice* for all in a country we love so deeply.

The old Setswana proverb has come alive with a fresh meaning for me at this point:

Mmangoana o tshwara thipa ka fa bogaleng

It means:

'The child's mother grabs the sharp end of the knife'.

Nkosi Sikelel' i Afrika
God Bless Africa.

South African Black Women Medical Doctors Qualified 1947–1981

Dr M.S. Xakana (Late)	University of Witwatersrand	1947
Dr H.N.L.N. Mahabane (Late)	University of Witwatersrand	1949
Dr O.B.Z. Bikitsha	University of Witwatersrand	1949
Dr M.M. Chuene	University of Witwatersrand	1951
Dr H.N. Jezile	University of Witwatersrand	1955
Dr R. Tsele	University of Witwatersrand	1955
Dr N.N. Mashalaba	University of Witwatersrand	1956
Dr A.P.M. Masibi–Langa	University of Witwatersrand	1956
Dr R.D. Shuping	University of Witwatersrand	1958
Dr M.S. Mbambo (Late)	University of Natal	1958
Dr L. Piliso	University of Natal	1958
Dr V.W.N. Matebese	University of Natal	1959
Dr L.H. Ngobese	University of Witwatersrand	1959
Dr S.J. Mjali	University of Witwatersrand	1960
Dr A.N. Luthili	University of Natal	1960
Dr C.A. Hlatshwayo	University of Natal	1960
Dr V.N. Mjombozi (Late)	University of Natal	1960
Dr M.N. Mlotjwa	University of Natal	1960
Dr P.P.N. Noah	University of Natal	1961
Dr E. Blakie	University of Witwatersrand	1961
Dr L.B. Dibe	University of Natal	1962
Dr N.M.E. Malake	University of Natal	1963
Dr E.N. Ngwane	University of Natal	1964
Dr M.N.B. Magwai	University of Natal	1965
Dr A.T. Ntlabati	University of Natal	1966
Dr L.F. Matthews	University of Natal	1966
Dr C.A.M. Phakisi	University of Natal	1967
Dr L.N Magazi (Late)	University of Natal	1968
Dr H.N. Nhantsi	University of Natal	1970
Dr E.C.N. Mabuya	University of Natal	1970
Dr I.F.N.E. Manana	University of Natal	1970
Dr P.K. Dlamini	University of Witwatersrand	1970
Dr V. Hina	University of Natal	1972

Dr M.A. Ramphele	University of Natal	1972
Dr T.N. Mkula	University of Natal	1973
Dr L. Shongwe	University of Natal	1973
Dr I.N.B. Skenjana	University of Natal	1973
Dr O. Mbombo	University of Natal	1973
Dr V. Mashalaba	University of Natal	1973
Dr R.R. Bala	University of Natal	1975
Dr J. Nhlapo	University of Natal	1976
Dr P.Z. Njongwe	University of Natal	1976
Dr P.R. Madiba	University of Natal	1976
Dr D.I.S. Magongoa	University of Natal	1976
Dr M.R.G. Kobe	University of Natal	1976
Dr M. Hlekani	University of Natal	1976
Dr P.T. Mongeka	University of Natal	1976
Dr N.L.P.J. Nkosi	University of Natal	1977
Dr T.J. Nkosi	University of Natal	1977
Dr Z.A.P. Nogantshi	University of Natal	1977
Dr P.V.M. Seleke	University of Natal	1977
Dr M.T. Dladla	University of Natal	1978
Dr C. Mabuya	University of Natal	1978
Dr N.L. Hlongwane	University of Natal	1979
Dr B.A.S. Jolobe	University of Natal	1979
Dr B.P.H. Majozi	University of Natal	1979
Dr B.B. Mbulawa	University of Natal	1979
Dr L.V.T. Motsepe	University of Natal	1979
Dr T.T. Tueumuna	University of Natal	1979
Dr L.L. Kwinana	University of Natal	1980
Dr K.N.L. Linda	University of Natal	1980
Dr J.S.S.N. Makiwana	University of Natal	1980
Dr M. Moalusi	University of Natal	1980
Dr M.L. Msengana	University of Witwatersrand	1980
Dr Z.A.Z.M. Erkana	University of Natal	1981
Dr D.V. Moloi	University of Natal	1981
Dr S.N. Siwendu	University of Natal	1981
Dr G.L. Kumalo-Dlamini	University of Witwatersrand	1981
(Princess of Swaziland)		

South African Black Women Lawyers Qualified 1967–1982

Ms D.M. Finca	Attorney's Admission	Unisa	1967
Ms L.G. Baqwa	B.Jur	Fort Hare	1973
Ms G.N. Mapasa	B. Proc	Fort Hare	1974
Ms D.N. Dineka	B. Jur	Fort Hare	1974
Ms N.N. Vabaza	LL.B.	Fort Hare	1974
Ms K.N. Nyembezi	B.A.	Zululand	1974
Ms I. Msimang	B.A.	Zululand	1975
Ms T.A. Mahlinza	C. Com. LL.B.	Zululand	1976
Ms T.P. Phaleng	B.A.	Zululand	1976
Ms P.G. Msimang	B. Jur.	Fort Hare	1977
Ms N. Ngubo	B.A.	Fort Hare	1977
Ms N.D.B. Orleyn	B. Jur	Fort Hare	1978
Ms T.C. Burhali	B. Proc	Fort Hare	1978
Ms N.C. Kumalo	B.A.	Zululand	1978
Ms N.N. Nyangiwe	B. Proc LL.B.	Fort Hare	1978/81
Ms L.P. Hamutenya	B. Proc	Fort Hare	1979
Ms N.S. Cuba	B. Proc	Fort Hare	1979
Ms N.B. Nomjana	B. Proc	Fort Hare	1979
Ms N.N. Ntsinde	B. Proc	Fort Hare	1979
Ms D.B. Moloko	B. Proc	North	1979
Ms A.M. Moside	B. Proc	North	1979
Ms A.T. Thoka	LL.B.	North	1979
Ms N.P. Mngqibisa	B. Proc	Fort Hare	1980
Ms L.B. Ngwane	B. Proc	Fort Hare	1980
Ms N.J. September	B. Proc	Fort Hare	1980
Ms N.J. Tshabalala	B. Proc	Fort Hare	1980
Ms H.V. Theyise	B.A.	Zululand	1980
Ms A.T. Ngobese	B. Proc	Zululand	1980
Ms F.P. Rabotapi	B. Proc	North	1981
Ms M.F. Thubisi	B. Proc	North	1981
Ms K.D. Motlana	LL.B.	Witwatersrand	1981
Ms V. Buthelezi	B. Proc	Zululand	1981
Ms V. Hlongwa	B. Proc	Zululand	1982